PRAISE FOR
HILLBILLY NATIONALISTS
RACE REBELS, AND BLA

"This is movement writing at its best—an accessible, critical, and compelling account of an exceptional organizing coalition that continues to fire radical imaginations today."

—ELIZABETH CATTE, AUTHOR OF *WHAT YOU ARE GETTING WRONG ABOUT APPALACHIA*

"*Hillbilly Nationalists* recovers the voices of white, working-class radicals who prove abolitionist John Brown's legacy is alive and well. Over ten years, Sonnie and Tracy have collected rare documents and conducted interviews to fill a long-missing piece of social movement history. Focusing on the 1960s–70s and touching on issues just as relevant today, these authors challenge the Left not to ignore white America, while challenging white America to recognize its allegiance to humanity and justice, rather than the bankrupt promises of conservative politicians."

—ANGELA Y. DAVIS, AUTHOR OF *ABOLITION DEMOCRACY: BEYOND EMPIRE, PRISONS, AND TORTURE*

"In our world, 'white, working-class anti-racism' is considered an oxymoron, or at best a pipe dream. Amy Sonnie and James Tracy prove these assumptions wrong, excavating a forgotten history of poor white folks who, in alliance with black nationalists, built a truly radical movement for social justice, economic power, and racial and gender equality. They have written a beautiful, powerful, surprising account of class-based interracial organizing; I expect *Hillbilly Nationalists* to inspire a new generation of activists who understand that a true rainbow coalition is not only desirable but our only hope."

—ROBIN D. G. KELLEY, AUTHOR OF *FREEDOM DREAMS: THE BLACK RADICAL IMAGINATION* AND *THELONIOUS MONK: THE LIFE AND TIMES OF AN AMERICAN ORIGINAL*

"This book gave me hope."

—ADAM SMYER, AUTHOR OF *YOU CAN KEEP THAT TO YOURSELF: A COMPREHENSIVE LIST OF WHAT NOT TO SAY TO BLACK PEOPLE, FOR WELL-INTENTIONED PEOPLE OF PALLOR*

"Gifted storytellers Amy Sonnie and James Tracy offer a timely portrayal of the Young Patriots and other poor white radical organizers who stood in alliance with, and learned from, the Black Panthers' revolutionary service model. Ten years after its initial publication, Hillbilly Nationalists continues to challenge students and will bring nuance to classes in Ethnic and Feminist Studies, Political Science, and Sociology. The opening photo says so much: the Young Patriots standing in their Confederate flag jackets alongside the Black Panthers in Oakland in 1969. Oral histories and interviews capture their allied struggles against racism, economic marginalization, police, and the state with detail and insight not usually found in academic writing. This book is a precious resource that offers sustenance and a model for today's activists struggling to build anti-racist intersectional coalitions."

—SUSANA GALLARDO, WOMEN, GENDER & SEXUALITY STUDIES SAN JOSE STATE UNIVERSITY

"Their writing is thoroughly captivating, providing the reader with a gripping glimpse into a lost world of possibilities of solidarity and struggle from below." —RAVI MALHOTRA, UNIVERSITY OF OTTAWA

"*Hillbilly Nationalists* is the urgently necessary and compelling history of poor and working-class white revolutionaries forging an interracial movement with Black Power activists and Third World liberation against ever-escalating police terror, relentless counterinsurgency, and the predations of racial capitalism. Sonnie and Tracy explode the tepid refrain of white allyship and instead vividly chronicle the militant work of solidarity in struggle."

—ALYOSHA GOLDSTEIN, PROFESSOR AND DIRECTOR OF GRADUATE STUDIES DEPARTMENT OF AMERICAN STUDIES UNIVERSITY OF NEW MEXICO

"Amy Sonnie and James Tracy have provided us with that most relevant of movement histories. *Hillbilly Nationalists* not only addresses a vast gap in the social movement literature; it complements what we do know about the nationalist aspirations of Third World Marxism as well as a labor and organizing history traced elsewhere."

—BEN SHEPARD, CITY TECH CUNY

"Solidarity may not be the coolest term in today's world. It's a timeless ideal, and it's rarely been explored with as much heart and soul as Sonnie and Tracy do in *Hillbilly Nationalists*. Within their historical and theoretical rigor roars a simple plea: The American working class, all races included, must join forces once again to realize their common goals and collective power. Ten years after its initial publication, this book still rings true—a profound reminder that working-class solidarity isn't just crucial, radical, and attainable. It's beautiful."

**—JASON HELLER, AUTHOR OF *STRANGE STARS*
AND *THE TIME-TRAVELER'S ALMANAC***

"This book is, without question, the definitive resource for scholars, students, and activists interested in some of the most innovative and understudied coalitional politics of the New Left."

**—DARREL ENCK-WANZER, EDITOR OF
*THE YOUNG LORDS: A READER***

"Sonnie and Tracy are master storytellers whose stories of working-class, interracial solidarity chart a new direction in the history of the modern freedom movement. Based on dozens of oral histories and previously untapped personal records of movement activists, this book offers an inspiring and largely invisible history of poor and working-class whites who built a 'vanguard of the dispossessed' with Black Panthers, Young Lords, and others in the radical movement for racial and economic justice. Written with nuance and power, this is a major contribution to the study of civil rights, social justice, working-class communities, and the politics of whiteness in the United States."

**—JENNIFER GUGLIELMO, AUTHOR OF *LIVING THE
REVOLUTION* AND *ARE ITALIANS WHITE?***

"*Hillbilly Nationalists* is the story of reformers and revolutionaries, dreamers and doers, who remind us of a transformative organizing tradition among white, working-class communities. Inspired by Black Power and global events, these organizers did what only poor folks can do: they pooled their resources to build a vibrant social movement that escapes easy classification. Sonnie and Tracy combine first-rate historical research and extensive oral histories to capture the legacies of those unsung heroes and heroines who battled for the hearts and minds of working-class Americans in the 1960s and 1970s."

—DAN BERGER, EDITOR OF *THE HIDDEN 1970s: HISTORIES OF RADICALISM*

HILLBILLY NATIONALISTS, URBAN RACE REBELS, and BLACK POWER

Interracial Solidarity in 1960s-70s New Left Organizing

AMY SONNIE
JAMES TRACY

MELVILLE HOUSE
BROOKLYN • LONDON

Hillbilly Nationalists, Urban Race Rebels, and Black Power:
Interracial Solidarity in 1960s-70s New Left Organizing
© Amy Sonnie and James Tracy
Foreword © Roxanne Dunbar-Ortiz

All rights reserved

First Melville House Printing: September 2011
Updated and revised edition: July 2021

Melville House Publishing
46 John Street
Brooklyn, NY 11201
and
Melville House UK
Suite 2000
16/18 Woodford Road
London E7 0HA

mhpbooks.com
@melvillehouse

ISBN: 9-781-61219-941-2
9-781-61219-008-2 (e-book)

Library of Congress Control Number: 2021938196

Printed in the United States
10 9 8 7 6 5 4 3 2 1
A catalog record for this book is available from the Library of Congress

Rest in Power:
Bob Lee, Gil Fagiani, Carol Coronado,
Doug Youngblood, and Bobby Joe McGinnis

Contents

Foreword
BY ROXANNE DUNBAR-ORTIZ

I first met representatives of the New Left at San Francisco State College (now University) in the Spring of 1961, my first semester there. I was twenty-two years old, having moved to San Francisco from Oklahoma with my husband. During 1960, my first year living in San Francisco and working full-time in an office machine repair factory, I followed the television images of the burgeoning Civil Rights Movement in the South and all over the country and I was ripe for recruitment to the Movement. In particular, I closely watched the local anti-death penalty sit-ins at San Quentin prison to prevent the execution of author-inmate Caryl Chessman, and followed the student demonstrations against the House Un-American Activities Committee at San Francisco City Hall as police attacked hundreds of students with batons, blasting them with fire hoses and arresting dozens. I wanted to meet those brave young people.

I had long hungered to go to college and now it seemed like a way to get involved with the Movement too—I was thinking less about the risk and more about my excellent typing skills. So, that day on the San Francisco State campus when I saw an information table about the Mississippi Freedom Rides, I thought, "Finally!" After a full year in San Francisco, this was the first seemingly public invitation to join.

Back in Oklahoma I came from a childhood of rural poverty. For my last year of high school I moved from "the sticks" to work full time in Oklahoma City, which meant I attended the trade high school, secretarial track of course. It was the first year of school desegregation in Oklahoma, a year after the Supreme Court decision, *Brown v. Board of Education*, which ordered the desegregation of public schools. I attended the first public school in Oklahoma to integrate. It was no accident that the single wholly working-class white school received that honor. Predictably, there were acts of white racist violence against the few Black students. I began to pay attention to the sit-ins at local drugstore counters. I read the local extremely right-wing newspaper, because that was the only one available, but the photographs spoke for themselves about the violence being meted out against Black people all over the South. Then, I married into a family that abhorred racial discrimination. My father-in-law, a New Deal Democrat, had been a leader in efforts to desegregate the local crafts unions. From my in-laws' point of view, "lower-class" whites were the racist culprits, the kind of people I came from. I nearly held my breath for three years until I could leave Oklahoma and my past forever. I hoped San Francisco would be free of "racist low-class" white people.

In San Francisco everything seemed possible. Attending college was a dream come true and here, during my first semester, I found the noble activists I hoped had all the answers. Without knowing it, they intimidated me to the core. Behind the table sat two handsome young white men wearing jeans and plaid shirts. Standing behind them were two young women with long, straight blonde hair, dressed in black turtlenecks, skirts and leotards with shiny black boots. They were all laughing and talking with each other. I felt thrilled, as if a whole new world lay before me. I was also panic-stricken, not knowing what to say. (I look back and see, through their eyes, this working-class young woman dressed in the style of the new first lady, Jackie Kennedy, in a pastel linen shift and matching cardigan sweater with matching purse and medium high heels, panty hose, of course, and a bouffant hairdo. And then, out came the pronounced Okie accent when she got up the nerve to speak). I fingered a flyer on the table that asked for donations to send freedom riders—Black and white students on northern buses—to Mississippi to protest segregated interstate transportation. It seemed a brilliant but dangerous program. They also had a sign-up sheet for volunteers. How I wanted to sign!

Suddenly, I heard my voice asking if they were going to talk to poor whites in the South. They seemed stunned by the question, perhaps thinking I was joking. But, my surely terrified face and trembling hands must have made clear that I was serious, and that I was myself one of the poor whites. Immediately, I wished I could take back the question and start over. Then, one of the young men said, "No," and added that they weren't recruiting them either. It seemed I had spoiled my attempt to somehow join the cause.

It took several years before I tried to get involved again—only after I had successfully gotten rid of my accent, changed my way of dressing, grown my hair long and driven the working-class rural Okie girl underground in order to be accepted by the Movement. My experience is perhaps exceptional, but only because most individuals from my kind of background instinctively avoided putting themselves in positions of such humiliation and rejection.

I am glad I persisted in my radical commitment, but the truth is that the Movement was, and still is, mired in class hatred. One of my mentors, the late Anne Braden, related to her biographer a new

problem facing white organizers who had "gone South" for the freedom rides and voter registration drives in Black communities. Once
they were asked to address racism in their own white communities,
they balked: "They just didn't like white people!" said Braden. "You
can't organize people if you don't like them."[1] Braden thought it
was because they had seen so much white violence against Blacks
and fellow white activists in Mississippi, but I think it was class
hatred. As an early leader in the Women's Liberation Movement, I
soon felt the same stifling around feminist activists as I did from
the young man at that table. I realized that the absence of class consciousness was a fatal flaw of the New Left. I became aware that the
experience these now-feminist women had gained in the southern
Civil Rights Movement was based on a class privilege that I could
not even imagine.

Yet this was not the whole story of the Movement. It was with
great excitement in 1968 that I heard about organizing projects
with Appalachian migrants in Chicago: JOIN Community Union
and the Young Patriots. I spent a few days in August 1969 talking
with Peggy Terry, one of the remarkable leaders featured in this
book. I had not before met anyone in the Movement from a rural, poor white background like mine. Not only that, Peggy originally was from Oklahoma and part Cherokee like me. She opened
a whole new world of possibilities for me. Peggy introduced me to
one of the young SDS organizers she mentored to show me around
the neighborhood. The young white woman, Gerry, impressed me
with her organizing skills and her ability to relate to the poor white
youth. She seemed to know and be respected by everyone. It was
quite a contrast to the SDS project I'd visited in Cleveland where
the SDS organizers seemed completely isolated from the impover-
ished Black community in which they had lived for several years.
Gerry took me into a pool hall filled with unemployed young white

Appalachians who wore their hair in ducktails and pompadours. I talked to them about their organization, the Young Patriots, and its relationship with the local Black Panther chapter, led by Fred Hampton, who would be murdered by the Chicago police only four months later. The young white men were also harassed by the police and had organized neighborhood patrols. To find poor whites organized in an alliance with poor Blacks was thrilling.

A few months later, I moved to New Orleans to organize poor white and Black women into a labor consortium, while my companion at the time worked to set up a Patriots chapter. We invited the Chicago Patriots to send a delegation to help us get started. When William "Preacherman" Fesperman arrived, he commented, "Who'd ever have thought the Patriots would get hitched to a women's lib outfit. Regular bunch of Mother Joneses. Now don't get me wrong. Wait till you meet my wife—she's a women's libber all the way."

I told Fesperman and the other Patriots I met that I objected to their use of "Patriot," explaining it was reactionary and supported a racist mythology dating back to Andrew Jackson and Indian killing. To me, the very definition of patriotism was patriarchy. I asked if they were teaching their members about past white populist movements in which anti-government sentiments were merged with Jew hating and racism. They argued that getting the poor white kids hooked up with Blacks and Puerto Ricans and Indians dissolved their racism. The historian in me knew that this was the same argument made by the Progressive Party until political expediency became a reason to ignore racism. However, I felt that things might be different this time. The Patriots represented the first poor white organization I knew of who took their cues from Black leaders.

We organized a meeting of Movement organizers, including members of the Republic of New Afrika (RNA), for the Patriots delegation. At the time, the New Orleans chapters of the Southern

Conference Education Fund (SCEF) and the RNA were working together supporting a strike by pulp mill workers in Laurel, Mississippi, not far outside New Orleans. Virginia Collins, the local RNA leader and one of the organization's founders, told the Patriots about the white and Black workers who had been enemies before the strike but were now working together. She shared that the local Klan actually provided security for the SCEF and RNA organizers when they came to hold meetings, and that sometimes they met in the Black Baptist church, sometimes in the white Baptist church.

A few weeks later, I visited a new Patriots chapter in Eugene, Oregon, where the members were mostly descendants of migrant "Okies," very dear to my heart. I had relatives who worked as loggers in nearby Cottage Grove. I stayed in the Patriots house, in a rather tense atmosphere, as the police had recently raided it. I stayed up most of the night talking with angry young white men and women whose families had migrated from the Southwest during the Dust Bowl. They were extremely alienated from their families and the rural, poor white culture in which they'd grown up. They were angry that the only work available to their fathers was cutting down the ancient redwood trees. Creedence Clearwater Revival's "Fortunate Son" played repeatedly on the stereo. I heard myself, saw myself, in them. It gave me hope and a mission, which I have never abandoned, to organize poor whites, however difficult.

....

The men and women we meet in *Hillbilly Nationalists, Urban Race Rebels, and Black Power* weren't the first working-class radicals to grapple with the racism's roadblocks. Hundreds of workers' movements have crumbled because of it. As Karl Marx famously explained, "Labor cannot emancipate itself in the white skin when in the black it is branded." But this insight was not original or new with Marx. It was first enunciated decades earlier by Scots-American socialist, labor organizer, abolitionist and feminist Fanny Wright in the 1820s, as well as the abolitionists who multiplied a decade later. However, what neither Marx nor the abolitionists nor later leftists and oppressed nationalities in the United States have fully grasped is the reality of the United States as a colonizing state in which, as historian William Appleman Williams phrased it, empire has always been a way of life.

No country has pursued this goal more successfully and ruthlessly than the United States, which, at its founding, announced its intention of conquering and eliminating all the Indigenous peoples west from the original thirteen states to the Pacific Ocean. The United States spent the next hundred years at war against Indigenous nations, thereby building the foundation for the most aggressive and violent military machine in human history. Soon after the founding of the United States, as the Spanish American colonies became independent republics, the "Monroe Doctrine" proclaimed the intention of dominating the whole hemisphere. By 1848, half of Mexico was annexed to the United States, which extended economic dominance over the rest of Latin America. These events secured for the settler nation a place among world empires. After World War I, the United States was recognized by the European imperialist powers as an equal, and after World War II, a superior.

When we imagine the consequences of this process, it had to be deeply corrupting of the European settler and his descendant, the American settler—so deep it is not even consciously acknowledged or interrogated. White supremacy and empire were normal. And, in this process, generations since its colonial beginnings have been corrupted or confused, often self-hating, not understanding why. Violence resulted at every level, from individual white supremacy to regeneration of the white republic through violence against non-white peoples. The identity politics born in the Sixties were just a temporary solution to the burden of the past. Now, we are stuck, having played out the multicultural program. All the while, the origin myth of the United States has remained intact, as virginal as the myth created by the colonizers, that they were claiming virgin land, unpopulated, in its original state. Gone is the truth of vast territories populated and transformed by Indigenous farmers for millennia who built towns and governments, perfected crops, managed ecosystems, fished, hunted, traded, practiced sacred rites.

These Indigenous farmers were easy to kill, by burning or stealing their crops and storehouses of food, or stealing the food. It's always been easy to kill farmers, but until the rise of capitalist-based colonialism, no one wanted to kill farmers, because the farmers fed everyone. Conquerors required tribute in food from the farmers. Yet, people still had to eat under capitalism, so the colonizers enslaved Indigenous African farmers and brought them in chains to the Americas. They also brought destitute British and European farmers who had been evicted from their farms through the enclosure of the commons. Once the Indigenous American communities were reduced or removed, these two groups—poor whites and enslaved Africans, who also intermarried with Indigenous individuals—made up the majority of the population of the British colonies in North America.

In these thirteen colonies, around 20 percent of the population of 2,780,400 were Africans at the moment of independence. There were 200,000 enslaved Africans in Virginia alone, more than in any of Britain's twenty-two colonies in the western hemisphere. By 1820, an estimated 20 percent of the nine million U.S. Anglo settler population lived west of the Appalachian/Allegheny mountain range. By 1860, the U.S. settler population was thirty million, and half of them lived west of the mountains.[2] This was one of the most rapid transfers of human populations in history. But it was not a natural migration. It was government-planned colonization with Indigenous territories cleared of their inhabitants by the military, and settlers given the land, resulting in markets guaranteed to the farmers by the government that was backed by its Navy and Marines. During the 1840s and 1850s, millions of white settlers were recruited to immigrate from Europe and given passage, tools and land, to people the territories taken. Sometimes this process is described as a rush of land-hungry farmers, in a democratic setting, forcing their government to destroy Indigenous villages and remove the survivors so that white settlers could have land. But that is not how it happened.

At the onset of the industrial revolution, millions of Indigenous Irish fled the famine in their British colonized homeland. The rapid development of industrial capitalism in the United States brought the opening of immigration to southern and eastern Europeans, many of them Jews fleeing pogroms and socialists fleeing persecution. Chinese and Filipino males were also recruited as cheap labor. Mostly European immigrants found jobs in urban areas, but many also worked in the mines in remote regions. This period of rapid development during the second half of the nineteenth century, and the formation of a huge immigrant industrial workforce, coincided with the wars against the Indigenous nations in the Plains and the annexed Mexican territory in the west and southwest parts of the continent. The establishment of the oppressive reservation system on reduced portions of their original territories left the Indigenous population living in the conditions of war refugees, totally dependent upon the occupying country.

This is the context within which we need to place and evaluate the role of "poor whites," "white trash," "rednecks," "crackers," "hillbillies," descendants of the original landless or land poor settlers, the ones that kept moving westward with the United States, squatters sent to fight the native inhabitants. Under Andrew Jackson in the 1830s, the process was institutionalized with the Homestead Act. The small farmers, those frontier trekkers, the foot soldiers of the United States project of imperialism, have been blamed for a lot, but they were not in control of their destinies, although they committed many crimes. They seemed to know it. Those westward "pioneers" practically drowned with alcohol consumption, the men at least. The men and the women fed their guilt into feverish evangelism, waves of it from the 1790s on into the 21st century with the "Tea Party" movement.

These descendants of the early settlers, those with little or no land or other property, have long been a problem for the U.S. ruling class, while being invisible or a blur to the urban population. Why a problem? They are evidence of the failure of the "American Dream." The mythology that they have some rights, some prominence in the national story buys the population's loyalty to the state, even though they have no say in its affairs. They are the people who give the lie to the Jeffersonian ideal of a rural republic of yeoman farmers, of the bootstraps paradigm. They were the foot soldiers of British and United States colonization in North America. They have been the point men on the front lines, killing Indian farmers to take their land, only to be displaced by land companies turning the land into real estate, later coal companies, oil companies, timber companies, agribusiness, cities. The displaced poor whites often moved on to repeat the pattern in Tennessee, Missouri, Arkansas, Oklahoma, parts of Texas, and even the fruit fields and cotton fields of the California Central Valley. The Appalachian poor whites relocated to Cincinnati, Chicago and other industrial cities for jobs in factories. All along, they have made up the majority of the military, still cannon fodder, but feeling righteous and "patriotic."

History is made up of stories, but those stories are meaningless or even distorting without an analytical context within which the narrative plays out. Many of the dedicated and brave organizers of the 1960s did not think of their work within this larger historical context. And that remains a fundamental problem today.

This essential book documents a moment in time when a group of radical organizers in Chicago, in cooperation with the Black Panther Party and other radicals of color, recognized a revolutionary potential in young, displaced Appalachians and other poor whites descended from the old settlers. These people were the Achilles heel of the U.S. origin myth and the "American Dream." These organizers attempted, for over a decade, to cut at the tendon of that myth. Given the invisibility of this history, this book couldn't be more timely and more necessary.

Poor whites are here today . . . to make ourselves visible to a society whose continued existence depends on the denial of our existence. We are here today united with other races of poor people, Puerto Ricans, Mexican-Americans, Indians, and Black people in a common cause. That common cause is freedom!

—Peggy Terry at the Poor People's Convention
Washington, D.C., June 19, 1968

Panthers and Patriots together at the United Front Against Fascism Conference, Oakland, CA, July 1969.

(Photo by Stephen Shames)

Introduction

In July 1969 a dozen self-identified hillbillies showed up to a Black Panther Party conference in Oakland, California with Confederate flag patches sewn to their ragged jean jackets. Just above the flag, three hand-painted letters identified their radical outfit: YPO, the Young Patriots Organization. To outsiders, the Panthers' reputation for self defense combined with the very real violence committed under the Southern Cross might seem to guarantee a nasty brawl. Instead, prominent Panthers welcomed the members of the Young Patriots Organization as revolutionary brothers and sisters—with a fist in the air and "All Power to the People!"

The Young Patriots had come to Oakland for the United Front Against Fascism Conference. They arrived from Uptown, a Chicago neighborhood home to thousands of economically displaced Appalachians, mostly white, who had turned the area into a bastion of southern culture. Their families had moved North in search of work after mining and agriculture jobs started to disappear. But only a few found anything steady. The rest scraped by on day labor, hustling and domestic work. By one estimate more than 40 percent of the neighborhood was on some form of welfare. The *Sunday Tribune* deemed them a "plague of locusts" descending on the city. Yet, Uptown's residents also represent some of the lesser-known protagonists in the Sixties New Left.[1] As one Patriots member put it, "We are the living reminder that when they threw out their white trash, they didn't burn it." That trash was picking itself up.

The Young Patriots were part of a new alliance with the Chicago Black Panther Party and a Puerto Rican street-gang-turned-political-organization called the Young Lords. Under the banner of the "Rainbow Coalition" they formed a vanguard of the dispossessed. While ultimately short-lived, the Rainbow Coalition created by these groups had deeper roots and a longer legacy than even their FBI tailgaters might have imagined. And yes, J. Edgar Hoover's FBI had tabs on them from the beginning. This was half the reason they traveled together to Oakland in July 1969. Called by the Black Panther Party, then at the peak of its fame, the United Front Against Fascism Conference addressed two urgent concerns: community control of police who were terrorizing poor neighborhoods, and mutual protection against the federal government's escalating attacks on the Left.

The three-day conference drew more than two thousand self-styled revolutionaries from across the nation. Black Panthers in their black berets and sleek leather jackets stood shoulder-to-shoulder with the Young Patriots wearing the flag of the Confederacy—a symbol they soon discarded. Joining them in the cavernous Oakland Auditorium were American Indian activists on the verge of their famous Alcatraz Island takeover, members of the Young Lords flying the bandera of Puerto Rico, Chicano farm workers wearing the Aztec eagle, sympathetic lawyers juggling a full docket of conspiracy trials, more than a few police informants, and members of

Students for Democratic Society (SDS), who were in the middle of a fierce organizational split that led to at least one fistfight before Panther leaders told the factions to "freeze on that shit" for the rest of the weekend.

Outside the auditorium, Panther members and sympathizers watched their kids play while serious-looking radicals floated in and out listening to speeches by Panther defense lawyer Charles Garry, Penny Nakatsu speaking out about Japanese American internment during World War II, and an especially moving message from jailed Panther Ericka Huggins read by Elaine Brown. At the mic, the Young Patriots' chairman, William "Preacherman" Fesperman, even let some heartfelt gratitude show in between jibes about the "pig power structure" when he explained how the Patriots came to be at the conference: "Our struggle is beyond comprehension to me sometimes and I felt for a long time [that poor whites] was forgotten . . . that nobody saw us. Until we met the Illinois chapter of the Black Panther Party and they met us and we said let's put that theory into practice." Summing up why they had all come to Oakland, he added, "We want to stand by our brothers, our brothers, dig?"[2]

For the leftists gathered that July, a life or death battle was unfolding. While the depths of the FBI's covert counterintelligence program (COINTELPRO) wouldn't come to light for years, dozens of movement activists had been killed, and others sat in jail facing serious legal charges. Among them: Panthers cofounder Huey Newton, several leaders of the Sixties student movement, and renowned icons of the Yippie youth counterculture Jerry Rubin and Abbie Hoffman. Though the government reserved its most vicious attacks for Black and Brown radicals, by 1969 nearly every sector of the U.S. Left was caught in its crosshairs. The conference in Oakland reminded movement leaders that unity was going to be their most effective defense strategy. As Chicago Panther Fred Hampton put it, "You can jail the revolutionary, but you can't jail the revolution . . . You can murder a liberator, but you can't murder liberation."

Hampton, it turned out, had written his own elegy. The Rainbow Coalition, spearheaded by Hampton and fellow Panther Bob Lee, lit a spark in the movement but ignited a fuse with deadly outcomes. Less than six months later Chicago police murdered Fred Hampton in his bed. The nighttime raid was orchestrated with the help of a local informant and the direct involvement of the FBI. Hampton had been drugged so he wouldn't wake up to fight.

....

With the 10th anniversary edition of *Hillbilly Nationalists, Urban Race Rebels, and Black Power,* we return to this history during a parallel moment of danger and possibility. Since 2011, we've witnessed the rise of authoritarianism across the globe, and of white nationalist movements in the United States. We've seen, once again, a fiercely reactionary conservatism take center stage in U.S. politics alongside a dangerous mainstreaming of far-right ideas. The brutalities of racial capitalism are on full display as poor communities worldwide have been hit first and worst by crisis after crisis: the tightening grip of climate change and a global pandemic that has killed millions and left millions more sick, homeless, or unemployed. At the same time, we see the legacy of the Panthers in the resurgence of mutual aid networks, community self-defense, and calls to defund the police.

Over the last decade, we've welcomed the growth of extraordinary, multi-issue movements led by Indigenous, Black, and immigrant communities sparking some of the largest mass mobilizations in history. We've begun to reckon with endemic racial and gendered violence, and welcomed a new wave of intersectional feminism and queer/trans liberation politics, reflected in the global Movement for Black Lives and beyond. As in 1968, we are at a turning point. This generation's new Left has the opportunity and imperative to build a united front against fascism for the 21st century.

Given these conditions, there is no better time to learn the lessons of racial solidarity, class struggle, and feminist leadership that was seeded in the Sixties, and especially to learn about the "rainbow politics" that defined the era's most visionary alliances. We focus here on the leadership of working-class white people who organized alongside communities of color to determine their own destinies and call for revolution. To understand how "hillbilly nationalists" came to stand arm-in-arm with the Black Panthers, we must understand the longer legacy of rainbow politics in Chicago and beyond, starting in the early Sixties and lasting well into the Seventies. Beginning with Jobs or Income Now in Chicago, and continuing with the Young Patriots Organization, Rising Up Angry, and its two sister groups on the east coast, White Lightning in the Bronx and October 4th Organization in Philadelphia, this book traces a historical arc among five community-based organizations that directly challenged white supremacy while struggling for the class interests of poor and working-class white people.

The seeming contradiction of Confederate flag-waving revolutionaries in deep dialogue about Black Power and Third World Liberation is less extraordinary than the fact that anyone doubted poor and working-class whites' participation in the first place.[3] Yet, they did. White workers' revolutionary potential was debated and doubted. Some members of the New Left dismissed poor whites as too narrowly focused on their immediate problems. Many sixties-era revolutionaries assumed poor and working-class whites were inherently more conservative, ignoring the radical history and potential in poor white communities and absolving themselves of the responsibility to understand their own middle-class communities' role in upholding structural racism. In the mid-Sixties, SDS president Paul Potter warned the student movement away from over-emphasizing the "problems of the dispossessed." Potter believed that the movement needed to take growing middle-class frustrations more seriously. "It is through the experience of the middle class and the anesthetic of bureaucracy and mass society that the vision and program of participatory democracy will come—if it is to come," Potter argued.[4]

Until recently, the narrative of the Sixties largely excluded serious mention of poor and working-class whites who formed or took over radical organizations.[5] Instead, historians have tended to focus on the oppositional role of white workers—Teamsters, construction workers and carpenters—who violently confronted anti-war protesters, disregarded the plight of fellow Black and Brown workers, and cajoled labor's support for U.S. military actions in Vietnam and Cambodia. Yet woven among the watershed events of the Sixties and Seventies are dozens of examples of poor and working-class whites who propelled racial justice rather than opposing it. These men and women understood that ending racism was not a threat or an act of charity, but a part of gaining their own freedom.

Out of necessity and strategy these men and women experimented with their own way to organize populations the broader Left had failed to reach. Their constituents included disaffected white youth, the chronically unemployed, welfare recipients, recovering drug users, day laborers, blue-collar workers, and white ethnic communities.[6] Inspired by the Black Power movement's call to "organize you own" and part of a longer legacy of progressive populism in the United States, these poor white revolutionaries carved out a community organizing approach that addressed poor people's immediate concerns—health, welfare, housing, jobs, drug addiction and police violence—while paying strategic attention to civil rights and multiracial coalitions. This approach opened direct links to similar struggles in communities of color, allowing poor and working-class whites to participate as actors, not just allies, in the struggle for racial and economic justice.

Theirs were the neighborhoods turned upside down by federal urban renewal programs and local neglect. Their families were the newly arrived Italian, Irish, and Polish émigrés; the poor whites living alongside Black, Native American and Latino neighbors; the white factory workers who counted the Wobblies as their forebears; and the "dislocated hillbillies" who were just as poor in the North as they'd been in the South, and even more maligned. For this reason and others, the "nationalism" of the hillbilly nationalists differed in every way from the white nationalism of today. Theirs was a nationalism focused on multiracial collaboration among working-class people, inspired by anticolonial struggles across the globe, and in step with the revolutionary internationalism and socialism of the original Rainbow Coalition.

....

Then, as now, their stories are largely invisible. In the United States we have seen so few mirrors of this reality that it's hard to imagine a broad Left movement that includes white poor and working-class people as radical change agents. Instead, poor and working-class whites occupy a unique place in the North American psyche. Whether presented as rednecks or trailer trash, or as Steinbeck's noble proles, depictions of struggling whites depend largely on the prevailing social need for either a hero or scapegoat.

Beginning in the early Sixties, the image of poor whites emerged as an especially pliant marionette for the nation's postwar blues. A decades-long tidal wave of 20th-century internal migrations crested in the early Sixties with millions moving from rural towns to urban centers . . . and so did the anxieties of businessmen who bankrolled popular culture and news. *West Side Story* and *The Young Savages* dramatized the mounting ethnic conflict in changing US cities. Turf war dramas neatly illustrated senseless urban tragedies offering only two remedies for the mean streets—federal urban renewal programs to displace the poor, and strong-handed law enforcement to keep the rabble in line. Those who could afford it escaped to the suburbs or at least the outer edges of the city. Enter TV's blue-collar everyman, Archie Bunker, who became the nation's number one racist-next-door. His armchair epithets mimicked white anxiety in the post-civil rights era, but reassured viewers of a harmless shift from direct racial violence to private bigotry and ballot box demagoguery.

Hillbillies and rednecks, of course, made for the most sensational characters in the national identity crisis. A slapstick comedy about hillbillies who strike it rich and move to Beverly Hills nicely obscured the massive industrial collapse and government neglect that actually forced millions of southerners to big cities. Lest anyone get comfortable with lovable illiterates, though, the media issued sinister warnings about their rough country cousins, still poor and unwilling to assimilate. Chicago's *Sunday Tribune* advised readers that opium dens made safer hangouts than neighborhoods "taken over by clans of fightin,' feudin' Southern hillbillies and their shootin' cousins." Worse, the film *Deliverance* offered one of the rare cinematic moments when the racial script of the savage gets flipped. The film fanned fears of backwoods, inbred predators lurking in the shadows. It supplied a disturbingly brutal warning to city slickers not to buck the march toward "progress."

In the early Sixties, Michael Harrington's exposé on poverty, *The Other America*, woke the country from its fable of universal prosperity. It was a threadbare myth to begin with. "The very rise in productivity that created more money and better working conditions for the rest of society" had been "a menace to the poor," Harrington wrote.[7] The coal miner automated out of a job, the farmer forced off his land, the poor woman working in a munitions factory told to return to homemaking even though she had been doing paid labor since age fourteen—each joined previous generations of Black and white migrants, Native Americans and newer immigrants looking for a fighting chance in urban economies. As a result, the racial makeup of urban neighborhoods changed rapidly during the Sixties and Seventies, escalating ethnic conflicts in some areas, and creating opportunities to heal racial divides in others.

There's a reason *West Side Story* tells a tale of true love tragically divided. Would anyone believe the plot if the Sharks and the Jets had joined forces to fight the police and open a community health clinic? Popular history gives us so few of these stories that tales of racial unity seem romantic at best, propaganda at worst. Just as likely it's because there is no easy theatrical resolution for the problems of poverty and racism. Instead, the media spotlight found a new character in poor and working whites. This time they were antagonists in highly publicized resistance to school busing, neighborhood integration and affirmative action. Unfortunately, this white backlash was real. But so were the lesser-known attempts people made to transform their communities and unite across lines of difference and division. So was the decade-long effort of Philadelphia's October 4th Organization to support neighborhood integration and work alongside Black and Puerto Rican women for guaranteed health care. So was the story of the Young Patriots chapter when it became the "Committee to Defend the Panthers."

In Chapter One we share several of these transformations, most especially the story of a southern migrant named Peggy Terry, whose sympathies for the civil rights movement evolved into a lifelong radicalism rooted most deeply in her years at JOIN Community Union in Chicago. Founded as a project of Students for a Democratic Society, JOIN is one of the few organizations in this book discussed in any depth by other scholars. Few have told its history from the perspective of leaders such as Terry, who was influenced by the best aspirations of the student Left and the emerging Black Power Movement. JOIN's work directly inspired the formation of the Young Patriots and Rising Up Angry in 1968 and 1969. In Chapters Two and Three we trace these two groups' unprecedented work and the role each played representing the "white arc" in the now-famed Rainbow Coalition. Their work took shape during years when white radicals searched for meaningful ways to support the goals of Third World Liberation while continuing to fight for concrete improvements in their own communities. This search sent them looking to other cities for models as well. Chicago's Rising Up Angry, in particular, forged strong relationships with two east coast groups organizing working-class whites. In Chapter Four we trace the distinct stories of October 4th Organization in Philadelphia and White Lightning in New York as they responded to a deepening recession and growing right-wing backlash throughout the 1970s.

In different ways, JOIN, the Patriots, Rising Up Angry, October 4th Organization, and White Lightning made two radical propositions through their work. First and foremost, they suggested that poor and working-class whites should be taken seriously as a base for revolutionary change. Second, they put forward the idea that poor whites experience the benefits of institutional racism differently and, therefore, class-based organizing must account for those differences without ever ignoring the reality of white supremacy. Through trial and error these groups engaged residents around bread-and-butter concerns, while nurturing a deep dedication to common cause politics that linked them across racial divides. Like most revolutionary projects of the period, they didn't always succeed. Yet their experimental alliances shed light on a largely unexamined dimension of urban radicalism in the United States. Amid the turbulence of the Sixties and recession of the Seventies, their projects offer hope that an interracial movement of the poor could undermine injustice and division.

We studied these organizations because we believe they engaged honestly with the complexities of racialized capitalism in the United States. Racism has long been used to divide workers and impede solidarity and social change. History provides a depressingly long list of movements started and then broken by race-baiting. But the end result is never the whole story. There have been times, as in the long arc of these formal and informal "Rainbow Coalitions," when poor and working people have come together in recognition of a common goal. Whether this political tendency constitutes a significant success depends largely on how one judges the outcomes they achieved given the conditions of the time. We believe it does. We've done our best to present the forces and debates shaping their work, along with the decisions participants made under those circumstances. Some are inspiring, others difficult to comprehend.

As authors we came to this project as activists, two individuals who—through the course of our own community organizing—sought answers to today's challenges in movements of the past. As part of reconstructing this buried history we relied largely on interviews with movement participants. Most of them are still active in community, labor, electoral and educational organizing. To all who have given their time, opened their homes and turned over their personal archives, we extend our deepest thanks. Their insights are woven throughout this text and so we chose not to footnote each instance. Quotations without footnotes come from these interviews and other original research.

Since the first edition ten years ago, several new resources have greatly expanded on this history. Excellent books by Jakobi Williams on the Chicago Black Panthers and Johanna Fernández on the Young Lords joined extensive archival work by Cha Cha Jimenez at Grand Valley State to capture more about the original Rainbow Coalition, while Ray Santisteban's powerful PBS documentary *The First Rainbow Coalition* brought the story to life. We are especially grateful to Chuck Armsbury and to Young Patriots co-founder Hy Thurman, whose recent memoirs added immensely to our understanding; and to Daniel Tucker whose "Organize Your Own" project inspired artists nationwide to explore the themes presented in these books. Even with its obligatory Hollywood distortions, Shaka King's *Judas and the Black Messiah* acknowledged this history as part of Fred Hampton's enduring legacy and the Panther's visionary politics.

We have been inspired by countless conversations with students, organizers, scholars, and—most of all—veterans of these movements as we have traveled the country sharing these lessons of interracial unity. We hope our work here inspires others to look for hidden histories to inspire today's Rainbow Coalitions and freedom fighters. Their stories are history in the making.

—Amy Sonnie and James Tracy, March 2021

HILLBILLY NATIONALISTS, URBAN RACE REBELS, and BLACK POWER

CHAPTER 1

· · · · · · · · · · ·

The Common Cause Is Freedom: JOIN Community Union and the Transformation of Peggy Terry

I come from the South / I followed the route
To Chicago, a big old town.
But I found me hard luck / Couldn't make me a buck
All I got was the run around.
If we're gonna get / What the poor ain't got yet
Gotta keep on the Firing Line.

—Popular folk song sung at JOIN,
adapted from "Good Old Mountain Dew"

In 1962 a southern-born white woman named Peggy Terry walked into the Chicago headquarters of the Congress of Racial Equity (CORE) and asked how she could help. For a daughter of the South, whose grandfather took her to a Ku Klux Klan rally at age three, this moment was immense. She didn't entirely know what to expect, but she knew CORE was one of the oldest and most respected civil rights organizations in the country.[1] By the end of Terry's first day she and dozens of other activists landed in jail for blocking an intersection outside the Chicago Board of Education in protest of the city's segregated school system. Terry looked around her jail cell marveling at the courage of her new friends. She was humbled to be a part of it and felt—for the first time in her life—a mutual respect from people she admired. It was exhilarating and a little overwhelming.

Terry moved to Chicago just a few years earlier and was keenly aware that most northerners viewed southern whites, especially poor whites, with cautious suspicion or outright animosity. She felt this more from bosses and landlords, of course, but who would blame Black civil rights leaders for thinking the same given the white racist violence erupting anywhere people of color organized? She hoped her commitment to civil rights would be apparent enough to overshadow her obvious southern drawl. She threw herself into local civil rights work, adopting a comfortable behind-the-scenes role. Over her two years in CORE, she mostly kept quiet about her past and her struggles living in one of Chicago's poorest neighborhoods.

All that was about to change. Before the turbulent Sixties came to a close Peggy Terry emerged as the voice of the invisible white poor in a nation experiencing major revolts against race, class and gender oppression. She spoke on national stages with famed civil rights leaders, held kitchen conversations with reluctant white neighbors, and shared the 1968 presidential ticket as running mate to Black Panther Eldridge Cleaver. She focused her entire vice presidential campaign on countering segregationist George Wallace and his fearmongering message to the white working class. Her story, however, is not one of exceptional celebrity. Peggy Terry's personal transformation is one of hundreds shaped, first, by the universal inspiration of the civil rights movement and, second, by deliberate local organizing that engaged working-class whites in the New Left through the prism of their own experience.

For Peggy Terry and dozens of others that personal transformation took place in an experimental new organization called Jobs or Income Now (JOIN). Initiated by young intellectuals from the country's rapidly growing student movement, JOIN was the pilot project for an ambitious organizing effort in poor urban neighbor-hoods. Initiated in 1963 by Students for a Democratic Society, the project set out to win "short run social reforms" that would cre-ate conditions for leadership and participation beyond campuses and the South. Anticipating a spike in joblessness and a recession, JOIN's founders were looking beyond their campuses to locations where a truly bottom-up organization might dovetail with the civil rights movement and growing radicalism among discontented middle-class youth. To the project's founders community organiz-ing seemed both logical and necessary, yet to some on the Left the poor white slum where Terry lived seemed an unlikely place to find willing volunteers.

While the civil rights movement started to expose many promi-nent lawmakers as witting enemies of racial justice, the public largely viewed angry white citizens as the primary agents of racial violence. When Alabama Governor George Wallace publicly pro-fessed allegiance to Jim Crow, his "segregation forever" maxim po-sitioned him as the protector of hardworking whites who had little to spare and everything to lose if Black southerners gained a social or economic foothold. He adopted this position midway through his political career in order to win the top state office, and he suc-ceeded. Wallace and other southern politicians cast the "Common Man's" concerns—and therefore righteous violence—as a century-old, grassroots effort to protect the Heart of Dixie against federal intrusions on state and local autonomy. If politicians were simply racism's insurers, the public saw poor and working-class whites as its mechanics.

While Peggy Terry began to see the fallacy of this logic, she certainly knew the voters who propelled Wallace to the governor's office. Born in Haileyville, Oklahoma, and growing up in Pa-ducah, Kentucky, she rarely came into contact with people of color as a child, even when the poor white and Black sections of town stood literally back-to-back. Segregation was a given in her southern towns, reinforced by silence and heated family gossip about her aunt's marriage to a Choctaw man. Terry's cousin Delbert, born from that marriage, was her only relationship with a person of color until she joined the civil rights movement three decades later.

Controversial as her aunt's marriage was, segregation between Blacks and whites created a far thicker smoke. While her father always "spoke out and stuck up for the workingman," he clung to the meager warranty of white supremacy with every breath. Terry's grandfather was a member of the Ku Klux Klan, her father a sympathizer. They brought her along as a child on rides through the Black section of town to "shoot off chimneys." When she was just eight years old she watched her father flatly refuse roadside assistance from a Black man, opting instead to leave his family stranded in a roadside ditch. It was a bitterly cold winter on the route between Kentucky and Oklahoma. Her pregnant mother tried to balance herself in the front of their lop-sided Model T, while Terry and her siblings huddled in the backseat to stay warm. When the passerby asked Lon Ousley if he needed a hand pulling the car out, her father commanded the man to get his "black ass on down the road." The irrationality of his racism was lost on Terry, but not on her mother, who muttered something about cutting off his nose.[2]

Terry left school after fifth grade. When she was fifteen, she left home and married her first husband. They hitchhiked from town to town looking for work. She labored alongside Mexican workers in the Rio Grande Valley picking grapefruits and worked the cotton fields in Alabama alongside Black workers, but she never spoke to them. Even the laborer's makeshift tent camps were segregated. Occasionally, a loaf of bread would appear when there wasn't enough food in one of the other camps, but few ever discussed it. Terry stuck with the Irish and Scots, failing to see any commonality with the other men and women who, like her, traveled from town to town, season after season, working, living, giving birth and raising children under plastic tarps that provided little shelter from the dust, heat and rain.

During World War II, Terry found her first stretch of steady employment in Kentucky working alongside her mother and sister in a weapons factory. Kentucky was the one place she considered home, but after the war, work dried up again. By the mid-1950s Peggy Terry reached a stop in her migration that altered her path forever. That town was Montgomery, Alabama, and in 1956 the Montgomery Bus Boycott shattered Peggy Terry's complacency. For ninety years Jim Crow laws upheld the southern *corpus juris* of "separate but equal," which reinforced vicious attacks on the minds and bodies of Black southerners. While Terry had heard rumors about the tempests brewing across the South as Black southerners began organizing against segregation, she certainly had never seen Blacks standing up for their rights, on the job or elsewhere. She worked in enough factories to understand the power of a strike, but this was different. This was Black people doing something on their own, demanding dignity, in the town where she lived.

The 381-day rider strike marked a highly publicized assault on Jim Crow and a push to finally challenge the specter of white supremacy in the United States. In a systematic effort to thwart the boycott, participants were fired from jobs, threatened and beaten. Local businesses denied car insurance to volunteer drivers who helped Black residents get to work, and city police jailed or fined participants for hindering lawful business. As the boycott gained momentum, though, the mass coordination of Black residents seemed a victory in itself. Before any legal victory was won, flyers announced, "Jim Crow is Dead!"[3] Speaking volumes about the cloud of privilege shrouding white southerners, Peggy Terry saw the signs and wondered who Jim Crow was and how he died.

Despite her ignorance about segregationist vernacular she knew the boycott was a big deal. Several weeks into the protest Terry and a group of girlfriends took a bus to the city jail to check out the spectacle. A number of boycotters, including the movement's budding emissary, a young pastor named Martin Luther King Jr., had been arrested for interfering with city commerce. As King exited the jail, a gang of white vigilantes grabbed him. Terry watched in disgust as they beat him in front of a crowd of onlookers. King's nonviolence in contrast to the mob's brutality shocked her most. At thirty-five years old, she saw the injustice of racial violence with new eyes. While it took a few years before she joined the freedom movement, that day forever altered her thinking. As she would tell her grandson's history class years later, "It marked the beginning of my becoming a better person."

....

Becoming a lifelong radical rarely occurs overnight, and in Terry's case it took years, first, as an observer of a different way of being and, only later, as a leader of organized action. A year after the boycott, Terry moved to Illinois with her three children. She also married her longtime friend, Gil Terry. It was Gil who provided Terry her first experience seeing a white person treat a Black person with respect. Gil was active in local politics and a member of the Communist Party. One evening he invited a Black friend to their home for dinner. Terry was nervous. "I didn't want it, but I didn't make a fuss," she said. As the front door opened, Gil greeted their guest and offered to take her coat. Terry froze. She didn't know how to act or what to say. She had never in her life seen a white man hang a Black person's coat. How did such a simple act seem so impossible? Of her own racism, Terry later said, "How can you be raised in garbage like that and not stink from it. You walk through garbage, you stink."

Over the next few years, the Terrys attended local labor and political meetings and she joined her first radical organization, a group called Women for Peace that was opposed to redbaiting, nuclear testing and U.S. action against Cuba. By the time Peggy Terry walked into CORE's headquarters in 1962, she had come to realize that racial discrimination was connected to a much bigger system, upheld through exclusionary practices of northern businesses and politicians just as efficiently as it had been back home. The laws were just a little less obvious. Chicago's mayor paid lip service to better education for Black children, but had no intention of changing the fact that 90 percent of the city's schools were physically and educationally segregated.[4] After Black communities forced the district to address disparity and overcrowding, public school officials erected $2 million worth of aluminum trailers outside Black schools rather than permit integration into white schools with empty desks. An influential Black community group dubbed the trailers the "Willis Wagons" after then-Superintendent Benjamin C. Willis.[5]

Terry learned most of this on her first day at CORE. Some of it was shocking. Other facts were familiar. She reflected on conditions in her own daughter's middle school with its falling plaster, outdated books, broken pipes and crowded classrooms. She had embarrassed her young daughter, Margi, on more than one occasion by marching into the school to confront teachers and administrators about the conditions and the lack of real opportunities for learning. She could scarcely imagine how a Black child would learn anything sitting in a tin box. With a protest planned for that afternoon, she had little time to think about the prospect of arrest. All she knew was she had to do something.

Despite the camaraderie she gained from her political involvement, Terry largely kept quiet about her own struggles living in the city's white slums. Her southern accent, clothing and address in Chicago's maligned Uptown neighborhood came with little esteem and even outright disdain from caseworkers, bosses and customers at the restaurant where she waitressed. Terry never experienced anything like that in the South where, as she put it, "the wool pulled over poor whites' eyes" gave men like her father a sturdy sense of worth and security. Feeling one's own poverty was relative to the nearest riches and in her youth there had been few displays of wealth to covet. Where the sting of poverty surfaced, a communal feeling that you were still better off than someone else usually compensated. In the North, though, the fabric of her privilege felt thinner somehow. Still, she worried that talking about her personal hardships would distract from the Black struggle for freedom. She adopted a behind-the-scenes role at CORE even though it proved a thin mask for the shame she carried. She was shocked and humbled when, after meeting Martin Luther King Jr. for the first time, he asked her about her experience as a poor white woman. How did he know? He asked her how other poor whites might become involved with the movement. Having thought little about this, she had no idea what to say.

Two years after she joined CORE, Terry's friend and civil rights leader Monroe Sharp encouraged her to face what she'd been hiding. She had long imagined herself rebelliously working against her own interests in the struggle for others' freedom. She had no idea what it meant to consider her own. Monroe Sharp knew she had much more to offer than she could at CORE. Peggy Terry had a natural way of connecting with people. Plus, she was whip smart. Sharp was working closely with the white student leaders organizing voter registration projects in the South and with Students for a Democratic Society, which had just started setting up community projects in northern cities. The Chicago project was in Terry's neighborhood and Monroe suggested she join. Terry wanted nothing to do with it. She found it hard to imagine what possible good might come of a mostly white organization, let alone one filled with poor white southerners and started by college students. She left Sharp with no choice. He all but dragged Terry to the JOIN office, leaving her there with the friendly admonishment, "This is where you belong. . . . You have to really know who *you* are before you ever know who *we* are."

After years crossing town to "help Black folks get their freedom," Peggy Terry looked around her own neighborhood trying to imagine the work ahead. Chicago's Uptown section was alternatively known as "Hillbilly Heaven" or "Hillbilly Harlem" after the large numbers of Appalachian families who moved there in search of work between 1930 and 1960. Like neighborhoods in Boston, Detroit and Cincinnati, Uptown started to change when the southern economy convulsed. Beginning with the Great Depression, the Appalachian region saw one of the greatest out-migrations in U.S. history. After automation decimated the mining industry and federal policy curbed the region's agricultural mainstay, people began migrating by the tens of thousands from mining towns and mountain hamlets.[6] During the Great Depression alone, nearly one million white southerners left the South. The "Great White Migration," as history remembers it, had a distinctly economic impetus for European descendents, while both economics and severe racial oppression propelled the massive out-migration of Black southerners during Reconstruction and again in the early twentieth century.[7] Even decades into the exodus, most who left intended to make their way back home, but this proved nearly impossible as entire towns from West Virginia to northern Alabama to the western Carolinas succumbed to the economic fallout.

By the 1960s nearly seven million southern-born whites lived outside the South. Uptown received economically displaced southerners by the busload. Although the 120-block area on Chicago's North Side was never exclusively white or southern, white southerners made up nearly 40 percent of all newcomers, accounting for more than 60 percent in certain census tracts.[8] To profit from the influx of a new laboring class, speculators had transformed the formerly middle-class enclave of Uptown by subdividing stately homes into small, ramshackle apartments. Landlords paid no attention to building standards; they left plumbing exposed, garbage on the streets and repairs unfinished. Housing conditions in Uptown were typified by single-room tenement-style apartments, dilapidated buildings, rat infestations, broken plumbing, peeling paint, missing locks and a constant, ominous police presence. Conditions in factories, on the railroads and in service jobs weren't much better. Northern business owners seized the opportunity to recruit a cheap, dependent labor force "who had empty stomachs and pocketbooks but strong backs."[9] Available work was hard and temporary.

A southern hillbilly identity surfaced nearly everywhere through community centers, barbeque stands, country music and religious institutions. To its residents the neighborhood was a piece of mountain life carved in the asphalt of the North, but few outside Uptown welcomed the cultural renaissance. The neighborhood's reputation as a bastion of southern culture stoked northern fears that indigent migrants would soon swallow the city. Uptown seemed the epicenter of northern anxiety. *Harper's Magazine* warned the nation about the ominous threat hillbillies posed to prosperity and sanctity in the northern United States. Invoking imagery of an invading army the magazine warned, "The city's toughest integration problem has nothing to do with Negroes . . . It involves a small army of white, Protestant, early American migrants from the South—who are usually proud, poor, primitive, and fast with a knife."[10]

Exaggerated as *Harper's* portrait might have been, Uptown gained a lasting reputation as the "most congested whirlpool of white poverty in the country."[11] When Bob Lee (later a leader of the local Black Panther Party) first visited Uptown as a volunteer, he described one of the most horrible slums imaginable. Many of Chicago's Black neighborhoods fared as bad or worse, but Lee never imagined white people living under such conditions. In the early Sixties, the North Side and the South Side were night and day, but for residents like Lee who managed a glimpse of both sides, the similarities were striking. They offered proof that the postwar boon did little to help the nation's permanent underclass.

The paradox for poor neighborhoods, of course, exists where systemic government neglect of people and infrastructure collides with overwhelming scrutiny by media, police, speculators and even sociologists fascinated by the primitive ways of the poor. In Uptown residents faced job discrimination, constant police harassment, invasive home visits by welfare counselors and the beginning throes of urban renewal. After the Housing Act of 1949 authorized local governments to demolish and redevelop areas deemed as blighted, areas like Uptown started to see changes, not all of them good. Invariably blight was in the eye of the beholder and most often found on valuable urban land occupied by low-income people. In Chicago the Act simply accelerated the process of displacing working-class communities. Between 1941 and 1965, 160,000 Blacks and 40,000 poor whites were displaced from their homes by freeway construction and city development projects. Only 3,100 received replacement public housing.[12]

Urban renewal programs treated poor neighborhoods like chessboards, chopping up neighborhoods to build new housing residents could no longer afford and forcing them to move into other poor neighborhoods or out of the city entirely. It was here that northern segregation persisted through an entrenched web of laws, regulations, and the informal practices of Chicago real estate agents, the Federal Housing Association, and neighborhood groups intent on curtailing Black homeownership. Restrictive zoning laws prevented public housing construction in any place other than existing ghettoes, while proposed highway construction decimated working-class neighborhoods including Italian and Greek ethnic enclaves.[13] In these circumstances the politics of white flight took a particularly bizarre turn. A real estate agent might offer to locate a Black family in a white ethnic area and simultaneously whip up fears among whites of an impending invasion of their neighborhood. For the whites that could leave, the agency would offer to sell them a house in the suburbs.

In Uptown the poor were left to fight for their homes and make sense of growing racial tensions that came with neighborhood integration. However, conflicts between new neighbors took second shift to the area's other ongoing battle: police brutality. The neighborhood was a hotbed for conflict between police and residents. According to witnesses, police in Uptown used anti-riot tactics and brute force to squelch even petty crime.

As mother to two sons, Peggy Terry tried in vain to keep her boys from ending up in jail—or worse, murdered. In one incident her thirteen-year-old son was nearly shot in the back as he ran home ten minutes past curfew. When an onlooker asked why they shot at the boy an officer supposedly reasoned, "He had to be running from something." Terry told anyone who would listen what Uptown residents knew all too well: police shot first and asked questions later. She pointed to the bullets lodged in the tree outside her apartment. From the concrete beneath Chicago's el tracks to residents' front doors, shell casings and bullet holes were more common than playgrounds.

Uptown in the Sixties belied the myth of the American Dream, and naturally social service agencies flooded in with programs to uplift and appease the poor. Most preached the benefits of assimilation in northern culture. Some blamed laziness and liquor. By the mid-Sixties there were dozens of agencies vying for "a share of the humanitarian good works."[14] Among the largest were the Montrose Urban Progress Center and the Council of the Southern Mountain. They represented two sides of the same coin. The Urban Progress Center was run by welfare administrators who placated the poor by promising residents a voice in local services, while the Council was run by conservative business owners hoping to protect their investments in the neighborhood. Both businesses and city officials worried social unrest would spread as demographic changes reshaped the region. Between 1950 and 1970 Chicago's white population declined by more than 20 percent, as its Black, Latino, Asian and Native American populations grew cumulatively to 35 percent.[15] By the end of the Sixties even Uptown became a more multiracial neighborhood. But as employed and middle-income whites fled to the suburbs, poor whites and more recent European immigrants had few avenues out of the city. Fearing rebellions, the city's elites saturated the neighborhood with do-gooders hoping to curb "political liberalism and the perceived threat of socialism."[16]

That perceived threat crystallized in 1963 when the North Side received a new group of migrants: student radicals. Even before the Vietnam War draft took direct aim at their generation, progressive student activism surged. No organization captured the youth movement's idealism, outrage and aspirations in greater numbers than Students for a Democratic Society (SDS). The group's early gatherings included an all-star cast of civil rights leaders, academics, influential authors and young intellectuals: Bayard Rustin, James L. Farmer Jr., Michael Harrington, Tom Hayden, Bob Ross and Sharon Jeffrey. Each shaped some of the Sixties' headlining events: from Harrington's detailed exposé on poverty in *The Other America,* to the first pivotal March on Washington, to the televised clash between protestors and police at 1968's Democratic National Convention.

SDS and its leaders were on the verge of making history, though no one could have predicted the group would grow into the most well-known student organization of the 20th century.[17] Their rapid growth, in no small part due to their vision and leadership, also owed a great deal to other movements of the era. In the South, the Student Non-Violent Coordinating Committee (SNCC, pronounced "Snick") was collaborating with CORE and King's Southern Christian Leadership Conference to train northern supporters in community organizing and nonviolent civil disobedience. SNCC grew out of the lunch counter sit-ins of 1960, when four black members of the National Association for the Advancement of Colored People's youth council refused to leave the "whites only" section of a restaurant in Greensboro, North Carolina. SNCC quickly became the leading force for the youth and students in the southern civil rights movement. Thousands of college students from all around the country descended on the southern states, participating in voter registration, freedom schools, sit-ins and direct actions. Within just a few months, more than 50,000 people either participated in or supported the campaigns including almost all of SDS's early members.

Combining the energy of the civil rights movement with a thorough analysis of mid-century ills, SDS outlined a platform for a wholesale transformation of purpose and values in the United States. The nuance and political import of their arguments might have been obscured by the decade's numerous manifestos if their proposal hadn't been so politically insightful. In a document dubbed

The Port Huron Statement, SDS leaders argued that industrial automation, foreign competition and Cold War military spending set in motion fast rising unemployment and the need for perpetual war to spur the economy. As solution, they proposed federal expansion of public sector employment and public housing as remedies for poverty, and called for the complete elimination of racial inequity. To finance social welfare, they called on the U.S. to abandon the arms race. Their analysis combined the wisdom of the Left's old guard and labor movement with the participatory vision and unflinching humanism of the civil rights movement.

While the document became one of the most well known of the decade, SDS struggled during its early years to show its theories had traction beyond the green lawns of the university. For a handful of students, campuses began "to feel like a cage."[18] Despite serious internal conflict over the group's focus, a vocal set of SDSers argued for a community action project. With upwards of thirty million people living in poverty and an estimated one-third facing substandard housing conditions, proponents of the move off campus felt organizing the urban poor provided a logical next step. *Port Huron* opened the door to such a strategy. In it, SDS adopted the principle of participatory democracy as both guiding theory and practical model. This commitment led to notoriously long debates—on everything—but it also laid a footpath toward the kind of broad participation modeled by the civil rights movement. If participatory democracy was praxis, wasn't it necessary to include the people most disenfranchised by the current political system?

In a way, the impulse toward community organizing also resolved longer-term plans for student radicals who only temporarily enjoyed membership in a campus community. Some SDSers never attended college in the first place, and others were dropping out to enlist themselves in the vocation of radicalism fulltime. Among those who completed their degrees, there was campus work during the year and then movement work to do each summer. A Harvard-Radcliffe student named Jean Tepperman took this decision very seriously. Even before she joined SDS, she recognized an important fork in the road ahead of her. The moral example of civil rights workers had curbed any possibility that she'd spend a leisurely summer near her parents' home in Syracuse, New York. She couldn't imagine just standing by.

Tepperman was a shy eighteen-year-old when she traveled with a college friend to the 1963 March on Washington. The two had seats on a bus departing from Manhattan with dozens of seasoned radicals, "old people" to her, mostly in their fifties and sixties. Tepperman looked around at everyone who seemed so comfortable and settled into their roles as lifelong activists. She wanted to be like that, but wasn't sure how to get there. Later, as she stood there listening to Josephine Baker, Bob Dylan, SNCC's John Lewis and finally Rev. King, she was struck by the astounding commitment people had made to the cause. When one of the speakers asked the crowd to take a collective step forward if they would commit their lives to the struggle, Tepperman hesitated. Could she really make that promise? She recalls the color and texture of the pavement under her feet as she paused, then stepped forward. That step ultimately led her to SDS's community organizing project.

Students for a Democratic Society dubbed its new effort the Economic Research Action Project, or ERAP. The group was hopeful, if not naïve, about its capacity to engage the poor masses and redirect both attention and resources toward domestic policy change.[19] Young SDS leaders envisioned, at first, an interracial organization of unemployed workers ready to demand federal economic reforms. One of their chief goals would be shaking up "quiescent populists in the ranks of labor-liberalism."[20] Proponents of the

ERAP project understood that economic resentment provided a powerful catalyst for white reaction, a reaction trade unions and liberals at best ignored and at worst encouraged. As the pace of desegregation proceeded, there was obvious potential for a permanent and deepening animosity between Blacks and whites, not just in the South but also across the nation. In a pamphlet circulated to announce the ERAP program, Tom Hayden and a Swarthmore student named Carl Wittman offered a clear prognosis: "The alternative [to an interracial movement] is more likely to be fascism than freedom."[21] A program for economic changes of tangible benefit to Black, Brown and white workers provided the best tool to unite the working class and win real changes.

The ERAP concept emerged during a pivotal moment for the New Left, as members of a highly organized Black struggle started to wonder aloud whether integrated organizations must wait. Just two days after the March on Washington, Tom Hayden and SDS member Lee Webb met with SNCC's Stokely Carmichael to talk about their strategy for building an interracial movement of the poor. Carmichael expressed enthusiasm for the concept with one caveat: SDS should focus on mobilizing the white community, in particular poor whites, around their own demands. The "organize your own" message reflected the informal beginning of a racial "division of labor" within the Left that eventually marked the tactical difference between the civil rights and Black Power movements.[22]

The strategy addressed two problems facing the Black movement during the mid-sixties. First, SNCC had supported projects to organize poor whites in the South, but found it took energy away from their work.[23] They also had trouble convincing white volunteers to live in white communities where the pace of change was far slower and it was increasingly difficult to keep civil rights workers safe anywhere, let alone outside the fold. Second, the growing presence of white volunteers in Black-led organizations was starting to take a toll. The practice of integrationism inside the movement reflected a tentative hope in the possibility of unified struggle, a transformation of society modeled within the movement itself. Since the number of white volunteers never exceeded 20 percent during the movement's early years, the balance of whites to Blacks remained in check. But by 1963-64 the racial composition of volunteers in the South started to change. Good intentions notwithstanding, Black movement leaders started to wonder if the presence of so many white volunteers was robbing southern Blacks of the movement's more implicit goals: dignity and self-determination.

It was on the porches of Southern Blacks that the chasm between a better world and the immediate one became most apparent. Both Black and white organizers discovered quickly that white supremacy existed as a psychological construct as much as a legal one. Student organizer Carl Davidson, then just twenty years old, recalls one time an eighty-year-old man he registered to vote called him father. SNCC leader Charles Sherrod highlighted one concrete cause for fellow Black activists' frustration over the deference given to white volunteers. Black organizers devoted months, sometimes years, trying to get people to come to a meeting, then watched in frustration as white kids with little experience came in and filled a church hall after one conversation.[24]

There was no denying the fact that an interracial movement required a deliberate attempt to address white anxiety and interest. As Richie Rothstein wrote of the ERAP concept, "What better allies are there than those organized around their own needs and demands, a functional and not merely charitable alliance?"[25] But this was easier said than done. Without sacrificing ERAP's broader goals, the students agreed that white radicals had an important job to accomplish, and they would try. Organizing poor northern whites toward a lasting interracial coalition could address a major gap and provide the surge of SDS volunteers with some meaningful work of their own. Since ERAP's leaders hadn't intended to limit which population of unemployed workers they would reach, they had to rethink locations and make an effort to reach populations of disenfranchised whites.[26] They used unemployment and poverty data, local connections and a bit of guesswork, much of which proved unreliable since urban demographics were changing so rapidly. Chicago, however, was a clear choice.

ERAP opened its flagship office on Chicago's North Side just a few doors away from the city Unemployment Compensation Office. The chapter called itself Jobs or Income Now (JOIN), a name that succinctly focused attention on their demand for full employment or guaranteed wages. SDS member Joe Chabot dropped out of the University of Michigan to become the project's first paid organizer in 1963 and was soon joined by New York organizer Dan Max. The pair planned to focus attention on unemployed young men, figuring their alienation and frustration might easily translate into collective action. Youth across the country, after all, were emerging as clarions for cultural change on and off campus. Among white working-class youth that cultural rebellion had started in the 1950s and usually involved fast cars, street gangs (often more social than criminal), and a hardened distrust of police, government and liberals. As the decade progressed they added "freaks" and hippies to that list. Whether the arriving SDS radicals were friends or foes depended on whom you asked. While not all of North Chicago's white youth fit this mold, it's not hard to imagine how a new organization might struggle to build trust amidst the region's growing list of speculators and do-gooders.

During its first few months JOIN struggled but managed to reach several hundred men, some of whom took on leadership roles.[27] They established a grievance committee to hear individual problems and solved them through collective action. When one man had his unemployment check withheld from him, an entire delegation went to the unemployment office to demand it. Still, joblessness failed to rouse mass interest. For one, the promise of government-guaranteed employment evoked suspicion among the disenchanted young men Chabot and Max talked to. They were, after all, not used to seeing anyone around them achieve the security of a steady job and the prospect of government job programs seemed dicey. On the flipside, many older white workers still had faith that the system would eventually work in their favor. Even if they doubted this, the shame of being out of work inhibited many men from organizing in full public view. Most showed up to JOIN once and never came back.

The focus on federal job guarantees also offered few opportunities for women in the community. While poor women were no strangers to paid labor, they often worked domestic and temporary service jobs for which there was no guarantee of state benefits or job security in the first place. And more importantly, joblessness hadn't reached the staggering levels SDS predicted for the early part of the decade, especially among white workers who were faring far better than workers of color—even if they didn't know it.

Joe Chabot's patience for immersion organizing wore thin. Reporting back to SDS, he wrote, "Just to understand the slang would be a matter of probably six months. If I try to be accepted by some gang, it would probably be a process involving at least a year, and needless to say I don't have time for any such luxuries."[28] A year into the ERAP experiment Chabot left Chicago deciding that the task of organizing poor whites beyond their immediate needs was an impossible dream. Intentional or not, his decision reflected the student Left's struggle with its own identity and a failure to define short- and long-term successes for its organizing experiments. Faced with the failure of a liberal administration to pay more than lip service to civil rights and the sixfold increase of troops in Vietnam, the movement for peace and justice seemed poised for rapid growth or major setbacks. No one knew which yet. Whether in meetings or more subtly, Chabot and others questioned whether the cycle of poverty and entrenched racism created too great an undertow for any meaningful organization of the white poor in that moment.

Fortunately not everyone shared Chabot's sentiments. The volunteers Chabot left behind refocused their efforts, coming back to the heart of participatory politics. Could middle-class organizers build a movement of the poor without believing in the people they were organizing? The answer was, unquestionably, no. Would it take time to gain people's trust? Yes, but it was possible. No one believed this more than ERAP's national coordinator Rennie Davis who moved to Chicago to head the chapter. Under Davis ERAP had become a hub of constant activity and Davis earned a reputation as one of SDS's most tireless leaders. His enthusiasm for expanding the movement's grassroots base proved infectious and soon dozens more organizers joined the community projects. In Chicago, organizers realized that fulfilling the potential of their project required a shift in both location and strategy. In early 1964, JOIN moved its office to Uptown and dropped the single-issue focus on unemployment. The students moved in too, sharing railroad flats in Uptown's neglected buildings. Over the next several years some of the Sixties' more infamous radicals spent time in Uptown, including actor Harry Belafonte who paid the group a visit in Spring 1965. More importantly the organization gave dozens of members a chance to cut their political teeth.

Out in California student Mike James heard good things about the effort to organize white southerners in Chicago, but he was skeptical too. The year before, James grabbed a summer opportunity working for an anthropologist studying white migration from Appalachia. James moved into a one-room apartment in the heart of Uptown and spent the next few months hanging out on street corners and front stoops. With guitar in hand, he learned some country tunes—a badge of entry to the neighborhood—while learning to roll cigarettes and cook a mean southern biscuit. Mike James was just one of Uptown's newcomers who saw a deep appreciation of local culture as a hallmark of good organizing.

James was planning to join one of the ERAP projects once he graduated, but he wasn't totally sold on returning to Chicago. There were projects in Newark, Cleveland, Baltimore and elsewhere, though most were located in predominately poor Black neighborhoods. At a benefit concert in San Francisco, James casually mentioned to Stokely Carmichael that he would either end up with Tom Hayden in Newark or with Rennie Davis in Uptown. Carmichael gave consistent advice. "Work with white people," he said. Given James's experience in Uptown the prior year, this made sense. He'd seen the conditions there and made a few friends. After college graduation, he drove east.

. . . .

JOIN's first notable success came from really listening to poor whites' concerns and turning them into actionable projects. Organizers spent weeks surveying Uptown residents about priorities. Confronting intrusive welfare agencies and greedy landlords rose to the top of agenda, along with poor housing conditions, day care and the need for community parks. This strategy drew criticism within SDS. Critics derided the new approach as "GROIN," a snide acronym for "Garbage Removal or Income Now." They argued that JOIN's original demand of "full employment" was being watered down by narrow local concerns disconnected from a national program.[29] Others worried this approach, coupled with JOIN's base in a white community, would go the path of Saul Alinsky's Back-of-the-Yards Neighborhood Council, which centered on community decision-making but steadfastly avoided issues of integration and civil rights.

A major force in progressive Chicago, Saul Alinsky was widely regarded as the godfather of community organizing. In 1939 he founded the Back-of-the-Yards Neighborhood Council (BYNC), so named for its location behind the former Union Stock Yard and meatpacking plants. He spent the next several decades building his archetype for a progressive populism in the neighborhood author Upton Sinclair had branded "The Jungle" in his 1906 novel.[30] Alinsky believed in people's fundamental decency and understood their alienation from politics as a symptom of machine politics, not inherent laziness. This was something New Leftists agreed with, but the Back-of-the-Yards version of participatory politics put process ahead of outcomes, even if that process yielded racist and reactionary results. In the late 1950s, Alinsky balked when asked to take a firm stand around integration. Ever cautious, he proposed a quota system to slowly integrate Blacks into white neighborhoods and circumvent violence. This proposal never gained traction, but Alinsky's decidedly non-ideological style clearly left wide gaps when it came to addressing racism in white communities.

By the mid-Sixties this approach became a dividing line between Alinsky's projects and younger radicals. Many saw Alinsky's belief in democratic reform as a problem. By 1964 members of the New Left began to view democratic politics and simple "American Dream" patriotism as an endorsement of a corrupt system that required radical reinvention rather than reform. The young radicals accused Alinsky of being stuck in the past, failing to confront racial discrimination among whites. Alinsky, meanwhile, viewed many in the New Left as hopelessly idealistic and out of touch with the desires of people whose neighborhoods they occupied. Adding to the generational divide, the New Left's beginning flirtations with communism and Third World Marxism angered Alinsky who had been critical of Stalinism for decades, not just ideologically but also for its corrosive and regimenting grip on the United States Left.[31]

In JOIN's early days labor leader Ralph Helstein brought the student leaders to meet Alinsky. The intergenerational confab was a disaster, ending with Alinsky harshly ridiculing the students for their criticism of the consumerist aspirations of everyday people.[32] Both sides had a point. JOIN would eventually confront this culture clash when neighborhood leaders started to challenge SDS control within the organization, but for the time being JOIN set out to prove that poor and working-class whites could jointly address poverty and racism. An alliance with Alinsky was out of the question, despite the respect most had for his other successes. Organizers did establish partnerships with Alinsky-affiliated projects, though, most notably Helstein's United Packinghouse Workers and The Woodlawn Organization, one of Chicago's leading Black community groups.

· ·

During JOIN's first few months in Uptown, a few progressive residents helped the neighborhood's newcomers gain a foothold. Mary Hockenberry raised all six of her children in Uptown. She'd never been directly involved in politics but sympathized with progressives ever since Eleanor Roosevelt spoke up for civil rights and women workers in the 1930s and 1940s. It helped that SDS members brought incredible knowledge to their efforts. This was clear from the first day Mary Hockenberry met Rennie Davis at the welfare office. Davis asked her if she knew her family was entitled to medical care along with a welfare check. She didn't, of course, since few recipients got this kind of helpful information from their caseworkers. When Davis asked if she wanted to do something about it, Mary Hockenberry felt valued, relieved and newly hopeful. Within two weeks she was helping plan meetings and knocking on her neighbors' doors with Davis and other staff members. Hockenberry literally opened those doors for JOIN. The year of state college she'd attended as a teenager made her a good bridge between Uptown's residents and SDS activists. She understood the students' rhetoric well enough to translate it for neighborhood people, and her neighbors trusted her enough to check out at least one meeting.

Along with other emerging leaders, she helped JOIN set itself apart as a real force for change in a neighborhood. People were fed up, but suspicious of newcomers promising solutions. Joining the mix of existing agencies pacifying needy migrants in Uptown, President Lyndon Johnson had just declared an all-out "War on Poverty." The war came with an onslaught of new government services like Job Corps, Head Start, and Volunteers in Service to America.[33] Under the Economic Opportunity Act of 1964, Johnson promised a participatory role for poor people in decision-making through local Community Action Centers—exactly what SDS demanded in Port Huron. Unfortunately service agencies usually confined this input to informal, non-binding dialogue. In Chicago politicians channeled these funds into existing agencies leaving the bulk of decision-making in the hands of administrators and social workers, not community representatives.

This came as no surprise to most Uptown residents. Chicago was ruled by the iron fist of six-term Mayor Richard J. Daley—whose intense political machine was efficient and everywhere. Democratizing city services wasn't exactly his style. The elder Daley created a legacy of gerrymandered school districts, segregated housing, and separate and completely unequal access to public resources. Few Chicagoans missed the message about Daley's tyranny. His grip extended into the ballot box, too. In neighborhood after neighborhood, precinct captains doled out patronage and failure to support Daley or his anointed candidates could cost a resident "a job, a needed license, intense inspection by city building inspectors, or other municipal punishment."[34] Precinct captains had a foolproof method of knowing how a citizen had voted: They, or a lackey, accompanied citizens to the polls. In one of the worst and most public incidents, the West Side's first Black alderman, Ben Lewis, was shot execution style after showing political independence from Daley on issues like housing policy, garbage collection and school segregation.

Given the fact that the federal government was intensifying poverty by destroying thousands of homes through urban renewal programs, Uptown residents had long known "The Great Society" was a charade. So, in 1965, when JOIN launched a "community school" including a class on the city's corrupt political ecology, members filed in, albeit cautiously. Among them, Mary Hockenberry and a very hesitant new member: Peggy Terry.

....

Peggy Terry had only come to a few JOIN meetings. As her friend Monroe Sharp pointed out, she still had a great deal to learn about herself and her own people before she could hope to organize anyone else. She was skeptical until JOIN's community school cut through her apprehension. Run by gifted educator Richie Rothstein, the community school covered the gamut of local and national issues, from urban renewal to the Vietnam War. More importantly it revealed the breadth of JOIN's analysis (and SDS influence) in connecting Uptown's problems to the forces driving national and foreign policy. Terry was impressed. The JOIN Community School put theory and words to the causes she cared about: the industrial automation that hurt the southern economy and city practices that created de facto segregation. Rothstein's class on Chicago's political corruption cemented her decision to get more involved. Terry had her own experience being roughed up by Daley's minions. She was once attacked on a street corner while conducting voter turnout for a candidate who hadn't received Daley's endorsement. Two men jumped out of a car, stole all of her flyers and knocked her to the ground. If JOIN was willing to stand up to Daley and address both racism and poor people's concerns, she might just stick around.

Weeks later Terry found herself in a car with Rennie Davis on the way to a large rally on the South Side. Though she doesn't remember what the rally was for, she distinctly recalls the moment Davis told her she'd be the one taking the stage. Terry protested. There was no way. She'd never spoken in front of so many people before. In her prior political work she remained comfortably in the background. What did she know about public speaking? Davis retorted, "What the hell do you mean you can't? You do it every day." Just as she recalled Sharp "dragging" her to JOIN, she insisted Davis "shoved" her up on stage. It didn't matter what she said or whether she said it right. What she remembers is how she felt afterwards: Like people valued what she had to say and folks on the South Side seemed to understand that they had some important things in common. She finally understood what it meant to speak from her own experience. It was the first time she publicly claimed her southern heritage and talked about her struggles with poverty.

After that Terry found herself in a flurry of work at JOIN. She and other new members—Little Dovie Thurman along with her aunt Big Dovie Coleman, Mary Hockenberry and a woman named

Virginia Bowers—had each taken up leadership roles. When SDS organizers asked them to create the agendas for weekly meetings and write demands for a protest at the welfare office, none of the women knew where to start. Despite her experience at CORE, Terry felt frustrated around some SDS leaders who seemed to take much for granted. Education made them more comfortable discussing history and theory, as well as writing things that would be shared in public. Terry and the other women became fast friends by helping each other figure out what the "SDS kids," as they called them, were talking about and openly discussing their own problems.

One of those problems was the mistreatment many of them faced at the welfare office. So when JOIN started a welfare committee, the five women formed its backbone. Most recipients had no idea they were entitled to reliable payments, basic household items and some amount of medical care. Committee members understood most caseworkers were simply overworked, not malicious. But well intentioned or not, the system was dehumanizing. The Montrose Urban Progress Center in Uptown operated a particularly invasive war on poverty program. Recipients were made to meet unreasonable requirements, they routinely had their homes inspected, and were denied important information and threatened with losing their aid or their children if they didn't comply. One member received a letter demanding she immediately go back to school or lose her benefits. She had attended three years of high school and just finished two years of night school. The letter was a mistake, but her caseworker told her there was nothing she could do about it. It didn't matter that she had no money for childcare or transportation. JOIN helped her appeal the requirement and the demand was withdrawn.

Cases like these helped members build their political confidence

one small victory at a time. When necessary, the welfare committee, along with JOIN staff, marched right into the welfare office
with their demands. During one march Rennie Davis announced
they wouldn't be leaving unless caseworkers agreed to log grievances from each recipient. Knowing they needed more than the
caseworkers' word to follow through, the welfare committee organized another march soon after. This time they commandeered the
caseworkers' welfare policy books. "The policies were hidden from
the public," Hockenberry recalls. "So we walked out with about
twenty books, and we danced and sang in the street." Soon after,
Terry began writing a regular column on welfare rights in JOIN's
newsletter and welfare committee members authored a 10-point
Welfare Bill of Rights demanding, among other things, a right to
write the rules of welfare dispensation, privacy, an end to threats
against their children, and the right to organize without fear their
aid would be revoked.

A few months later JOIN members picketed at the welfare office
demanding protections for day laborers as well. Terry considered
this one of the "most far reaching and important" actions because
they actually won a day laborer center in the Montrose Urban Progress Center. In contrast to predatory labor placement agencies like
Manpower that took half of workers' pay, the welfare committee organized for months to convince Montrose not to charge a fee at all.
Agencies like Manpower were also in the habit of yanking workers
just before they logged enough time to qualify for a job site's union.
The Montrose day labor program was one of the few times poor
residents ended up having a say in how city and federal dollars were
spent. The campaign helped expand the welfare committee, which
boasted dozens of active members and gave each of its founding
members a sense of leadership and purpose.

Coming into her own confidence, Terry began helping other poor whites wrestle with the fear of losing what little they had. For folks in Uptown, this was very, very little. Politicians stoked poor whites' fears that any gains for people of color would come at the greatest loss to them. The Cold War added even greater trepidation that social change meant austerity and sacrifice. Terry brought the sophistication to navigate these anxieties. For many of her neighbors she was the first person in the movement they could trust. At the time the Left was notorious for its esoteric debates about what people should be willing to give up for the revolution. Terry knew these arguments turned people off and, like Hockenberry, she understood her role as a bridge between the sometimes-alienating rhetoric and real values of the Left.

Conversations like these made all the difference. Terry spent hours in her kitchen just talking to people—a tactic far more effective in bringing poor people into the movement than any SDS manifesto. One evening Terry went to visit neighbors who had been around JOIN but reluctant to get involved. The Lalys lived in a tiny Quonset hut with salvaged furniture, including a very treasured teapot that someone passed down to them. Mrs. Laly confessed her reluctance about coming to meetings. She had heard people should be willing to give up their teapot if the people's army needed the scrap. Terry patiently listened before replying, "No dear, you don't have to give up your teapot. This isn't about you giving things up, it is about making more so everyone can live in dignity." With honesty and humility, Terry triumphed at a politics of the kitchen table at a time when the middle-class Left's messages failed miserably with most poor whites.

JOIN's success in changing individual attitudes was, of course, relative. Poor whites in Uptown experienced a tenuous security as insiders and outsiders in the United States. For Appalachian migrants, in particular, their outsider status was reinforced by dire poverty and harsh media stereotypes that trickled down to job sites, welfare offices and schools. A good number of Uptown's white poor succumbed to the double-edged sword of white supremacy, understanding themselves as more deserving than Blacks and Latinos, but also as victims—of police, bosses, politicians, the draft and, most divisively, of the economic promise civil rights seemed to offer communities of color. More than one JOIN member came into the organization railing against uppity Blacks who were looking for a free lunch, then showed signs of changing attitudes before ultimately retreating back to the safety of white superiority. There were notable exceptions, though, as dozens of residents made JOIN their political home and with it embraced coalition politics.

For many whites, the group provided their first direct exposure to Black and Latino experience. For Virginia Bowers, an active member of the welfare committee, Chicago had been the first place she ever saw Blacks and whites living and working together. "I didn't know what prejudice was," she recollected. As some of the few Blacks to live in Uptown, Dovie Coleman and her niece Dovie Thurman had a big influence on everyone at JOIN. Raised in the Pruitt-Igoe Projects in St. Louis, Thurman moved to Chicago when she was eighteen while her husband was in Vietnam. Like the poor white Appalachians who came to Uptown to live with extended family (someone knew someone who lived there), Little Dovie came to live with her aunt.

The Dovies, as they were known, provided dozens of their neighbors with their first chance to meet, let alone befriend, a Black person. For better or worse, these personal relationships often went the furthest in changing people's minds. One of the young guys from the neighborhood, eighteen-year-old Bobby Joe Wright, recalled how the Dovies and his new friendship with local Black youth cemented his growing repulsion at racial violence. "I started findin out all these things about black people bein' really fucked over for so many years, you know, and I also started findin' out about my own people bein' fucked over as much as they was, and like it changed my whole view about things."[35] The Dovies were highly respected among JOIN's members, both young and old, and it was their leadership in the welfare committee that turned it into one of the group's most lasting and fully community-led projects.

....

Despite this headway, some SDS leaders were questioning the success and sustainability of projects like JOIN. By 1965 the Vietnam War pulled organizers' attention to the national arena and created new challenges in working-class communities. In just two short years draft calls quadrupled, pulling nearly half a million young men, mostly from low-income families, into the fray. SDS played a defining role in organizing the anti-war movement's mass mobilizations and campus actions, which grew in frequency and scale, eventually attracting hundreds of thousands of people. Split in too many directions, JOIN's parent program, ERAP, dissolved in the lead up to those first anti-war demonstrations. According to SDS's Tom Hayden the political potential of pro-active community organizing was doomed by escalation of war in Vietnam. "Once again the government met an internal crisis by starting an external crisis," Hayden observed.

Even without the anti-war effort, coordinating a national network of local projects proved challenging. In each city, local priorities were shifting constantly. Organizers tried to balance people's needs with shorter, winnable campaigns. But even those proved challenging. Some student organizers reported they felt "demoralized" in their attempts to organize the poor. Others were more blunt. They deemed ERAP a failure. Failure depended on how groups measured their goals, though. Richie Rothstein, who had spent two years at JOIN, authored a thoughtful examination of ERAP's limits. In creating the project, he wrote, "SDS people were convinced that their movement must be one that could end racist exploitation and imperialism, collectivize economic decision making, and democratize and decentralize every political, economic, and social institution in America."[36] Two years into the experiment, the projects had clearly failed to fulfill expectations on this scale. Yet they had started to produce important results, particularly in Chicago where JOIN built lasting alliances with labor—United Packinghouse Workers and the Independent Union of Public Aid Employees—as well as local Black and Latino community groups.

If the tumultuous Sixties proved anything it was that no single issue could feed the radicalism sweeping the country. While many Chicago activists stayed on, JOIN faced a crisis of purpose and undeniable opportunity after ERAP dissolved. The organization would continue and expand. In Uptown it wasn't enough to focus on welfare or even on poor women. Jobs, housing, police violence, racial tensions and the escalating war in Vietnam all begged equal attention. Out of necessity, political optimism and some degree of confusion about direction, JOIN tried to move on all fronts.

Where the welfare committee had been the group's center, JOIN's housing rights campaigns soon provided a crosscurrent connecting people across the city. JOIN evolved into a "union in the community," taking residents as its rank-and-file the same way a union would workers, and forming a steering committee of resident-leaders to govern the organization and plan actions. This idea translated well in a city long familiar with union activism and the tactic of the strike. Instead of withholding labor, organizers encouraged tenants to organize each building and collectively withhold rent monies when landlords failed to address housing violations. JOIN's first rent strike in April 1966 resulted in an historic collective bargaining agreement with notorious landlord Richard Gutman. Twelve of the fifteen tenants in the Gutman building were JOIN members, including Mary Hockenberry. After picketing for a week, tenants won a contract recognizing the union as the collective bargaining agent for the building. The agreement outlined a detailed grievance process and ordered Gutman to make more than a dozen immediate repairs. The contract was the first of its kind in the city's history.[37]

Two subsequent strikes also resulted in bargaining contracts. When landlords failed to uphold the agreement, JOIN supported tenants to take over the buildings. The tactic spread like fire as more tenants began organizing their own strikes. Some strikes ended poorly when landlords retaliated or, worse, when the person in charge of collecting tenant money to make their own improvements decided to take off with the cash. Cheated residents had little recourse for tracking the person down and there was only so much JOIN could do to hold each landlord to task. Still, those who participated in the Uptown rent strikes consider them some of JOIN's biggest successes because they so effectively built a sense of power for poor residents. Dozens of people came to see JOIN as *their* organization—building by building, block by block.

JOIN also made headway building multiracial solidarity through its housing campaigns. An estimated fifteen million people nationwide lived in deteriorating, overcrowded or undersupplied housing.[38] In Chicago these conditions created a public health crisis for the poor. Infant mortality, disease, lead poisoning and sanitation all presented urgent problems for Uptown residents, just as they did for surrounding communities of color. Because the landlords JOIN confronted often owned buildings across the city, there was clear cause to build coalitions that transcended neighborhood and racial divides. Implicit in JOIN's mission was its aim to prove that poor whites could become partners in class-based coalition with communities of color. By working with the Latin American Defense Organization, The Woodlawn Organization on the city's South Side and Kenwood-Oakland Community Organization, JOIN was able to coordinate bigger rent strikes demanding building improvements from slumlords. The groups often crossed town to support one another and, when urban renewal turned their neighborhoods into a game of dominoes, they were better positioned to jointly assert a voice for the poor.

Unlike community organizations reluctant to push urban whites on the race question, JOIN's organizers pressed the point at every opportunity. The group even mobilized members to support Rev. Martin Luther King Jr.'s campaign to desegregate housing in Chicago in the summer of 1966. The Chicago Freedom Movement marked the most ambitious civil rights campaign above the Mason-Dixon and may have been the first time since the unemployed workers' movements of the Thirties when a large section of a city's Black community focused its political attention on housing inequalities. Calling Chicago "the most segregated city in the North," King saw Chicago as the best place to call the Democratic Party to task for its inaction around racial discrimination. JOIN agreed. Peggy Terry, the Dovies, Jean Tepperman and other members marched in almost every one of the Open Housing Marches beginning July 10 when sixty thousand people marched to City Hall.[39]

Just over two weeks later, civil rights protestors marched through the all-white area of Gage Park to draw attention to real estate brokers' pattern of housing discrimination. A crowd of whites attacked the marchers in a hail of bricks, bottles and projectiles. Rather than back down, they held a second march in Marquette Park, just to the southwest. There, King was hit in the head with a rock thrown from among the jeering white crowd. Again, they pressed on. A third march was announced for late August to the suburb of Cicero, Illinois, notorious for its racial violence. After a closed-door meeting with Mayor Daley, King called off the march. Suspicious of King's compromise, local organizers carried on the Cicero march anyway. Peggy Terry, the Dovies and other Uptown organizers joined three hundred marchers who faced another angry white mob. Even though law enforcement officers outnumbered protesters ten to one, white reactionaries again attacked marchers at will. This time it was Big Dovie who was hit in the head with a brick. As Rev. King said, Cicero was indeed "the Selma of the North."[40]

While JOIN failed to mobilize more than two dozen or so supporters for the housing marches, those who did participate found a great deal of validation in the Chicago Freedom Movement's focus on local reforms and interracial coalition. For JOIN, the housing marches had been a chance to highlight alliances with Black and Latino groups and draw attention to the roots of reactionary white violence. JOIN soon began using its mimeographed newsletter to carry stories about the Black Power Movement, the war's impact at home, liberation movements in the Third World and the anti-colonial struggle in Ireland.

Even more effective than the newsletter or community school was JOIN's community theater, which involved just about everyone in the organization at some point. Through drama, JOIN members sharpened their analysis of sociopolitical problems and brought humor and flair to a community hard hit by the draft and urban renewal. Theater student Melody James came to Chicago in 1966 to visit her brother Mike. During her visit she spent hours at the JOIN office debating theories of change with SDS leaders. "Does social revolution have to be violent?" she asked of Rennie Davis. He never answered the question but asked one back: Would she move to Chicago to help build a popular theater project? Maybe, there, Uptown residents could wrestle with those questions together. Melody agreed. She found a job at the Montrose Urban Progress Center, a target of JOIN criticism but also one of the few ways organizers could get paid for political work. Little Dovie Thurman joined Melody as the project's co-director. Mary Hockenberry's daughter joined in and soon even neighborhood "tough guys" became regulars on stage. While some JOIN organizers thought the project would pull members away from "real" organizing, the theater built such momentum that it was eventually accepted as one of the group's most potent tools for political education.

Celebrating working-class culture also proved central for JOIN's growth. Over time JOIN evolved its own blend of southern, city-born and student customs. People sang protest songs and southern spirituals alongside classic country tunes. Favorites included Merle Haggard, Pete Seeger, Johnny Cash, Woody Guthrie, Phil Ochs and, of course, Bob Dylan. Dylan's "Only a Pawn in Their Game" about the murder of Medgar Evers pretty much summed up people's frustration about their social status and politicians' self-interested lip service to civil rights. Rennie Davis adapted the lyrics of the song "Good Old Mountain Dew" to reflect the hard times most residents faced in the North while paying homage to the trade unionism people took pride in from back home. The song became a kind of anthem for JOIN members and eventually inspired the name of JOIN's tabloid newspaper, *The Firing Line,* with Peggy Terry as its editor.[41]

The radical renaissance in Uptown wasn't limited to meetings and marches either. A culture of independence was emerging among Uptown's longtime residents. For all of JOIN's participatory politics many longtime residents started to feel SDS organizers were still generally calling the shots. Some activists in JOIN, like the New Left overall, had yet to fully understand the impact of classism within the movement and in their own work. In JOIN, power struggles bubbled up over who got paid staff positions, how decisions were made and where funds got spent. Most Uptown residents felt SDS volunteers and students in JOIN, even new arrivals, dominated decision-making and the organization's public profile. Residents also sensed some SDS activists' impatience with the pace of change in their community, and ultimately there was no overlooking the obvious contradiction that most middle-class organizers could leave whenever they wanted. In trying to build an interracial movement of the poor, many SDS leaders lacked a realistic plan for dealing with their own class privilege and the power imbalances it created.

Class tensions were only exacerbated by the fact that women, both longtime residents and student volunteers, started to have discussions about how they were treated by men in the organization. As early as 1964, JOIN women produced flyers calling attention to the treatment of women in meetings and the devaluing of welfare rights work. According to organizer Marilyn Katz, JOIN women were the canaries in the coalmine whether the issue was male dominance inside the organization, unemployment, substandard housing or the police violence impacting Uptown's sons. Women lacked access to birth control, legal abortions, childcare and health care. Naturally, women in JOIN talked about their troubles, but they soon created a women's group that met formally. Within JOIN and the community, this created conflicts as women's organizing threatened male control. Women students bore the brunt of the criticism and some men accused them of dividing the organization or pushing "college bullshit."

While young men from Uptown were generally the most vocal about this, their concerns weren't solely about women's liberation.

Many were rightfully "peeved with the way the students were running JOIN." In July 1966 a group of them decided to carve out a space with some autonomy. Naming themselves the Goodfellows, the youth group was a cross between a street gang and a loose-knit radical social club. Founded by Jimmy Curry, the group drew in Peggy Terry's son Doug Youngblood, Bobby Joe Wright and a talented local leader named Junebug Boykin, and the young men opened up a band hall and local youth hangout. They also made their political mission known: They intended to unite local gangs by turning street youths' attention toward the "real enemy." At a general level, this meant corrupt politicians, the war and capitalism, but the Chicago cops made for a more tangible and immediate target.

Jimmy Curry was a lifelong resident of Uptown who spent most of his teenage years in conflict with the police over loitering, curfew violations and just about any other infraction they could find. "The police just came here and beat people up for fun. Beat us up just as bad as the Blacks," says Curry. Jimmy Curry had a well-deserved reputation as the "toughest guy in Uptown," a fact that landed him in jail on more than once occasion. When he was seventeen, he was walking his girlfriend home when two police officers stopped the couple for being out after curfew. After one of the officers insulted his girlfriend, Curry "picked up a bottle and whacked him right in between the eyes." His partner responded, "You're dead," and Curry took off running. Police chased him into a dead-end ally behind an apartment building. Standing there with nowhere else to run Curry heard the officer's gun click. Suddenly, the building's landlord came out the back door. The police must have weighed the complication of having a witness, because they took Curry to jail instead.

Most young men in Uptown had been hassled by the cops, and so the Goodfellows became JOIN's de facto anti-police brutality committee, drawing support from local leaders Ralph Thurman,

Bob Lawson and Nanci Hollander who'd already started a police watch. One night the three JOIN activists came across police beating a teenage kid. Police confronted the nineteen-year-old and his mother as the two walked to the back of their apartment building to put away his bike. Shortly thereafter, officers entered the family's apartment to "see who was there." When the teenager gave the police some attitude, he was removed from the apartment, pushed down the outside stairs, beaten and arrested. His mother was also hit by the police. The JOIN activists on the scene wrote down badge numbers and took photos. Lawson was arrested. After that, the youth's mother got involved with JOIN and activists started a regular police watch. Armed with cameras and notebooks, they canvassed the neighborhood and collected affidavits from residents.

In many ways what happened in Uptown was nothing compared to the level of brutality in Black and Latino communities. As the Goodfellows sat down with local gangs to talk about unity, they heard story after story about brutal police violence in other poor neighborhoods. In June 1966 police shot and killed a young Puerto Rican named Cruz Arcelis, setting off the Division Street Riots in Humboldt Park, west of Uptown. Throughout the Sixties riots erupted as a particularly potent expression of urban outrage and desperation. JOIN's idea for its police watch was even borrowed from Black activists in Los Angeles who launched one after the 1965 Watts Riots that left thirty-four dead. The lore of urban unrest, particularly among Black communities, often stoked white anxiety about racial tensions, even though the worst damage from the uprisings occurred within communities of color. Media coverage did little to help. By dubbing uprisings "race riots," mainstream media made incidents sound unprovoked. While some seemed to spring from "nowhere," the media spin obscured people's demands for an end to slum conditions, police brutality and racial discrimination. JOIN's Bob Lawson and Mike James attempted to reframe the uprisings as examples of class struggle in an article for JOIN's newsletter, as did Peggy Terry who penned her own piece. But the message didn't carry as far as they hoped.[42] The Goodfellows took a different approach: They decided to launch a kind of street corner education project, reaching young men on the streets, in bars and in local pool halls.

By August 1966 JOIN and the Goodfellows came up with a way to focus people's outrage and bring them together. A march on the local Summerdale police station would draw Black, Puerto Rican and white youth, along with mothers, fathers, local religious leaders and all of JOIN. Jimmy Curry helped activists Ralph Thurman and Bob Lawson drum up support by talking to guys on street corners and reaching people coming out of neighborhood bars. They figured out which guys were most influential on each block and invited them to a sit down. Each agreed to tell their crew.

The protest demanded an end to police brutality, a citizen review board to address complaints and the removal of officer Sam Joseph, a particularly brutal cop. News reports announcing plans for the march—in supposed editorial oversight—erroneously conflated their message with that of angry white mobs in Gage Park protesting Dr. King's Open Housing Marches that summer. According to the *Chicago Sun-Times*, the march to the Summerdale police station was to be a protest against police mistreatment of white counter-protestors who had hurled bricks at civil rights marchers.

The Goodfellows message, while lost in the city press, was not lost on neighborhood residents who watched in horror as police violence and intimidation increased in the days before and after the march. It represented a different flavor of business as usual for the Chicago police, but something had to give. Like Terry's epiphanous moment watching Rev. King attacked outside a Montgomery jail, some of the young guys in the neighborhood began to see white racial violence and police brutality as mirrors of the same systemic problems. While police intimidated many residents not to attend the march, nearly three hundred people gathered at the JOIN office for the Summerdale march. The moral imperative of stopping police harassment had united families from different parts of town, rival gangs, young and old. Young men with nicely greased pompadours took the lead greeting neighborhood mothers, student activists and local youth, gathered together to demand "community control of the police."

The day also marked a turning point for internal tensions between SDS organizers and Uptown's longtime residents. In the hours before the march, several students sat around a table at a local bar discussing whether the community members were aware of the danger they were walking into. Goodfellows members, along with Peggy Terry and other local JOIN leaders, were done being underestimated. Not only had they already seen warning signs in the days before the march, they were fully aware that political organizing had consequences. Summing up the sentiment, Terry retorted, "Who knows better what the Summerdale cops will do to you than the people they been killing." The Goodfellows made the call to start the march without the students. "We just marched off and left them discussing whether they should tell us we might get killed," Terry said.

Despite the internal fissures widening within JOIN, all sides had been right about the threat that came with their more confrontational organizing. The expansion of their work into other neighborhoods and the Summerdale march focused police attention on the organization with dire consequences. Two weeks later police raided JOIN's North Sheridan office, along with the office of United People, a local organization that supported the march. Organizer Pat Sturgis walked into JOIN's office in the middle of the raid. Theater coordinator Melody James was on her knees with a cop holding a gun to her head. The office was destroyed. Police confiscated letters, files and newspapers. Before they left they arrested James, Richie Rothstein and Mickey Birger for drug possession. Across town at United People, police arrested Rev. George Morey, a Presbyterian minister, and local resident Jack Hollenbeck on similar charges. According to JOIN, police planted the drugs, including various narcotics, needles and syringes. Police turned the allegedly "anti-government" literature over to federal authorities. Everyone affiliated with the organization was "gripped with a paranoia," according to Sturgis, who had only recently arrived and felt some people held him suspect.

Two days later police shot and killed Uptown resident Ronnie Williams, brother of Goodfellow Kenny Williams, who was running from the cops after a fight with his brother. After shooting him several times, witnesses reported "an officer put a bullet in his head point-blank." As witnesses rushed up, one demanded an explanation. The officer responded, "Just another dead hillbilly." A half-dozen witnesses said Ronnie never fired at the cops. At the funeral home, the undertaker told JOIN organizer Nanci Hollander he found four bullet wounds: one in the arm, two in the back, and one in the head.[43]

This was only a small taste of what would come as Mayor Daley's contempt for New Left activists mixed with the FBI's push to dismantle dissent in the United States. Retaliation after the Summerdale march foreshadowed an all-out war on the Left from all levels of law enforcement. In fact, at least one informant was already hovering around JOIN and the Goodfellows. Raised in Uptown, Thomas Edward Mosher received a scholarship to attend Stanford University in 1962 but dropped out to join the civil rights movement in Mississippi. Mosher claimed he genuinely sympathized with the New Left's goals until later in the Sixties, but no one knows for sure exactly when he started spying on his former friends. Most JOIN activists remember Mosher as an extremely intelligent, charming and destructive individual. According to JOIN organizer Steve Goldsmith, Mosher was never up front about having gone to college, passing himself off instead as a regular "neighborhood guy" and frequently starting fights. Regardless of the chain of events, it's clear Mosher kept his ties to JOIN and the New Left until he testified about his activities before the Senate Internal Security Subcommittee in 1971, just as the extent of the government's program to discredit the Left was being uncovered.[44] In 1967 only one thing was clear: external forces were wreaking havoc on the movement. Few foresaw how much worse things would get.

....

Still reeling from the office raid and growing surveillance around their activities, organizers in Uptown were facing an uphill struggle. Events in the national arena only steepened the grade. Anti-war efforts had drawn the student movement's attention away from local projects, government crackdowns on radicals increased and civil rights organizations were facing tough internal questions. By 1966, members of the highly organized civil rights movement began more formally insisting white activists leave civil rights groups like SNCC and "organize their own." The racial division of labor Carmichael had suggested to ERAP's founders was no longer a suggestion, but an instruction.

The division of radical labor evoked controversy on all sides. Black civil rights leaders debated the costs and benefits of a racially integrated movement, with Rev. King standing staunchly opposed to the separation and Carmichael adamantly for it. It played out as a clash between old and young, calling into question whether the movement should maintain nonviolence and integration or claim a right to self-defense and self-reliance. As King later wrote, "I should have known that in an atmosphere where false promises are daily realities, where deferred dreams are nightly facts, where acts of unpunished violence toward Negroes are a way of life, nonviolence would eventually be seriously questioned."[45] For him, abandoning nonviolence marked a fatal misstep for the cause. For Black leaders on the other side of the debate, the question was not whether to endorse violence; it was whether Blacks could build any meaningful political and economic power without first defining their own needs and demands. Everyone agreed that uprooting racism in the U.S. required white communities to confront its source—in the minds, hearts and establishments of white America. This was an especially difficult new directive for white activists who had spent the better part of the Sixties working in integrated organizations like SNCC. Many felt the decision was wrong; others called out the ways gender and male dominance informed these internal power struggles.[46]

For JOIN's Peggy Terry, now fully aware of what Monroe Sharp meant when he dragged her to JOIN, the strategic separation made sense. Peggy Terry's experience at JOIN gave her a rare vantage point. She knew and respected King, but she easily related to the idea that Blacks weren't given the respect they deserved in integrated organizations. Watching middle-class radicals get the final word on everything in SDS and even JOIN had shaped her understanding of organizational power relations. More importantly, Uptown's small experiment in community organizing proved that it was possible to help whites see a vested interest in ending racism.

Peggy Terry was also one of few white activists to witness the birth of the Black Power Movement firsthand. In June 1966 a white vigilante shot and injured a Black activist named James Meredith who had set out on a solo "March Against Fear" in Mississippi. In the days that followed a dozen civil rights organizations gathered to continue Meredith's march. The event marked a turning point in the Black freedom struggle as leaders got into heated debates about whether whites should be allowed to join the march. At King's urging, the march proceeded under the banner of nonviolence and the united chorus "Freedom Now." White allies joined the procession, including Peggy Terry who had traveled down from Chicago to meet longtime friends from CORE and SNCC.

Once the marchers arrived in Greenwood, Mississippi, though, this chorus changed. Local police arrested SNCC's Stokely Carmichael for trespassing at the local school where activists had set up camp. As marchers waited, debates about the movement's direction and values reignited. The night of his release, Carmichael spoke to the crowds gathered in Greenwood and changed the course of the movement with a simple question. "What do you want?" he asked the crowd. Picking up on a phrase suggested by SNCC organizer Willie Ricks, they answered with a roaring "Black Power! Black Power!"[47]

Peggy Terry knew she'd been witness to an incredible moment. "We reached a period in the civil rights movement when Black people felt they weren't being given the respect they should have and I agreed. White liberals ran everything." She remembers heated debates in the marchers' camp at night, while she sat there wondering what all the fuss was about. "There was never any rift in my mind or my heart. I just felt Black people were doing what they should be doing." For the majority of JOIN organizers, the division of labor made sense. They were, in fact, already a model for what it looked like to organize your own. Shortly after the Mississippi march, JOIN's Mike James penned a message to fellow white radicals: "Given Black Power's challenge to white activists to go organize their own communities, JOIN provides an example to be emulated, for it is unfortunately one of the few attempts being made to organize permanent bases of radical opposition among whites in general, and poor whites in particular."[48]

The Goodfellows and the welfare committee, along with *The Firing Line* and aspects of the theater, each served as emblems of JOIN's success. And there was still plenty of work to do. JOIN's second and third rent strikes were successful in winning collective bargaining agreements with landlords and bringing in new members. At the same time, organizers were making plans to build a new council based on block clubs (with stewards elected from the community), open a food co-op, get the city planning commission to fund a playground on Clifton Avenue and turn their full attention to fighting urban renewal.

According to Gayle Markow, a white student who first visited Uptown through a federal VISTA program, "JOIN was where the action was at. In the movement, there was no one else that I knew of that said that poor whites weren't automatically racist." Like many volunteers who came to JOIN, Markow had no understanding of poor white poverty before she came to Uptown. She shared the common "suspicion that poor whites were probably the enemy of civil rights," but her experience at JOIN changed that perception immediately. JOIN's unique experiment proved that poor whites could be a part of social change and modeled an explicit commitment to race and class politics that attracted a dozen new volunteers.

SDS member Diane Fager planned to join the civil rights movement in the South after graduation, but as she wrote her final paper on the topic of Black Power, she couldn't escape the fact that the civil rights leaders she most admired were urging white progressives to organize working-class whites. She heard about JOIN from friends in SDS, but couldn't find any contact information, so in early 1967 she just packed up her VW and drove from New York City to Chicago. She arrived shortly after the police raid and JOIN was in chaos. Marilyn Katz offered her couch as a place to sleep, but one organizer cautioned Fager that there were already "too many students at JOIN." Most were aware that class differences between newcomers and longer-term residents caused ongoing tensions. New volunteers like Fager came into the organization with this in mind, bringing valuable experience and a good deal of humility. For a year Fager, along with Jean Tepperman and other white activists steered away from the South, delved into tenant organizing and supported the welfare rights committee.

Within the year, the balance between locals and students tipped. While many community residents held staff positions at one time or another, SDS still largely controlled the group's resources and major decision-making. The welfare committee struggled to set their own direction and Peggy Terry accused women students at JOIN of "mother henning." In May 1967, welfare recipients decided it was time to break away from JOIN. Dovie Thurman and Dovie Coleman led the effort to create an independent organization and the committee was officially renamed Welfare Recipients Demand Action with local women working to bring in new members from the South Side and other parts of Chicago.

The move alleviated some of the pressure and many of the women remained members, pressing for more resident participation in JOIN's other projects. Honest about their growing pains and responding to mistakes they saw among other radicals heading into white communities to "organize their own," several JOIN leaders published an article called "Take a Step Into America" cautioning activists to expect some culture shock and assume a period of learning from the community. "Take a Step Into America" made the immodest proposal that the Left needed to be relevant to the everyday needs of everyday people. Those everyday needs were not trivial, they argued, no matter how un-revolutionary it seemed to clean up garbage or address the need for health care. Moreover, they assessed that the role of community organizers in 1967 was to help working people develop political consciousness and confidence, however long that took. "Let's get it straight: all of us understand U.S. imperialism and we hate it," they wrote. "Those of us who didn't learn about it while sitting on the terrace at Berkeley . . . learned about it because we were organized."[49] The revolution was not going to happen just yet, they argued, but it could come if organizers now readied new leaders for tomorrow.

While the broader Left may have underestimated poor whites' readiness for radicalism, the SDS organizers who spent time in Uptown gave lie to this. Their mistake was in forgetting one of the main tenets of participatory democracy: the outside organizer should "be a catalyst, not a leader." Ultimately, the power struggles in JOIN proved irreconcilable. In December 1967, shortly after the "Take A Step" article was published, local leaders asked SDS students and other outside volunteers to leave. Accounts from all sides point to the fact that poor white Chicagoans felt this was the best way to assure an organization that truly reflected their own leadership. The Black Power movement provided undeniable inspiration. At the December 1967 SDS national convention, Peggy Terry delivered a blistering critique of SDS, informing student leaders that she and her neighbors would be relying on themselves and entering into alliances with student organizers very rarely. Under the banner "Tellin' It Like It Is," Terry stated, "We believe that the time has come for us to turn to our own people, poor and working-class whites, for direction, support and inspiration, to organize around our own identity, our own interests."

Beyond local control, Terry and other local leaders were hoping a working-class led organization could make a bigger impact on the national stage. Few political organizations spoke to poor and working-class whites' concerns and aspirations in any positive way. The KKK, White Citizens' Councils and reactionary politicians like Alabama's George Wallace stood among the few directly promising solutions to their problems. JOIN's new leadership hoped to make an intervention. "We believe that, given the understanding that comes only with working-class oriented organizing, we can change the direction in which many of our folks now seem headed," said Terry.[50]

JOIN's local leaders had no intention of isolating themselves from the broader movement, though. Peggy Terry's son Doug Youngblood actually dedicated himself to taking JOIN's lessons nationwide through a training program for middle-class organizers and campus activists. Youngblood reasoned that middle-class students weren't to blame for their inexperience working with poor people, but that students simply needed more training if they wanted to be effective. Hoping to prevent misunderstanding and offer concrete lessons, Terry and Youngblood carefully explained the reasons for the split. "No matter what background a person comes from, when he or she takes on the role of organizer their primary job is to find people to whom they can pass on their abilities, their skills. The job of an organizer is to organize themselves out of a job."[51] A poor-people-led JOIN, they argued, was proof that SDS organizers had accomplished their job. It was simply their "unwillingness, or inability, to fade from the scene" that caused tensions.

Terry and Youngblood also challenged the verbal separation between "organizers" (meaning students) and "community people," offering that all those in the new JOIN were community people and organizers both. Students genuinely willing to live as part of the community for the long haul would eventually have a place in the new organization. But ultimately, the split with SDS marked the beginning of the end for JOIN. Like the separation of white activists from civil rights groups a year earlier, the demand that outside organizers leave JOIN opened up both interpersonal and political contradictions. For many of the women student organizers, gender bias along with class tensions and issues over money—mostly controlled by male leaders—seemed to precipitate the split. The class questions were real, but the ejection of student organizers struck them as far more complicated.

JOIN organizer Pat Sturgis agrees that gender played a big role in the power struggle, but believes the decision to eject SDS organizations was based in an honest belief that working-class whites had to build their own base. With Peggy Terry as the community's spokesperson, few protested the extenuating dynamics. As Sturgis put it, Terry was an extremely smart woman who read just about everything coming out of the movement. She, along with Uptown's radical hillbillies, street youth and welfare recipients, found inspiration in the Black Power model and believed there was only one path forward. That path would be short but very eventful.

. . . .

JOIN kicked off 1968 with its first solo endeavor, the national Poor People's Campaign established by Rev. King and the Southern Christian Leadership Conference (SCLC) to address economic injustice. The campaign had been a contentious topic in JOIN prior to the split. Several SDS organizers felt the campaign reflected the kind of soft, reformist politics the movement could no longer afford. This was somewhat true given the growing state repression against the movement. But while King thought the "Black Power" slogan sent the wrong message, he was also taking increasingly radical stances on issues like Vietnam and the economy. King agreed with one of Black Power's basic tenets—the need for economic self-sufficiency—though he never embraced the racial division of labor. In a telegram inviting nearly eighty leaders to a planning meeting in

Atlanta, King wrote, "The time to clearly present the case of poor people nationally draws near. I hope you will agree with me that this can only be done effectively if there is joint thinking of representatives of all racial, religious and ethnic groups."[52] Peggy Terry joined representatives from some of the nation's largest membership organizations—César Chávez for the United Farm Workers, Reies López Tijerina of the Alianza de Pueblos Libres, Tillie Walker representing the Plains tribes of North Dakota, and Big Dovie Coleman on behalf of the National Welfare Rights Organization, among others—on the steering committee. Most everyone involved had high hopes about the project's potential. Before anyone made it to Washington, DC, however, those hopes and dreams were shattered.

On April 4, just weeks before the launch, Martin Luther King Jr. was assassinated at his Memphis motel. Peggy Terry heard the news on the television. She picked up her pen and recorded Uptown's heartbreak. "Big Dovie is moaning and crying. Doug is chewing his fingernails and I sit here in shock trying to capture this feeling of a moment in history so painful I will feel it for all my days."[53] More than one hundred cities erupted in protest and mourning, including Chicago. Three hundred thousand people attended King's funeral in Atlanta, Georgia. Former JOIN organizer Fran Ansley witnessed the heartbreaking scene at the airport as she, and thousands of others, arrived for the services. Writing to Peggy Terry, with whom she remained close even after the students' expulsion from JOIN, Ansley captured the moment's painful contradictions: "Two different hillbilly families sending boys off to Vietnam (the women crying, and the boys all in pimples trying to look brave). And then four beautiful black women from SCLC, with signs pinned on their blouses, greeting the black people who were arriving—at least one every five minutes. Black armbands. TV cameras. Hostile whites."[54] Grief, hostility, war and protest defined 1968.

In the wake of King's assassination, the Poor People's Campaign steering committee decided to go forward with the gathering in Washington. SCLC's vice president Ralph David Abernathy took the helm. On May 12, Mother's Day, the National Welfare Rights Organization kicked off the convention with a march that drew six thousand people. Soon, nearly three thousand poor people from across the country arrived to set up camp on the lawn of the National Mall, dubbing their new home "Resurrection City." They slept on the lawn for six weeks and held a massive Solidarity Day rally on June 19 that attracted fifty thousand people. Terry was asked to represent poor whites by giving a speech. She was still a reluctant speaker, but she recognized the rare chance to give poor whites a voice on the national stage. Even more, it was a chance to share JOIN's message, a message she had first learned from Rev. King when she finally met him at CORE—that ending poverty was part of that movement's goals and that poor whites had an important role to play in the struggle. That message transformed her life as it did the lives of thousands of others. So she did what she learned at JOIN and spoke from her own experience: "We, the poor whites of the United States, today demand an end to racism, for our own self-interest and well being, as well as for the well being of black, brown and red Americans who, I repeat, are our natural allies in the struggle for real freedom and real democracy in these, OUR, United States of America."[55]

Much of what's been written about the convention focuses on the infighting, SCLC's mismanagement and the utter misery in the rain-soaked camps. Several civil rights scholars have written it off as the end of the civil rights golden era and even the press at the time largely ignored the event or grossly exaggerated the crime and tensions.[56] Power struggles aside, the JOIN members who attended considered the experience transformative. In that moment all JOIN's drama in the prior year fell by the wayside. It was not a revolution, but it was theirs. "The important thing that is happening is going around the campfires," Youngblood wrote. "What I mean is that poor people from all over this land are sitting down together and talking about their lives and some of the things they've done and want to do about changing them for the better. . . . It may not be radical enough for some but to me it is one of the most radical events I've ever been a part of."[57] Youngblood acknowledged the campaign's limitations in a letter he wrote to *The Movement* newspaper, but shared the feelings of Uptown residents who felt they had participated in something rare and beautiful. The student movement, he argued, had gotten too far ahead of the people. Youngblood closed his letter with a direct challenge to elements of the New Left moving away from the masses: "Because I have faith in people I am willing to walk, work, sleep, fight, and even die at the pace they set."

....

The Uptown organizers returned home energized but under pressure to rebuild the infrastructure they had lost with SDS. Terry's apartment served as JOIN's office. A small group of local organizers kept up work to stop city urban renewal projects and started a health clinic. But after funds dried up and rumors circulated that monies earmarked for the Poor People's Campaign in Chicago might go to one of Saul Alinsky's projects instead, JOIN's fate seemed sealed. In August 1968 JOIN suspended its local work to take on one last campaign: Peggy Terry's run for vice president of the United States.

The Peace and Freedom Party (PFP), founded to capture the votes of the country's growing progressive electorate, nominated Black Panther Eldridge Cleaver to take on Republican Richard Nixon, Democrat Hubert Humphrey and southern Independent

George Wallace for the presidency. Both PFP and the Panthers saw their alliance as mutually beneficial. PFP publicized the Panther program, while the Panthers helped broaden PFP's voter base among communities of color and radical whites.[58] Some radicals saw the ballot box as a waste of time, but Cleaver and PFP believed putting radical candidates into the electoral arena would "illuminate the inadequacy of establishment politics" and incubate a unified front against racism and imperialism by specifically focusing on public education and outreach.[59]

Peggy Terry and Doug Youngblood were already working to sway southern white voters away from segregationist George Wallace, authoring articles and leveraging what contacts JOIN had. To those who knew her, Terry seemed a natural choice for running mate, but the decision was far from unanimous. At the PFP convention, Cleaver asked for the Yippies' Jerry Rubin or SDS leader Carl Davidson. When neither was willing, members put forward a range of names including Terry's. Cleaver wasn't satisfied. He called for a meeting with his top aides in private. JOIN's Mike Laly barged in with Panther founder Bobby Seale, exclaiming, "What could be better than running a black ex-con and a working-class white woman for president and vice president?" Cleaver's aides ejected the two, but Terry's advocates persisted from the convention floor. Eventually a compromise was struck. Peace and Freedom Party members could nominate their own vice president state by state. Of the thirteen states where the new "fourth party" qualified for a ballot slot, Terry appeared on the ticket in California, Minnesota, Iowa, Kentucky and Illinois.

Cleaver wasn't the only one who had misgivings about the pairing. Movement women were confounded that Terry had partnered with a convicted rapist who described raping white women as an "insurrectionary act" in his book *Soul on Ice*. Terry wasn't much of a Cleaver fan, nor did she ever expect to win office. She entered the race so she could go toe-to-toe with George Wallace for the allegiance of poor white communities.

After a failed bid for governor in 1958, Wallace's popularity skyrocketed when he embraced pro-segregation policies in the early Sixties.[60] During his first term as governor Wallace honed his racist rhetoric and argued that federal civil rights legislation violated "states' rights." He deliberately fortified his national reputation during a 1963 "stand in" against school integration when he personally blocked the entrance of two Black students to the University of Alabama.[61] Moving further and further away from his affiliation with the Democrats, by the time Wallace ran for president he had joined the American Independent Party and garnered the backing of the KKK and White Citizens' Councils across the South. As his campaign picked up steam, it illustrated that racism was alive and well far beyond the southern states. In New York, twenty thousand supporters filled Madison Square Garden. In Boston, Pittsburgh, San Francisco and San Diego he drew crowds in the tens of thousands.

Peggy Terry focused her campaign on confronting Wallace, while exposing the hypocrisies of the other candidates as well. On October 1, Terry invited Wallace to a national televised debate. The next day she followed with an official announcement about her plans to take on Wallace's deception of the people. "His 'little man' appeal has won over many white workers who are tired of their unions' cooperation with big corporations. But Wallace is not the answer to their problems. He is just another kind of boss," she wrote.[62]

Wallace never accepted Terry's invitation, but she kicked off her campaign anyway with former JOIN member Mike James as her campaign manager. It began at an Iowa drive-through restaurant with a gathering of welfare recipients, SDS activists and high school students who were organizing around a student bill of rights. The owner, disturbed at the large crowd, called the police. Terry and three other organizers were detained as they exchanged power fists and V-signs, for victory, with the high schoolers. The youth taunted the police until the activists were released. The chaos spilled over to the local high school where the principal was challenged for attempting to confiscate radical literature from students. At a supporter's home, Terry sat down with the students to answer questions and offer advice on everything from protest tactics to control of the curriculum.

Terry's forces were not so warmly received in all cities. In Louisville, Kentucky, just a few hours from her hometown of Paducah, students at a local high school heckled Terry's caravan and challenged her positions on nearly everything. Weren't they just draft dodgers? Why were they trying to start a riot? They asked Terry to leave their school, but not before a local reporter documented the incident and students' clear disinterest in Terry's message.[63] Terry persisted, making several other stops in Kentucky before heading to California. Cleaver, at just thirty-four years old, wasn't old enough to be president, so both California and Utah listed only his running mate on the ballot. As a neighborhood organizer with limited experience on the national scene, Peggy Terry was largely unknown among progressives in California or elsewhere. Her son Doug Youngblood worked hard on this aspect of her campaign, writing and speaking to progressives about the need to abandon middle-class tunnel vision. If PFP or the New Left overall hoped to outrank Wallace, let alone the "demopublicans," the movement needed to make itself more relevant to working-class people just as JOIN had argued all along.[64]

Terry, too, pled her case in a lengthy *Los Angeles Times* article, but ultimately the Cleaver–Terry ticket won just 0.4 percent (or just under 28,000) of the state's votes. Wallace garnered half a million.

His 6.8 percent of the vote was four times higher than the American Independent Party's membership in the state.[65] Nationwide Wallace received ten million votes and carried the total vote in five southern states. Nixon, of course, won the national election with 43 percent of the vote, only slightly more than Humphrey. Cleaver–Terry garnered less than one percent in every state. Though actually winning was never the goal, Terry's goal of inspiring poor whites outside of Uptown proved more difficult than she anticipated. In the end, Terry doubted whether working-class whites or even the PFP's liberal white membership understood her message.

Peggy Terry never considered the campaign a failure though. Like the long talks she had around her kitchen table in Uptown, the Peace and Freedom campaign was an opportunity for yet another protracted conversation, worthwhile if just a few people started to think differently. While an injury—sustained when a police officer kicked her in the back at a protest—required invasive surgery and took Terry out of the movement for several years after, she never ceased in her role as an educator and lifelong proponent of radical causes. Terry did what she did out of love for people. "I love people who aren't organized," she said. "But it's up to me to find a way—to find the words, to make them understand that there's more to life than today's pleasures." Laughing that she might sound a bit like a preacher "fired up to save souls from hell," she add, "I want to save them from capitalism."

In the end, JOIN Community Union saved more than a few. What set them apart from their contemporaries was the realization that it was futile to ask someone to challenge an empire if they didn't feel powerful enough to challenge their landlord, insist on their right to health care, refuse the draft or stand up to a corrupt police department. Projects like the welfare committee, housing strikes and Goodfellows illustrated their successes. After a series of joint actions with welfare organizations in other states, the Dovies and Welfare Recipients Demand Action helped to build the National Welfare Rights Organization (NWRO). At its peak in the late Sixties, the NWRO boasted twenty thousand members from hundreds of regional welfare groups.[66]

JOIN's welfare committee also laid the foundation for women's leadership in Uptown as local women forged their own vision of women's liberation dealing with race, class and gender oppression simultaneously. At a time when many middle-class feminists alienated poor women and women of color, Chicago's early feminist movement was deeply influenced by poor women's leadership, in large part because of JOIN and Welfare Recipients Demand Action. During their time at JOIN several women leaders also helped found the Chicago Women's Liberation Union, one of the oldest feminist organizations in the country.

Perhaps JOIN's biggest legacy is the number of organizers that, through their shared experience, became lifelong radicals. The inspiration they found and the outrage they experienced empowered a core of white radicals who "never left the Left," as Marilyn Katz put it. According to Jean Tepperman, whether students or dislocated southerners, "Nobody, well almost nobody, truly left JOIN." Their effort to build a sustained, progressive working-class movement in Chicago inspired new projects that eventually succeeded in changing the face of Chicago politics and the visibility of poor whites in the movement. Just months after JOIN closed its doors, the Goodfellows founded the Young Patriots Organization and formed an unprecedented alliance with the Black Panther Party. Within a year, JOIN's Mike James, Diane Fager and Bob Lawson also founded Rising Up Angry, an organization that spent nearly a decade organizing working-class whites across Chicago and forging partnerships with radical working-class whites in other states.

In 1983, Katz and others who had come through JOIN helped get Chicago's first Black mayor, Harold Washington, elected. Most saw Washington's victory as the culmination of two decades of work, beginning in the Sixties and continuing into the Seventies through the Young Patriots and Rising Up Angry. Their projects proved that barriers to progressive, multiracial alliances were not immutable, and that poor and working-class whites had a leading role to play.

CHAPTER 2

The Fire Next Time: The Short Life
of the Young Patriots
and the Original Rainbow Coalition

We've got to face the fact that some people say you fight fire best with fire, but we say you put fire out best with water. We say you don't fight racism with racism. We're gonna fight racism with solidarity.

—Fred Hampton, Chicago Black Panther Party, 1969

April 4, 1969, marked the one-year anniversary of Martin Luther King Jr.'s assassination and the urban uprisings that set hundreds of cities ablaze. In the year since, millions of U.S. residents changed their calls for equality to demands for a second American Revolution. At the helm of that movement was the Black Panther Party, widely regarded as the vanguard of the radical Left by 1969. While the Panthers were best known for asserting their right to "police the police" by carrying guns in self-defense, the group's national influence grew because of their exemplary work serving breakfast to hungry kids, their cogent internationalist politics and their commitment to building alliances. In Chicago, Panthers Bob Lee and Fred Hampton spearheaded one such alliance, knowing the move would garner more controversy than clout.

The Rainbow Coalition initiated by the Panthers united poor whites, Blacks and Latinos in a "vanguard of the dispossessed." In addition to the Chicago Panthers, its members hailed from the Young Lords, a group of mainland Puerto Ricans who turned their decade-old street gang into a radical political organization, and the Young Patriots Organization, poor "dislocated hillbillies" descended from JOIN Community Union's anti-police brutality committee.[1] The Young Patriots took pride in their southern roots and newfound independence from the middle-class Left. From afar these urban hillbillies looked like any other white street gang, young men in their twenties and late teens dressed in white T-shirts, black pants, and sleeveless jean vests or leather jackets with their group's signature hand painted on the back. Each wore perfectly greased hair, unless covered by a cowboy hat, and a clean shave. Up close there were telltale signs setting them apart from other neighborhood guys: buttons that read "Free Huey" and "Resurrect John Brown," another showing two fists breaking a set of chains. To hear them speak was even more telling; these cats were about something different. As one Patriot put it, "Before we are proud of who we are, let us be proud of who we are supposed to be."[2] For the Young Patriots, that meant "revolutionary solidarity" with oppressed people around the world, starting with the Black Panthers and Young Lords in Chicago. Also joining the early days of the coalition were members of Rising Up Angry, a not-yet-named radical outfit that also grew out of JOIN Community Union.

In Spring 1969, members of the Rainbow Coalition made their first joint appearance at a press conference on the anniversary of King's murder. Crowded around a long folding table, dressed in black leather jackets and dark sunglasses, they projected an image of ultimate revolutionary cool—albeit a male-dominated one. Black Panther Nathaniel Junior sat at the microphone to urge the city's poor to stop fighting each other and tearing up their own neighborhoods. Street rebellions grew from an understandable grief and rage, they argued, but only invited police retaliation. It was time to decrease petty turf wars and quell pointless violence. It was time for poor people to claim their rightful place leading movements for revolutionary change in Chicago and beyond.

The Patriots may have formed with or without the direct influence of the Chicago Panthers, but there is no doubt that the Black Panther Party lent primary inspiration, theoretical framework and a programmatic model to the Uptown organization. The Panther Party was founded in Oakland, California, in October 1966 by seasoned activists and community college students Bobby Seale and Huey Newton to address two of Oakland's biggest problems: police brutality and the city's dangerous neglect of poor neighborhoods.[3] One of their first actions highlighted the city's culpability in a child's death at a dangerous intersection where residents had long demanded a stop sign. Newton and Seale, with a shotgun in hand in case anyone tried to interfere, went to the intersection and installed stop signs themselves. As young black intellectuals who studied the writings of Marx, Lenin, Mao, W.E.B. DuBois, Malcolm X and Frantz Fanon among others, Newton and Seale also showed just as much dedication to revolutionary theory as they did to planning actions. Their study of theory, particularly around questions of socialism, nationalism and self-determination, inspired the Panthers' famous ten-point manifesto poetically outlining demands for community control, housing, health care, meaningful employment and an end to racist judicial practices. Embodying their call for self-determination it began, "We Want Freedom. We Want Power to Determine the Destiny of Our Black Community."

That freedom required, first and foremost, an end to the constant police harassment in Black neighborhoods. During their first few months the Black Panthers started community patrols to protect residents from police. They came armed with legal doctrine and firearms, letting furious officers know that citizen observation of police was protected under the law. In response, city and state officials decided to change the law, making it illegal for citizens to openly carry loaded firearms. Shortly thereafter, in May 1967, the Panthers catapulted into the national spotlight when they showed up to the Sacramento State House brandishing rifles. They certainly got the attention of lawmakers, including a young actor-turned-governor Ronald Reagan, but the Panthers' real target was the media. Frenzied reporters snapped photos of the shocking spectacle as thirty Black men and women, outfitted in sleek leather jackets, berets and shiny rifles marched across the Capitol lawn. For the mainstream public, the event focused more attention on the group's militancy than its message, but for radicals and even a few left-leaning liberals the Panthers' stand was a lightning rod, a dramatic and well-planned theater of the oppressed.

The Panthers' strong self-defense position garnered attention, but this wasn't what ultimately earned them the support of grandmothers in Uptown, actors Jane Fonda and Marlon Brando, famous musicians and more than five thousand Panther rank-and-filers. While the Panthers' history is filled with internal strife and its leaders were far from perfect, the media's sensational reporting obscured the group's biggest contribution: In city after city Black Panthers spent most of their daily energy on community service, a strategy they called "Survival Pending Revolution." In practical terms, they provided the basic services people desperately needed, including a popular free breakfast program, sickle cell anemia testing, legal defense clinics, literacy classes and schools that taught children cultural pride and Black history for the first time.[4]

More commonly referred to as the "Serve the People" approach, the Panthers' service model reached thousands of families each day. This approach changed the terrain for dozens of radical community groups. Inspired by the Panthers, many stopped waging long, resource-intensive campaigns to win paltry concessions from social welfare bureaucrats. Instead radicals increasingly created community-run solutions. Though this certainly wasn't the first time U.S. radicals had created autonomous social services, the Panthers' service-plus-organizing approach offered a necessary alternative for community organizers who had more than a few reasons to question the point of reforming a broken system. Soon Latino, Asian, Native American and white radicals were putting forth their own revolutionary platforms. By 1967 the Panthers model inspired dozens of other organizations from the Chinese I Wor Kuen to the Young Patriots and the Puerto Rican Young Lords Organization.

In Chicago, the Young Lords Organization started out as a street gang similar to the neighborhood social networks the Young Patriots grew from. Based in the city's large Puerto Rican community not far from Uptown, the Young Lords evolved into a political party under the leadership of Jose "Cha-Cha" Jiménez who developed a close relationship with movement groups including the West Coast Panthers. In 1967 the group launched its own service programs including drug education, food and toy giveaways and "Soul Dances" in collaboration with another local gang, the Blackstone Rangers, who had been a security force for Martin Luther King Jr. during the Open Housing Marches the prior year. Fred Hampton reached out to both groups about joining the Rainbow Coalition. The Lords agreed. The Rangers declined. While they supported the unity message, the Rangers ultimately drew the line at Left politicking and the groups' identification with Third World Marxism.

The Lords embraced it, expanding to other cities like New York and continuing to grapple with their own precarious circumstance as internationals whose homeland had been seized as a territory of the U.S. at the end of the Spanish-American War in 1898.[5]

. . . .

By the mid-Sixties, anticolonial struggles in the Third World lent tremendous inspiration to radicals in the United States. Rebellions by colonized peoples around the globe suggested that liberation movements among oppressed peoples in the U.S. were possible, even imminent. Stateside radicals watched national liberation struggles in China, Cuba, Vietnam, Mozambique and Guinea-Bissau closely, drawing lessons and confidence in the legitimacy of their own struggle. The Black Panthers and Young Lords, along with I Wor Kuen, the American Indian Movement and other groups, formed a growing nucleus of self-defined Third World Liberation movements within U.S. borders. As the descendents of colonized nations still living under an imperial thumb, they understood themselves as oppressed nationalities within the United States, an idea with roots much earlier in the 20th century and popularized again in 1962 by Harold Cruse in his essay "Revolutionary Nationalism and the Afro-American."[6] As "nations within a nation," Third World peoples within the U.S. claimed their right to real self-determination for their communities, while drawing strength from their part in an unprecedented global struggle.[7]

The growth of these movements represented a tactical shift from the integrationism of the civil rights movement. Civil rights reforms had failed to produce the wholesale change many envisioned, and racially integrated organizations had allowed white activists too much control. Expressed concretely in the call for Black Power, organizations like SNCC and the Black Panthers insisted on the need for organizational autonomy. During the latter half of the Sixties, radicals of color tried to define the short-term function and long-term goals of autonomous organizations. In doing so, they evolved different strands of nationalism. Where cultural nationalism centered cultural pride, most famously expressed in the refrain "Black is Beautiful," its adherents generally took a strict approach to ethnically separate movements. Revolutionary nationalism and revolutionary internationalism, while distinct from each other, each held a vision of multiracial collaboration, in theory if not in practice. It was versions of these two ideologies that most shaped the Black Panthers' and Young Lords' interest in working with the Young Patriots. Drawing inspiration from Third World Marxism and Maoism, the Rainbow Coalition in Chicago was the Panthers' most concrete attempt to put internationalism into practice. According to its leaders, the Rainbow Coalition was "the first living proof of a new revolutionary classless society in the making."

Standing beside the Panthers and Lords, members of the Young Patriots Organization set out to show that poor whites were ready to fight for this new society. JOIN Community Union had instilled a deep sense of radical purpose in these younger members. Their political coming of age in the Sixties forced them to reckon with more rapid social upheaval than almost any generation prior, and the dramatic civil unrest they witnessed changed more than unjust laws. It fostered an impetus toward change that burst forth with such momentum it completely reshaped the self-image of a generation. For Uptown's young organizers the movement promised a political home as important as any physical one. And just like they fought landlords for building improvements, they continued fighting for their own place within the broader Left. "We're sick and tired of certain people and groups telling us 'there ain't no such thing as poor and oppressed white people,'" the Young Patriots announced. "The so-called 'movement' better begin to realize, that—first of all—we're human beings, we're real; second—we've always been here, we didn't just materialize; and third—we're not going away, even if you choose not to admit we exist."[8]

Founded by former JOIN members Junebug Boykin, Hy Thurman, Bobby Joe McGinnis, and Doug Youngblood, the Young Patriots was an organization *of, by* and *for* poor whites, just the kind of independent project JOIN activists had hoped to create by splitting from SDS the prior year. Junebug Boykin had been one of JOIN's more respected young leaders. His experience at JOIN helped him grab occasional work in War on Poverty service programs around Uptown, but he always matched that with part-time work hustling in pool halls. The same strategic thinking that earned him considerable respect for his billiards skills also made him a pretty good organizer, and his relaxed self-confidence made him a likeable leader. Through him, the pool hall became one of the more reliable places to go if you wanted to chat about revolutionary politics.

Boykin and Doug Youngblood had been good friends for years, yet Youngblood was a much more private person who worked most of his ideas out in poetry and political essays. While he struggled with hotheadedness and often provoked a good heated debate, in other moments he revealed his softer side. He had his mother Peggy Terry's sense of justice and believed in meeting people where they were. Rather than admonish poor whites for being hesitant or even outright disinterested in movement politics, he took a long view of community organizing. His own path to radicalism had more than a few twists and turns. Youngblood was in his mid-twenties before he even warmed to the idea of civil rights. He was almost thirty by the time he found his purpose as an organizer and traveling guest speaker on class politics among middle-class leftists. At one rally in Uptown Youngblood revealed his own approach after fellow

organizers scolded a crowd of seemingly apathetic white southerners. "I can't get as mad as these people here," he said. "I went for
24 long years myself not caring, just looking out for myself, before
I finally saw the light. You just come on out for the clean-up party,
you hear? We'll have us a lot of fun."[9] And with that he reminded
everyone that radical progress with poor whites took both patience
and diligence. That day was a day for patience.

Through word-of-mouth the Young Patriots soon attracted
new members beyond the JOIN family tree. One Southerner,
Andy Keniston, ended his long search for a political home once
he found the Young Patriots.[10] A few days after King's assassination, Keniston drove out to an Ohio farmhouse for a gathering of
radicals concerned about the future of the movement. Emotions ran
high, but the meeting's main speaker, former JOIN member Mike
James, kept people focused on the potential still ahead of them.
James encouraged Keniston and his wife to move to Chicago and
organize. Keniston arrived a few months later, broke and unemployed, on Junebug Boykin's doorstep. Boykin almost turned him
away. For years most eager newcomers had arrived in Uptown looking for JOIN's well-known student leaders. With the exception of
Peggy Terry and Doug Youngblood, there had only been one or
two movement newspapers with any other poor white Chicagoans
named in the byline. Boykin assumed Keniston was looking for
Rennie Davis and the JOIN days of radical legend. Prevailing on
Boykin to let him stay a while, Keniston spent the next year helping
build the Patriots.

Following the Panthers' lead, the group released its own Ten-
Point Program, including demands for full employment, decent
housing, prisoners' rights and an end to racism. The original Patriots platform never used the word "white," but explained issues
of police brutality, unions, the war draft and run-down schools in

terms of class politics. A later version more closely echoed the Panthers' program, though, replacing the word *Black* with *white*. "We demand power to determine the destiny of our oppressed white community. . . . We demand an immediate end to police brutality and murder of oppressed white people, and that the people of our community control the police." In defining these oppressed white people, the Patriots asked questions of their audience: Were urbanized Appalachians a separate nation within a nation in the same way Blacks and American Indians were oppressed nationalities within the U.S.? The Patriots reasoned yes, they were. Influenced by the politics of the time, the Patriots asserted that oppressed whites, particularly poor white southerners, constituted "a people," and in doing so carved out a rare and controversial claim to white ethnic revolutionary nationalism. As "hillbilly nationalists" they claimed white southerners' right to determine their destiny and oppose the "pig power structure" that created slavery and the capitalist North–South divide. While the term was never thoroughly defined and it was never clear what they thought a Hillbilly Nation would look like if indeed the revolution ever arrived, it was clear they hoped to build a new brand of southern pride.

Despite the vagueness of their positions, the Patriots' message might be one of the few times in U.S. history that anyone uttered the phrase "White Power" as a rallying cry for racial justice. The Patriots' early leaflets highlighted the phrase on the cover to capture attention. Inside, the contents spelled out what they really meant. As the Panthers' slogan went: "Black Power to Black People, Brown Power to Brown People, Red Power to Red People, Yellow Power to Yellow People. . . . White Power to White People." The Patriots soon took this message a step further. "The South Will Rise Again," read one of their early manifestos, accompanied by the caveat, "Only this time in solidarity with our oppressed brothers and sisters." As proof of that solidarity, the Young Patriots devoted page after page of their new tabloid-size newspaper, aptly titled *The Patriot,* to the release of political prisoners including Panther founders Huey Newton and Bobby Seale. *The Patriot* appealed to whites to abandon racism, unite with the political vanguards of other oppressed communities and "fight the real enemy."

Both Patriots and Panthers saw new member William "Preacherman" Fesperman as the firebrand who might truly win over poor whites. As a student of theology from North Carolina, Fesperman was inspired by the Patriots' emphasis on reaching white southerners and immediately saw ways to take their message nationwide. Fesperman was a fiery orator with a magnetic charisma and the integrity to back it up. "Preacherman would have stopped a bullet for me, and nearly tried," Bob Lee recalls. "He was one of the best human beings I ever met." Every time he spoke, someone approached asking how they could start a Patriots chapter where they lived. He conveyed a rare clarity about white people's purpose in the fight and shared how hundreds of poor whites felt newly freed once they let go of learned racism. Confronting its machinations was not only logical, he said, but also empowering. "Check out what this country is," Fesperman wrote. "Let racism become a disease. I'm talking to the white brothers and sisters because I know what it's done. I know what it done to me. I know what it does to people everyday. And we're saying that's got to end, it's got to stop and we're doing it."[11]

With new members like Fesperman, the Patriots crafted their rhetoric and public image. In a decade when symbolism mattered like never before, most Left groups chose their radical dress code— whether the dignified suits of civil rights leaders or the sleek leather jackets of the Panthers—to consciously send a message. For a brief time, the Patriots adopted the Confederate flag as a symbol of southern poor people's revolt against the owning class. While they came to see this choice as a mistake, the Patriots initially argued that the Confederate flag would grab attention among their base and give them an opening to discuss the nation's history of capitalist land grabs and divide-and-conquer tactics. They argued that the Civil War was a pissing match between a feudalistic slave-holding southern planting class and the newly industrialized capitalist North. The divide between North and South, they argued, was not created by the common people, but rather by businessmen and wealthy politicians. By this logic the Confederate flag, originally a cultural symbol of the South, was no more offensive than the Stars and Stripes.[12] "From historical experience, we know that the people make the meaning of a flag," they wrote in their newspaper. "This time we mean to see that the spirit of rebellion finds and smashes the real enemy rather than our brothers and sisters in oppression."

Unafraid to ruffle a few feathers, the choice of the Confederate flag also raised a blatant middle finger to the student Left. Most Patriots took pride in their ability to rattle the cage of middle-class politeness. They also needed a radical uniform they could actually afford. Flag patches were cheap from the local military surplus store and sewing them onto jean jackets and berets seemed easy enough. As the Patriots sat around discussing their options, Panther Bob Lee weighed in with his full blessing so long as members were up for all the explaining they would have to do. Lee even spent his first three weeks breaking bread with folks in Uptown without telling Chairman Fred Hampton. Once Lee had something to show for his effort, he took the idea of the coalition to Hampton who "got the idea" right away. Not everyone responded as Hampton did. Members of the Panthers and Lords questioned the choice of emblem, and outsiders were simply confused about the seeming contradiction of Black radicals standing beside self-proclaimed hillbillies wearing Confederate flags. The Young Lords actually debated the matter at length when deciding whether to join forces with the Patriots. "It was really their choice to make," explains Cha-Cha Jiménez. "In order to understand it, you have to understand the influence of nationalism." The Chicago Lords ultimately decided there was enough shared vision to build upon, but demonstrating that camaraderie to their members took more time, however.

Late one spring evening Bob Lee, field secretary for the Chicago Black Panthers, stood in a North Chicago church where the Panthers and Patriots were supposed to spend the evening hammering out political points of unity. Instead, Lee and the Patriots spent the whole meeting trying to convince poor white residents that the Panthers were allies, not threats. The crowd of Uptown residents alternated between silence and vocal resistance to the proposal. Exhausted and knowing that the scene would be repeated on his own turf at a Panthers meeting later that night, Lee needed to get outside and walk.

Outside the church Bob Lee's instinct told him he was being followed. He realized he made a big mistake by leaving alone. Almost immediately two police officers approached him from behind. "You know what to do," they demanded. Lee put his hands up against the wall. Soon he was inside the squad car with a sneaking feeling he wasn't going to be cited and released down at the station. Looking up he saw Patriots chairman William Fesperman ushering men, women and children out of the church. Were they hurrying home? Did they see Lee in the squad car? They did. With no hesitation, the entire community surrounded the car and began to yell at the police, demanding Lee's release. Lee was awestruck as every single person from inside the church rallied in his defense. Despite their general fear about inviting Black radicals into their community and long-held misunderstandings about the intent of Black Liberation, there was one thing poor whites in Uptown understood: The police were a common enemy. The cops let Lee go. Unplanned and spontaneous, but fully aware of the risks, the Patriots' rank and file helped un-arrest a virtual stranger. As Lee put it, "I'll never forget looking at all those brave white motherfuckers standing in the light of the police car staring in the face of death."

This proved the first of many risks the Patriots took as they tried to carve out a militant opposition to racism and capitalism in white communities. Bob Lee, too, was fearless as he immersed himself in other communities, building rapport with razor-sharp insight and unwavering patience. For a few weeks he lived alongside the Patriots in Uptown. He advised them on setting up community programs and chipped away at people's ignorance one home-cooked meal at a time. "I had to run with those cats, break bread with them, hang out at the pool hall," Lee said. "I had to lay down on their couch, in their neighborhood. Then I had to invite them into mine."

Almost by accident, these early days of the Rainbow Coalition were immortalized in the independent film *American Revolution II*. Ironically, it started during a shoot for a Kentucky Fried Chicken commercial. As the 1968 Democratic Convention melee erupted in Chicago's Grant Park, Colonel Harlan Sanders stood just blocks away in a television studio filming a commercial for the restaurant chain. As the film crew broke for lunch, word arrived that protesters and police were squaring off downtown. Impulsively ordering the film crew to scene, director Mike Gray was alarmed as he watched police officers removing their badges and readying riot gear. Over the next three days the Film Group documented the chaos including many of the incidents that earned radicals a newfound national sympathy. The cops' overreaction was blatant. Gray and his film crew captured "Chicago Police wading into crowds of protesters and beating them senseless."[13]

Eyes pried open by the violence, Gray decided to explore the events leading up to the violent clash during the convention. He met with Bob Lee and convinced him to let him film the process of building the Rainbow Coalition. The grainy, black-and-white documentary captured both the potential and the awkwardness of the alliance, as neighborhood organizer Chuck Geary tried to explain the Panthers' program to community residents in Uptown. "This is Poor People's Park [referring to a local development campaign the Panthers, Lords and Patriots were fighting for] and that's what this little button is all about," Geary said holding a small, hand painted button of the rainbow for the crowd to see. He then introduced Bob Lee with the disclaimer, "He might be from another part of town, but he is fighting for a lot of the same things we are." The crowd sat silently, as if waiting for a better explanation.

In the film we see Lee in action, explaining in a confident, slow tone what the Panthers were really about. He asked people what it was they wanted to change. At first, residents shifted in their chairs, but gradually he got a steady stream of responses. Uptown had seen its own share of rats, roaches, police, poverty, pimps and promises, people said. While most residents stayed quiet, a man named John Howard, who had been an active member of JOIN since 1964, ex claimed, "I'll stick with the Black Panther Party if they will stick with me!" It was a start and with a small cadre of leaders the Rainbow Coalition grew stronger, in large part because of the quiet work Chuck Geary and Bob Lee did together to introduce people they knew to each other. Geary had a rare ability to work with all of Chicago's competing factions, and it was Geary who originally seized the imagery of the rainbow as a way to describe the unique brand of unity under construction.[14]

Despite its timeliness and dramatic footage, every major movie theater in Chicago refused to screen *American Revolution II* thanks to Mayor Daley's influence with the Screen Projectors Union. The filmmakers turned to one of the few theater owners in Chicago audacious enough to tell Daley to go jump in Lake Michigan. In April 1969, the film premiered at Hugh Hefner's Playboy Theater. The film caught the immediate attention of the mainstream media, earning a positive review in the *Chicago Tribune* and accolades from famed reviewer Roger Ebert, a former student radical himself, who believed the movie was necessary for every Chicagoan to see in order to make sense of the events of 1968.

For all its brutal honesty, *American Revolution II* got mixed reviews among its own subjects. Bob Lee thought it was an accurate snapshot of the complexity of the times, but also feared that it would attract the attention of law enforcement eager to shut down any viable alliance. Panthers co-founder Bobby Seale was more disturbed by what he saw. In between images of poor whites and Blacks finding common cause, a few Panther rank-and-filers went on the record advocating violence against white people—any white people. According to Seale, "These were the expressions of nonmembers or new members who hadn't learned of the party's guiding philosophy." Seale felt the main value of the film for the Panthers was to learn "how to combat this kind of thinking."[15]

For the most part, these debates stemmed from ideological differences among radicals of color about the kind of nationalism they felt they needed. While none of these organizations advocated random violence against white people, tensions flared over the question of working with white leftists. Some members disagreed with the organization's cozy relationship with white liberals; others questioned whether an alliance with the Patriots so soon would compromise the organization's nascent sovereignty. Even those who agreed that nationalism was a first step toward class-based unity debated the time and effort required to build such an alliance.

For both Panthers and Lords this proved divisive. Bob Lee knew fallout was inevitable and, as *American Revolution II* foreshadowed, the decision had consequences. Both the Panthers and the Lords lost members after the Rainbow Coalition was announced. For Cha-Cha Jiménez these exits were sobering. "There's nothing wrong with the process of building pride in yourself, your community, your culture and people," he says. "However, some people got stuck in that phase and never moved beyond it." Bob Lee was more blunt about it. "Some didn't like the Patriots; some just didn't like white people in general," he says. "To tell the truth, it was a necessary purging. The Rainbow Coalition was just a code word for class struggle."

The Patriots agreed, but respected their allies' need to go through this process with their membership. Reading Fanon and Mao themselves, they agreed with the Panthers' line on revolutionary nationalism wherein ethnic groups self-organized but collaborated, and given the history of white domination within Left movements, they understood why some members might hesitate. Being revolutionaries, though, they minced no words condemning pure cultural nationalism as self-interested and a boon for a capitalist system that now "makes millions on love beads, afro-shirts, and cowboy hats."[16]

. . . .

Despite its process-filled beginnings, the Rainbow Coalition did manage to put its vision into practice across Chicago. It became common to see Fred Hampton "give a typically awe-inspiring speech on revolutionary struggle, while white men wearing berets, sunglasses and Confederate rebel flags sewn into their jackets helped provide security for him."[17] Members of the Panthers, Lords and Patriots routinely provided protection for each other at public events, collaborated on political education classes and launched a "Rainbow Food Program" distributing free meals to thousands of families in Illinois.

Rainbow Coalition members also worked together on several local campaigns and informally drew new organizations into the fold. Under the banner of "rainbow politics," the Patriots and Lords organized alongside a broader Poor People's Coalition to halt the expansion of McCormick Theological Seminary, which required the demolition of nearby homes.[18] In protest they occupied several college buildings on Belden Avenue and demanded more than a half-million dollars to build low-income housing along with university support to build a daycare center. McCormick's president ponied up $125,000 to end the building takeover. After the university dropped the court injunction levied against protesters, the coalition members cleared out.

In Uptown, the Patriots applied the Rainbow Coalition's solidarity model to their other local work. They reached out to activists in Uptown's growing Native American community and linked their efforts to stop urban renewal. The neighborhood's Native American population had grown to well over a thousand residents by the end of the Sixties. In an effort to link newer urban displacement with ongoing Native sovereignty issues, American Indian activists from the neighborhood occupied a piece of vacant land near Wrigley Field where they wanted affordable housing built. Dubbed the Chicago Indian Village, groups eventually took over a vacant city-owned apartment building on North Broadway too. The Patriots put out a handbill explaining their support for the cause: "For years now we have seen buildings being torn down. We are glad to see these rat holes being demolished, because they are not fit for human beings to live in. . . . At the request of the Chicago Indian Village, the

Young Patriots Organization has assisted in occupying this building, and their action is the same as ours. We are not going to move until something is done about the problem of housing in Uptown."

Some of the Patriots' longest lasting campaigns centered on community health care and urgent care access at city hospitals. In the tradition of the Panthers' survival programs, the Patriots opened their own health center staffed by dissident doctors. For most residents, it was the first time they really understood what dignity and self-determination could mean for their daily lives. In their clinic, poor people were "treated with all the courtesy and dignity of a society matron going to the highest priced doctor you could find anywhere," recalled Peggy Terry who visited the clinic regularly and acted as a kind of mentor for Young Patriots on the community campaigns. "The doctors and nurses devote their time to the clinic. They fund us, they pay our rent, they pay the utility bills, things like that out of their own pocket." This might have seemed condescending at any other point, but these clinics weren't run on charity. They were run on mutual aid and everyone pitched in.

The independent health care centers faced constant harassment and the Patriots worked alongside other Rainbow Coalition members to defend their citywide network of free medical clinics. Police stopped patients exiting the buildings and took prescribed medicines from them. Sometimes they booked patients on illegal narcotics possession. Police disrupted meetings between medical volunteers and Patriots organizers, and one landlord was pressured into evicting the clinic and a Patriot-affiliated day care center. The Chicago Board of Health then moved to close the clinics through legal channels. The city adopted new rules mandating all free clinics to submit to stringent licensing requirements and provide immediate access to patients' personal medical records. One city official asked, "How do we know the Young Patriots aren't using their medical service at 4411 N. Sheridan to treat gunshot wounds, hand out drugs irresponsibly, perform abortions or give shots with unsterile needles?" At the time, Chicago boasted dozens of unlicensed free clinics. The volunteer-run clinics couldn't handle the barrage of new paperwork and most closed their doors. The Patriots' health center and the Jake Winters Clinic, run by the Panthers, refused to submit to the new regulations. In one clinic defense action forty-one Rainbow Coalition supporters landed in jail. The groups fought to keep their clinics open for more than a year, but eventually the city succeeded in shuttering the programs.

The free breakfast programs faced similar challenges. Like many survival programs, the actual services they offered existed elsewhere in the neighborhood. The Montrose Urban Progress Center had a food pantry, for instance, but the intake process was extensive. Recipients were even required to let social workers into their homes to prove there was no food. In the Serve the People programs, residents faced no bureaucracy and no judgment. Between them, they fed thousands of children each morning. With such high demand, the programs needed to be held in locations big enough for the crowds. The Patriots partnered with the local Hull House, a social service agency with roots going back to Jane Addams's settlement house movement. At its peak the Patriots' breakfast program served more than four hundred families per week. Initially the Hull House director was enthusiastic about the partnership. After several months, however, he called the Patriots in and simply said, "Can't do the breakfast program." According to Patriot Carol Coronado, someone had likely scared him away. It was a blow for the Patriots and their allies. "These programs meant the most to us," Coronado explains. "Even more important than the politics. They gave us a chance to serve our people and learn how to work with other communities."

Members of the Rainbow Coalition were facing several uphill battles, not least of which were threats to their programs and even their lives. Uptown organizer John Howard had been active in JOIN from its inception, serving as one of the few men on the group's welfare committee; he was a bit older than most Patriots members but sympathized with their goals. It was Howard who appeared in the film *American Revolution II* as one of the first community residents to express support for the Panthers. That appearance got him killed. On a trip home to Georgia in 1969, he was recognized as "the guy who works with niggers in Chicago." He was found the next day with his throat slit.[19]

And just that fast, the other shadows that followed the coalition from its beginning started to loom much larger. By the end of their first year, things devolved into the worst kind of nightmare.

. . . .

The Federal Bureau of Investigation had the Panthers in their cross-hairs from day one. That scope also included their close allies in the Rainbow Coalition. While the FBI kept files on almost everyone in or remotely associated with the New Left, Director J. Edgar Hoover nurtured a special animosity for the Panthers. In Hoover's own words they were, "The greatest single threat to the internal security of the country."[20] According to Bob Lee, "Once the [Black Panther] Party departed from the hate whitey trip" and got serious about real politics, Hoover clearly saw them as a far bigger threat. The Bureau's documents reveal a paranoid, almost apocalyptic quest to prevent the rise of a potential Black "messiah" who could "unify and electrify" not only the Black movement but the entire progressive Left.[21] "The Rainbow Coalition was their worst nightmare," says Lee. This scrutiny would soon prove lethal.

The aging Hoover had decades to perfect his craft. During

World War I, Hoover collaborated with Attorney General Alexander Palmer to organize the "Palmer Raids," a targeted attack on literally every single left-of-center organization of the era. The raid resulted in the deportation of every non-citizen activist, including renowned anarchist Emma Goldman. Beginning in 1956 Hoover channeled his ability to disrupt social movements into the Counterintelligence Program (COINTELPRO). Hoover's brainchild distinguished itself through relentless attempts to frame, arrest and discredit dissidents, including a young Rev. King. Under Hoover, COINTELPRO wreaked havoc on progressive organizations. Today there are hundreds of thousands of pages in the public domain detailing the federal government's targeting of the Civil Rights, New Left and Third World Liberation Movements. Catholic draft resisters, the Berrigan brothers, labor organizer César Chávez, Quakers and even the National Council of Churches all endured Hoover's constant gaze.

The Bureau's repertoire included brute force and more covert disruption. Infiltrators joined organizations specifically to propagate disinformation and exacerbate disagreements between individuals and groups. Agents planted false media stories, created fraudulent anonymous leaflets, and visited activists' parents, clergy, landlords and employers in what amounted to low-tech psychological warfare on the Sixties Left. The police and FBI targeted movement figures on false charges, both petty and serious, while the seemingly endless court trials reinforced the public perception of a movement populated by dangerous criminals. Whether or not there was an acquittal on the charges, the FBI's tactics drained personal and organizational coffers and sapped the energy of activists who built one of the most notable populist movements of the 20th century.

In Chicago, police repression kept Rainbow Coalition members on the defensive from the beginning. On May 4, 1969, off-duty policeman James Lamb shot and killed Manuel Ramos, a teen-age member of the Young Lords, and critically wounded member Ralph Rivera. Lamb maintained that Ramos initiated the attack, but witnesses and the medical examination disproved his version of events. Within a week, the Rainbow Coalition mobilized three thousand people to march to the police station on Chicago Avenue demanding a new investigation. The group also demanded Officer Lamb be charged with murder. State Attorney Edward Hanrahan initially agreed to meet with a delegation from the march but later cancelled. During the march members of a local gang called the Cobra Stones began tailing protestors, taunting them and waving weapons. When marcher Hilda Ignatin approached them to explain the goals of the march, one of them responded, "The police told us the Young Lords were helping the Panthers take over our projects." Realizing local police had intentionally lied to them the group joined the march as did other passersby and other local gangs. Local authorities weren't done spreading inflammatory rumors though. Following the Ramos slaying, word got around that police were going to attack the Rainbow Coalition. Members holed up in the rectory of a Lincoln Park church overnight, armed and fearful. The raid never happened, but the stress and paranoia continued to haunt the alliance.

It's impossible to know whether or not the Ramos killing was meant to curb the growing unity of Rainbow Coalition members. Activists certainly thought it was. According to Jiménez, "Repression certainly came down much stronger after the Rainbow Coalition was formed." While those incidents gave them something to rally around, government scrutiny—both through legal and illegal means—put a stranglehold on their efforts. Seemingly groundless rumors festered into long arguments. Accusations were sometimes petty, and other times they were deadly serious. A whisper campaign against the Patriots accused them of links to the Ku Klux Klan, and a steady stream of anonymous letters cast aspersions on political loyalties and interracial liaisons, and turned personal disagreements into deadly conflicts. Still, nothing prepared them for the fact that one of the decade's most public assassinations was about to take place in their backyard.

On December 4, 1969, the State of Illinois committed a now-infamous double murder in the city of Chicago. To do so State Attorney Edward V. Hanrahan convened a collection of federal, state and local law enforcement agents aided by an informant. The day began with an early morning raid on the Panther Party office. Before sunrise, two Panther leaders, Chairman Fred Hampton and eighteen-year-old member Mark Clark, lay dead. Four other Panthers were shot: Ronald "Doc" Satchel, Blair Anderson, Verlina Brewer and Brenda Harris. Police arrested all survivors including Hampton's fiancée, Deborah Johnson, who was sleeping next to him and eight months pregnant. At a press conference following the murders, Sergeant Daniel Groth maintained that he knocked on the door several times and identified himself as a police officer. When the Panthers failed to open the door Groth said he gently shoved the front door open as shots were fired from inside. Over the next several days, independent crime scene investigators easily debunked Groth's story. More than eighty bullet holes were found in the apartment. All but one came from police weapons. The lone bullet coming from Mark Clark's gun hit at an upward angle leading investigators to wonder if he fired as he fell to the ground after being shot once in the heart. Hampton was shot twice in the head, at point blank range. According to his fiancée, he never woke up.

Hanrahan held a press conference defending Groth's version of events and using the incident to further criminalize the entire Panther Party. "The immediate, violent criminal reaction of the occupants in shooting at announced police officers emphasizes the extreme viciousness of the Black Panther Party," he said during a televised press conference. The Panthers responded by conducting public tours of the blood-soaked rooms. Thousands of people arrived to see with their own eyes. Reporters, legal experts and neighbors found a scene of unprovoked slaughter. One *Chicago Sun-Times* reporter quit his job after his editors initially buried his story about what he saw inside that apartment. An elderly woman visiting the scene named it for what it was, "a Northern lynching."[22]

An independent autopsy later found barbiturates in Hampton's system. Everyone close to Hampton insisted he never did drugs. A sense of despair gripped the neighborhood surrounding 2337 West Monroe. Spray-painted messages of revenge sprung up on walls. For days hundreds kept vigil near the home. Speaking later, Deborah Johnson underscored the state of siege surrounding the Panther membership at the time. "They had destroyed our movement, not just in Illinois," she said. "Just like this [snapping her fingers]."[23] But the event also brought the Black community together. In the wake of Hampton's blatant murder, the Panthers gained even more supporters.

The Patriots were expanding too, but for some, Hampton's assassination cemented the need to break away from Chicago community organizing and build a stronger national presence. Without a strong national network, and without more members, some Chicago Patriots wondered whether the group would survive. The snail's pace of community services and local campaigns started to seem trivial in the face of such deadly repression. Local work remained important, but attack and infiltration were guaranteed. Chicago lawyer Jeffrey Haas, who worked closely with Rainbow Coalition members, recounted how the groups' joint efforts against urban renewal had suffered. "This project, which had been many months in the making and had successfully brought together black, Latino, and white community groups, suddenly seemed distant and insignificant."[24] The group's original founders, though, who'd seen the changes JOIN had inspired in their neighbors, disagreed with the idea of abandoning community work and suspected there was more ego involved in the suggestion than strategy. Another split was in the making.

By early 1970 the Young Patriots Organization severed into two groups. The Young Patriots remained in Chicago to continue local organizing, while the newly formed Patriot Party, under the leadership of William Fesperman, took the Patriots' message to the national stage. The group's newspaper explained the division as an ideological disagreement between those who supported community organizing and those who felt it was time to build a Left Party. Such divisions were nothing new, but Andy Keniston was disturbed by the events surrounding the Patriots split. Fesperman had disappeared for a few weeks, returning with a man named Arthur Turco whom none of the Chicago Patriots had ever met before. The two men convened the Patriots, telling everyone the West Coast Panthers were displeased with the Chicago branch and expected the Patriots to distance themselves from it. "This was extraordinary," explained Keniston. "We had a very good method of communicating with the Panthers through Bob Lee." Since there was never any reason for leaders to rely on information from anywhere else, Keniston felt certain the group had been infiltrated and remained suspicious of Turco. To him the Patriots' fate had been sealed. "From that moment on, I felt as if the deed had been done—that we were pawns in a drama we had little control over."

Keniston stayed in Chicago with Youngblood and the original Young Patriots members. With Chuck Geary they continued fighting urban renewal in Uptown, and several put their energy into a new group called Rising Up Angry, another JOIN spin-off started by Mike James. As for the Patriot Party, Fesperman and Turco franchised the group in a half dozen new cities and, for a short while, boasted dozens of new members. In 1970 they established headquarters in Manhattan and set up small branches in Eugene, Oregon; New Haven, Connecticut; Washington, D.C., and other cities. The group made a strong start on the East Coast, attracting two hundred people to a meeting against urban renewal in Yorkville, New York. The momentum proved hard to maintain, though. FBI files assert that their John Howard Free Breakfast Program in New York fed less than a dozen children daily. Poor white families seemed to be staying away from the program and operations were soon turned over to the New York Young Lords. Similarly, a free health clinic offered by the group received few visitors because other local clinics provided identical vaccinations for free if parents were unable to afford the service. Soon the group's housing campaigns in New York were confined to showing up at meetings organized by pre-existing resident advocacy groups. By spring 1970, Patriot Party efforts in New York were mainly confined to selling copies of their newspaper.

Internal strife also dogged the Patriot Party from the start. In New Haven, Connecticut, police targeted Patriot Tom Dostou while he was trying to set up a breakfast program. He was charged with possession of drugs (the Patriots maintained it was a bottle of vitamins) and non-support of his family, despite that fact that his wife and two children were in the car at the time of his arrest. With little explanation other than the claim Dostou was "provacateuring," the Patriot newspaper announced that Dostou along with four other members had been expelled. In the coming year, Patriot activities focused almost entirely on legal battles, both their own and those of Black Panther leadership. The Patriot Party, like the rest of the movement, found it hard to carry on any pro-active organizing with so many disruptions. Today, COINTEL-PRO documents available under the Freedom of Information Act confirm their suspicions. The FBI tracked every move the Patriots made from the moment they started working with the Panthers. In one agency document, the list of informants stretches for three full pages, line after line of redacted names, addresses and phone numbers. For a good portion of the Patriots' existence, there were actually more people watching the group than there were members.

. . . .

In the District of Columbia, activists attempted to build a Patriot Party chapter, but it was quickly swallowed by the campaign to defend the local Panthers from the ongoing FBI crackdown. Bob Simpson was born in D.C. and got involved with Students for a Democratic Society while attending the University of Maryland. Simpson was the product of a working-class family that moved to the suburbs during the first wave of white flight. At the University of Maryland he submerged himself in solidarity work with the southern civil rights movement, which eventually put him into the orbit of the Patriots and the Panthers.

As the global tumult of 1968 unfolded, the University of Maryland chapter of SDS turned its attention to supporting the campus workers' union of mostly Black low-wage employees. In Maryland, still very much a Jim Crow state, mutual distrust had prevented lasting collaboration between white and Black students. The same went for the workers. Most white employees enjoyed higher wages and occupied white-collar positions. Blacks worked in the cafeteria and janitorial jobs. One dorm housekeeper, Gladys Jefferson, a leader in the American Federation of State, County and Municipal

Employees Local 1072, was known for both her organizing savvy and patience in building alliances between campus radicals in SDS and the Black Student Union. Through Jefferson's example, Simpson found a practical way to address civil rights locally and undermine racism on his own campus.

Energized by the planned arrival of the national Poor People's Convention in the capitol, Simpson worked behind the scenes building the stage that Martin Luther King was to speak from. King was assassinated before he could deliver that speech. Simpson was devastated. The murder let loose a dam of hopelessness. Many, like Simpson, retreated from activism in the months that followed. Some never found their way back. Fortunately, Simpson did. Fred Hampton's assassination and the national outrage that followed convinced him that they had been on the right path. They needed a much stronger multiracial movement. The Rainbow Coalition was a sign that the civil rights movement's vision of the beloved community was still possible, if in a different formation. He was less certain, though, about sticking to the path of nonviolence.

Simpson contacted Dick Ochs, a friend from Maryland SDS, to ask how white radicals could best support the Panthers. Through Ochs he learned that a new Patriots chapter was starting in Washington, D.C. The small chapter mixed some familiar SDS members with working-class whites from the area including Danny Embry, an ex-Marine, who had survived Vietnam without a scratch. He walked with an intense limp, though, after being tossed around a police van. Embry had been arrested while supporting picketing furniture workers and was handcuffed in the back of a paddy wagon when the vehicle flipped over due to heavy rain. His wife, Elise, was from Kentucky. Like so many other activists who'd grown up in poor and working-class communities, her firsthand experience made her confident white southerners could get onboard a revolutionary movement, if only the movement spoke to them. The Patriots were still one of the only organizations in the nation trying to do this.

Crafting such a message to the white working-class took a backseat for obvious reasons. Locked into a constant dance with local authorities that regularly raided their offices, arrested members and disrupted activities, activists were permanently on the defensive. In the wake of Hampton's and Clark's murders, the Panthers' strategy of armed self-defense seemed the only realistic option to the D.C. Patriots. They remained a small cadre, operating independently of the original Chicago chapter and its hillbilly origins. This had one upside. Bob Simpson couldn't reconcile himself to the use of the Confederate flag, and the relative autonomy of the new Patriots chapters meant he didn't have to. That mischosen symbol was also the least of their worries. Several Baltimore Panthers had just been arrested on suspicion of killing a snitch, and the Patriots' Arthur Turco was also implicated.[25]

In 1970 many Panther leaders were still on the run or in court. The prior spring in Manhattan, police had rounded up twenty-one New York Panthers, accusing them of a plot to use explosives to destroy police stations, high schools and even the Bronx Botanical Gardens. It took two years, but eventually the Panther 21 were all acquitted.[26] In New Haven, police alleged that Bobby Seale ordered the murder of a suspected informant, Alex Rackley. His trial began at the same time that the U.S. started bombing missions in Cambodia to destroy National Liberation Front outposts. In order to reach out to white people in the area, the Panthers asked the Patriots to come to New Haven for the "Free Bobby Seale and Stop the War" rally. The National Guard brought a full force to control the rally. That evening, a fundraising dance was scheduled for a local skating rink. As Simpson and his wife napped in the parking lot, an explosion rang out. The bomb went off before the dance had officially started. No one was seriously hurt, but the Panthers were blamed for the blast.[27]

Panic descended on the Panthers and the Patriots. The number of movement people shot or in prison piled up. Both groups assumed there were informers in their midst, but they were hard to identify—some members' disruptive nature seemed just as likely to be personality or a medical issue. At many points it was impossible to tell friend from foe. It was also impossible to sustain any real community programs. Activists were always coming in and out of hiding. The D.C. Patriots' dream of creating breakfast programs, health clinics and liberation schools was overshadowed by the need for their own survival. One afternoon Simpson arrived at the 17th Street Patriot-Panther offices to discover police had the offices on lockdown. Most members were arrested. A few weeks later, Patriot Party member Jenny Stearns finally decided to call things for what they were: The Patriots had become "The Committee to Defend the Panthers." After less than a year the D.C. Patriots were no more.

Back in New York, fortunes were no better. For the majority of the Patriots, their own experience with political repression was nowhere near the punishment meted out upon Black radicals. Still, a mass arrest of the entire Patriots central committee led to the dissolution of the organization. On February 22, 1970, New York police raided the group's 2nd Avenue headquarters. According to witnesses, officers held guns to the heads of children, threatening to kill them if they didn't stop crying. William Fesperman and Larry Moore were taken downstairs. Simultaneously, police stopped a carload of Patriots traveling across town. They arrested twelve Patriots and charged them with illegal possession of weapons and guns as well as interfering with arrest. Police hinted to the press that the

Patriots had a hand in the bombing of a judge's house and assorted sniping of police. The twelve were held on bail totaling $34,500. While the charges were eventually dropped, the bust just added to mounting legal troubles for Oregon-based Patriot Chuck Armsbury who was in town visiting. After spending weeks in a New York jail his legal counsel, lawyer-turned-tabloid-reporter Geraldo Rivera, who also represented the Young Lords, simply handed him over to federal officers to face firearms charges pending in Oregon.

The Eugene, Oregon, chapter of the Patriots was fairly new, but West Coast activists had their own share of problems. Two weeks earlier an armed gunman had attacked the Patriot Party office and targeted individuals. "He had shot openly at a young Black student, shot openly at a white woman in our party, right near the campus," Armsbury explained. According to former Black Panther Jaja Nkruma who relocated to Eugene as a youth from Southern California, the Panther presence in Eugene was virtually responsible for the creation of a Black community in the town and not everyone was happy about it. Seattle Panther chair Aaron Dixon hoped to consolidate alliances up and down the West Coast. To do so, he had several dozen Panthers relocate from Compton, California, combining with a small group of Black students there. Howard Anderson, who previously worked in Mississippi and Alabama with CORE and SNCC, became captain of the Eugene Panther branch. The Panthers created a breakfast program and a liberation school, with Armsbury and his wife helping out and building a new Patriots chapter.

It didn't take long for local racists to stake their opposition to the alliance. Shortly after the targeted shootings, another assailant fired on Patriot Party headquarters. To Armsbury, the reason was self-evident. "Back then, there were the Minutemen militias who weren't too happy about whites and Blacks in a rural area cooperating with one another." In Eugene, whites opposing racism were considered race traitors, making them open targets for white vigilantes. Crossing the color line had pronounced consequences. Since the 1920s, several of rural Oregon's mayors and police chiefs had connections to the Klan. White supremacist organizations lay in wait for opportunity, confident in the relative protection of local law enforcement. Soon after the attack on Patriots headquarters, an "unknown punk" assaulted ten-year-old Lani Wright, daughter of a Patriots member, in a local drugstore. The child was knocked unconscious and spent multiple weeks in the hospital.

....

When the Black Panthers began asserting their "right to bear arms," the gesture had been equal parts symbolic and defensive. In rural Oregon, Second Amendment protections evolved far beyond symbolic meaning. Self-protection was a necessity, but it also made radicals immensely vulnerable and provided a distraction for reporters who wanted to write about violent radicals rather than studied revolutionaries. Just before Armsbury's trip to New York, local police stopped a car carrying six Patriots, ostensibly for a noisy exhaust. Officers noticed two firearms on the floorboard of the backseat. Police ordered Armsbury out of the vehicle and asked him to pull back his jacket, revealing a .45-caliber pistol. According to the police report, the confiscated weapons were fully loaded and a notebook belonging to Armsbury was full of "Revolutionary Theory."[28] Police arrested the driver of the car for driving with a defective muffler. The Patriots maintained the guns were solely for self-defense and warranted given the recent attacks on them, which included two attempted murders, an assault and attacks on their office. It did no good. The bust started a multi-year prison odyssey for Chuck Armsbury.

Only a few years earlier Armsbury seemed destined for academia, not prison. Born in Kansas, and raised by a single mother in Eastern Washington, he worked as a meatpacker before attending college at the University of Oregon, Eugene. It was there that he met his first wife, Sonja Brooks, a Black woman who later joined the Panthers. Armsbury was one of those working-class organizers who could move easily between Eugene's poor white community and the town's university. Although he earned a degree in sociology and came to the University of Oregon to teach, he was always more at home with fellow workers. His early political action included a run for mayor of Eugene in 1968. Soon after, Brooks took him to a Panther convention. The Black Panthers' vision transformed Armsbury's politics, and the Young Patriots he met at the convention completed them. Listening to William Fesperman address the crowd, Armsbury felt there was finally someone in the movement who not only wanted to reach poor whites, but also could do so. "There really wasn't much encouragement from most of the Left for poor white people to do much about their situation," Armsbury recalls. The Patriots filled that gap and Fesperman seemed a reliable leader.

Armsbury had no way of knowing that his new affiliation would lead to a ten-year prison sentence. At the trial for the Eugene weapons charges, the arresting officer showed up to testify in full Marine Corps uniform; he had returned to the Marines after being discharged from the police force for failure to turn in confiscated property. The proceedings were also marred by a series of bombings in the Portland and Eugene areas. The judge allowed speculation about Armsbury's involvement in the blasts to come up in court. Some activists suspected authorities might have perpetrated the attacks themselves, but they could never prove it. Throughout the trial, no evidence surfaced that Armsbury took part in any bombing. Nonetheless, in August 1970 U.S. District Judge Alfred

T. Goodwin sentenced Armsbury to two concurrent ten-year prison terms. At sentencing, Goodwin said he anticipated the conviction could be reversed on appeal and so, he reasoned, giving Armsbury the maximum sentence would assure jail time but give the court flexibility to alter the sentences—that is, if Armsbury showed signs of rehabilitation.

Sent to McNeil Island Federal Penitentiary in the southern Puget Sound, Armsbury immediately mounted an appeal and petitioned for bail. Judge Goodwin denied his bail request stating, "I think Armsbury is a little unstable. I was worried that he might decide to blow up something." Goodwin also accused Armsbury of writing him threatening letters, something the judge later downplayed when questioned about it by the press. Goodwin justified his actions by citing a pre-sentencing investigation alleging Armsbury's links to other bombings in Eugene during May 1969. The unsubstantiated bombing allegations resurfaced throughout his appeal and parole efforts. Both Patriots and Panthers suspected the judge may have been playing a waiting game, giving prosecutors time to put together a case around the bombings. Richard J. Oba, who was convicted in the bombings, received an immunity offer in exchange for testimony against Armsbury. Rejecting the offer because he believed immunity laws too new and untested, Oba was sent to jail. Arthur Cox, an expelled member of the Panthers, was the one to testify that he had been at a meeting where Oba and Armsbury conspired about the bombings. Cox himself had been convicted of two unrelated felonies.

For Armsbury organizing didn't end at the prison gates. Rainbow Coalition politics were just as necessary inside prisons, maybe even more so, and Armsbury began organizing fellow prisoners immediately. The conditions at McNeil Island led prisoners to believe they were part of a controlled social experiment designed to amplify inmate-on-inmate violence.[29] The fall of 1970 was particularly brutal at the prison, with inmates suspecting guard collusion in a hit-squad death, several stabbings and deteriorating conditions. Things came to a boiling point in November following the fatal stabbing of prisoner William Carter by fellow inmate Eddy Sanchez. Inmates and guards all knew that Sanchez had a poorly treated mental illness and was prone to sporadic violence. In this instance Sanchez announced his intent to commit murder merely two hours prior, but guards made no effort to separate him from other prisoners. Armsbury sought the collaboration of Paul Bailleaux, an inmate litigator, to craft a response. The duo met in the Portland U.S. Marshall's office. Bailleaux was a lifer in transit to federal custody from Oregon State Prison. President of the lifers' club there, he had earned the ire of prison officials for his steady stream of lawsuits challenging prison conditions. The Old Con and the Young Radical became solid friends. Throughout December, the two drafted a lengthy document they named "The Genocide Complaint."[30]

Neither Bailleaux nor Armsbury had illusions that any court of law would side with prisoners alleging genocide by the federal government. Rather the suit was an attempt to build multiracial prisoner unity and galvanize support from outside the walls. "Rarely had writ-writers purported to file a cause of action alleging the whole damn top-down management of McNeil Island prison was hell-bent on our common destruction," Armsbury later wrote. To bolster their charge of "terrorism and murder" at McNeil, the plaintiffs pointed to several other suspicious inmate deaths, including Larry Mastne, Troy White and Roy Rodriguez. Arguing that prison officials had ample knowledge and opportunity to prevent each death, the complaint urged officials to segregate violent, mentally ill inmates from the population. The Genocide Complaint went further, too, as its authors outlined racially based "divide and conquer" tactics used inside prisons. The complaint described the engineering of racial hostility through "racial name-calling and the granting of preferred treatment based solely on skin color and nationality." They also deconstructed the prison's two-tiered system of favoritism. McNeil paid an hourly wage for prison industry labor and none to dining room, kitchen, laundry and maintenance staff. Pointing to prison officials' own public assertions that they were fully in control of everything that happened inside, the lawsuit argued that officials were clearly responsible, then, for the abhorrent conditions, favoritism and deaths at McNeil.

At first, it seemed some of the lifers had a better chance of leaving McNeil than seeing the Genocide Complaint succeed. Guards in the visiting room prevented the complaint from reaching a Portland attorney who planned to file it in a Tacoma court. A prison counselor offered to mail it through the formal prison mail system, but the complaint was promptly lost. Bailleaux had anticipated this and prepared a facsimile, managing to sneak the document to supportive lawyers on the outside. When finally filed in January 1971, the suit assembled a rainbow coalition of its own with six lead plaintiffs. Willie Brazier, a Seattle Panther member, Gerald Thompson, Larry Crews and Armando Vargas joined Armsbury and Bailleaux in charging federal officials with a thinly veiled genocide behind prison walls.

According to Armsbury, prisoner reaction to the complaint was a victory in and of itself. The suit opened a space to discuss racial unity and divisive favoritism. Small indignities, like not being able to kiss your wife more than once during a visit, were linked to larger ones, such as guards' lethal decision to release Sanchez back into the general population. One evening, while Armsbury studied in the writ room, he was summoned to the warden's office and presented with a letter allegedly signed by "real inmates" condemning the plaintiffs for working with "pinko fag" lawyers. It included a death threat against Armsbury. He laughed it off and returned to the writ room, secure with the fact that McNeil's prisoners stood behind the Genocide Complaint.

As preparations for court proceeded, McNeil whirred with rumors of an unrelated labor strike. McNeil prisoners were paid wages for their work assembling cables for Polaris submarines used by the U.S. military. Though initially planned as an anti-war action, those prison workers added the Genocide Complaint issues to their list of demands. Bailleaux recoiled at the thought of a strike. He believed that any sort of work stoppage, especially one linked to the anti-war movement, would bring greater repression than the inmates were prepared for. Armsbury concurred. He had come to think that explosive and chaotic actions were ultimately futile and allowed provocateurs the opportunity to attack. The strike went ahead anyway. For ten days prisoners refused to leave their cells. During the strike all prison staff, including the prison chaplain, wore full riot gear. Guards eventually broke the strike through a combination of intimidation, bribery and loss of privileges. In the end, giving inmates access to the more desirable two-man "flat" cells, broke the strike faster than brute force.

Shortly thereafter, the Genocide Complaint was unceremoniously dismissed. Even though Armsbury actually counseled against the strike, the Genocide Complaint was viewed as its catalyst. When the strike failed, the momentum died, and Armsbury was sent to isolation for orchestrating the events. Then one morning a guard took him to the waiting area with no explanation. He was abruptly transferred to the Marion Penitentiary. To his surprise Eddy Sanchez was there too.

Armsbury's supporters continued a public campaign for his release. In spring 1971 the 9th Circuit Court upheld his conviction, but just before Christmas, Judge Goodwin ordered his parole. The judge set a five-year parole and prohibited Armsbury from possessing firearms. In 1974, Armsbury returned to prison once more for harboring escaped convict Carl Cletus Bowles, in prison for a double kidnapping and murder, who had escaped while on a social pass and killed Deputy Carlton Smith in Eugene. Armsbury admits to being blinded by his own feelings at the time that all prisoners were simply victims of the government and capitalism. He had underestimated Bowles' potential for violence. "He was completely raised by the state, and I didn't understand what that could do to someone." For this, Armsbury served four years of another ten-year sentence before being paroled in 1978.

By the time Armsbury was released, the Patriots and the Rainbow Coalition had long since passed. While Armsbury remains involved in community politics along with Bob Simpson, now a history teacher, and Andy Keniston, few other Patriots have stayed involved with progressive activism. William Fesperman returned to China Grove, North Carolina. Doug Youngblood and fellow Patriot Carol Coronado started a family and, along with Junebug Boykin, mostly retreated from public organizing. They remained in occasional contact with former JOIN members and in 2005, at his mother's memorial, Youngblood spoke favorably about their years of work in Chicago. He focused mostly on the JOIN years. The Patriots era left deeper scars. Like many of the people who lived through this time, privacy became a treasured possession. Youngblood remained in Illinois until his death in 2008.

....

In 1972 Raymond Tackett, a Chicago Patriots member, had described the devastation that shattered the organizations in the Rainbow Coalition. "Every time one of us were arrested, we could see our pictures hanging on the wall of the police station and the pigs aiming darts at them." Tackett also worked with the Patriots sister group, Rising Up Angry, and did his own stint in prison. "All there was left was the power structure of the pigs who had destroyed everything else," he wrote.[31] Tackett was killed in 1973. Under circumstances eerily similar to John Howard's murder, Tackett returned to his home state of Kentucky to organize in the mining town of Evarts. He was in the process of starting a Serve the People–inspired free clinic when he was killed. Although the police arrested a suspect in his murder, Tackett's family alleges he was killed by a hired assassin, paid for by the police.[32]

While the Young Patriots and Patriot Party only receive passing mention in most histories of the New Left, their alliance with the Panthers has been held up as proof of the era's revolutionary vision.[33] A group of poor white guys—some former gang members—working alongside the Black Panthers and Young Lords contradicts biased notions about poor whites as either hopelessly racist or reliant on the Left intelligentsia for a radical reeducation. To Jaja Nkruma, the Patriots were obvious allies because they were truly grassroots. "In order to be grassroots you have to reach your community in the beauty shops, barbershops, grocery stores, factories, sawmills and cabinet factories," he said. To outsiders the Patriots–Lords–Panthers partnership may have seemed unlikely, but to its founders it was an inimitable political alliance—unique and difficult, but necessary. Theirs was a project molded in the image of other multiracial uprisings in U.S. history, and like the work of Carl and Anne Braden in the South and JOIN Community Union in Chicago, the Patriots boldly suggested that the white children of the Southern Diaspora might claim an identity separate from the legacy of racism and help realize the promise of rainbow politics for the entire nation.

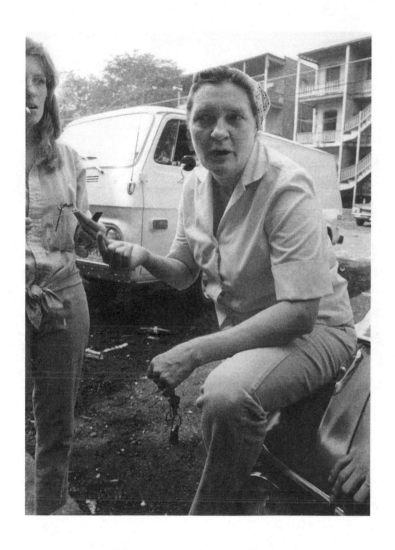

Peggy Terry on Clifton Street, Chicago, Illinois, Summer 1967.
(Courtesy of Wisconsin Historical Society)

Actor Harry Belafonte visits JOIN, from left to right: Ralph
Thurman, Evelyn Arnold, unknown, Harry Belafonte, Virginia
Bowers, Dominga Alcantar, Peggy Terry, Spring 1965.

(Photo by Nanci Hollander, courtesy of Wisconsin Historical Society)

Dovie Coleman at the JOIN office.

(Photo by Burton Steck, courtesy of Mike James)

JOIN march against urban renewal, 1966.

(Photo by Nanci Hollander, courtesy of Bob Lawson)

Organizer Bob Lawson gives Mayor Richard J. Daley
a copy of JOIN's paper *The Firing Line.*

(*Photo by Nanci Hollander, courtesy of
Wisconsin Historical Society*)

Jimmy Curry and Junebug Boykin at Goodfellows'
march to the Summerdale Police Station, 1966.

(Photo by Nanci Hollander, courtesy of Mike James)

Peggy Terry, Hy Thurman, and friends, at Resurrection City,
Washington, DC, June 1968.

(Courtesy of Highlander Research and Education Center)

Young Patriots members outside their free
community health clinic, 1969.

(Courtesy of Mike James)

Junebug Boykin outside JOIN's office.

(Photo by Nanci Hollander, courtesy of Jean Tepperman)

Doug Youngblood at a rally for a new playground in Chicago's Uptown neighborhood.

(Courtesy of Wisconsin Historical Society)

William "Preacherman" Fesperman, Patriot Party.

(Courtesy of Wisconsin Historical Society)

Fred Hampton, chairman of the Illinois Black Panther Party, speaking at rally to support the Chicago 8, October 29, 1969.

(AP Photo/Staff)

Puerto Rican activists and members of the Rainbow Coalition take over a building to honor Young Lords member Manuel Ramos, who was killed by an off-duty police officer in May 1969.

(Courtesy of Mike James)

In Chicago, the Young Lords lead residents in a march against police brutality and the local Red Squad. Cha-Cha Jiménez, bottom right, wearing beret.

(Courtesy of Mike James)

Eugene, Oregon, Patriots and Panthers at a protest again conditions at Attica State Prison.

(Courtesy of Chuck Armsbury)

Patriots and Panthers family photo in Eugene, Oregon.

(Courtesy of Chuck Armsbury)

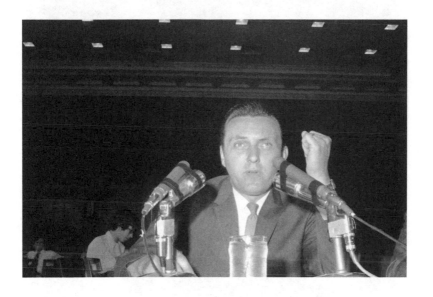

Just months after the Rainbow Coalition formed, William
L. Olsen, commander of the Chicago "Red Squad," tells a
Senate investigations subcommittee that the Black Panthers
have created similar groups among Puerto Rican and poor
white radicals. July 1, 1969.

(AP Photo/Henry Griffin)

Mike James (right) with unidentified man in Fairborn, Ohio,
on the day Rising Up Angry got its name
from the theme song of the film *Wild in the Streets*.

(Courtesy of Mike James)

Rising Up Angry's first group photo, 1969.

(Courtesy of Mike James)

Anti-war rally supported by Rising Up Angry as part of the national "People's Armed Farces Day," May 1972.

(Courtesy of Bob Lawson)

Neighborhood kids volunteering at the Rising Up
Angry health clinic, circa 1973.

(Courtesy of Bob Lawson)

Rising Up Angry members hold pictures of housing violations in the home of Margaret Burton. The action helps Burton win her case at Chicago's housing court, October 1972.

(Courtesy of Bob Lawson)

Rising Up Angry's Diane Fager, Victory Kadish and Norie
Davis at a Chicago Women's Liberation Union / Rising
Up Angry abortion rights rally.

(Courtesy of Bob Lawson)

October 4th Organization protesting a Philadelphia city council bill allowing a Model Cities housing site to be used as a truck-loading terminal, Kensington, 1971.

(Photo by H. Earle Shull Jr., courtesy of Temple University, Urban Archives McDowell Collection)

Final issue of JOIN newspaper, *The Firing Line*, during Peggy Terry's campaign for vice president of the United States, Fall 1968.

The Patriot, volume 1, number 1. March 21, 1970.

Rising Up Angry, volume 5, number 11. February 1974.

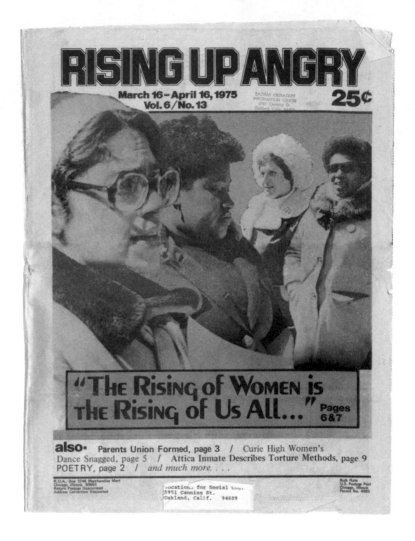

RISING UP ANGRY

March 16 – April 16, 1975
Vol. 6 / No. 13

EASTBAY LIBERATION
INFORMATION CENTER
2951 Canning St.
Oakland, Calif.

25¢

"The Rising of Women is the Rising of Us All..." Pages 6&7

also· Parents Union Formed, page 3 / Curie High Women's
Dance Snagged, page 5 / Attica Inmate Describes Torture Methods, page 9
POETRY, page 2 / *and much more. . . .*

R.U.A., Box 3746 Merchandise Mart
Chicago, Illinois 60654
Return Postage Guaranteed
Address Correction Requested

Location. for Social City.
5951 Canning St.
Oakland, Calif.   94609

Bulk Rate
U.S. Postage Paid
Chicago, Illinois
Permit No. 4985

Rising Up Angry, volume 6, number 13. March–April 1975.

October 4th Organization's *A Single Spark!*, Fall 1973.

A Single Spark!, Winter 1974.

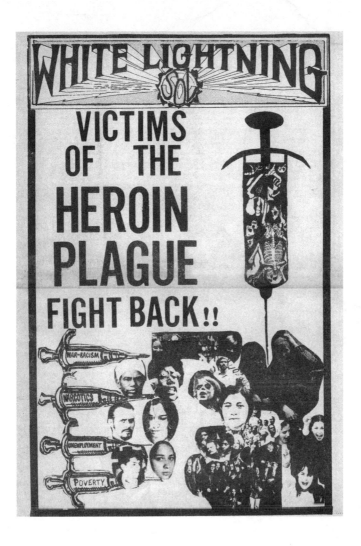

White Lightning newspaper, 1970.

White Lightning, number 23. March 1974.

CHAPTER 3

· · · · · · · · · · ·

Pedagogy of the Streets:
Rising Up Angry

There's a new sun / Risin' up angry in the sky
And there's a new voice sayin' / "We're not afraid to die"
Let the old world make believe / It's blind and deaf and dumb
But nothing can change the shape of things to come

—Davie Allan and the Arrows, "The Shape of Things to Come"

On December 6, 1969, five thousand people filed into the First Baptist Church to pay respects to murdered Black Panther Fred Hampton. It was unusually warm for a December weekend in Chicago. One of the mourners, fifteen-year-old Paul Wozniak, felt his anxiety level rise when he entered the church. As a white kid from Northwest Chicago, Wozniak had only a few Black acquaintances at his Jesuit high school and none from the all white, blue-collar neighborhood where he grew up. The 41st Ward of the Far Northwest Side was the only ward with a Republican city council member and was home to Chicago's cops, sanitation workers and firefighters. They lived on the farthest possible edge of the city, penned in by a law requiring municipal workers to live within city limits. Wozniak's neighbors in Norwood, Jefferson and Edison Park adopted a fierce protectionism typical among residents in the city's white enclaves. If they were being forced to stay, they planned to police their borders and keep out the riffraff, by which they meant hippies, commies, spics and negroes.

For these residents, putting the fear of God in their children seemed a good way to erect the barbed wire fences they couldn't build down Montrose Avenue. Many of Wozniak's childhood friends were sons of police officers. The boys spent their time recounting stories they heard from their fathers about violent, wanton Blacks and Puerto Ricans. They had been told how one guy stabbed a friend over a cheap bottle of wine; another guy committed suicide with a shotgun in the mouth. Wozniak and his friends took such stories as proof that "those people" lacked common sense. To them, they were just as crazy as the monks in South Vietnam who protested the war by burning themselves in the street. Pointless, they thought. But something in Wozniak's worldview started to shift by his teen years. Some of his newer friends were considered the bad kids, the motorcycle-riding greasers and dropouts who made up Northwest Side gangs. They raced cars, shot pool and listened to soul, Motown and the Rolling Stones. Depicted most famously in books like *The Outsiders*, greasers got their name from the pomade sheen of their slicked back hair. They dressed in three-quarter-length black leather jackets and baggy blue or gray work pants and earned their reputation from hanging out on corners, smoking, shooting the shit and fighting whenever someone threatened them. The first time Wozniak saw pictures of the Black Panthers he noticed that they wore the same black leather jackets and heavy boots as the white greasers he knew. By the time he met the Panthers in person Wozniak realized they shared more than a working-class sense of style.

Wozniak first heard Hampton speak at a Federal Building rally just months before his murder. The gathering attracted thousands calling for the release of the Chicago 8, including JOIN's Rennie

Davis and Panther Bobby Seale, on trial for conspiracy to start a riot at the 1968 Democratic National Convention. From the platform, a twenty-year-old Hampton laid out the vision of the emerging Rainbow Coalition. The message drew in Wozniak, who arrived at the rally that day after meeting members of a new organization called Rising Up Angry, launched in summer 1969 by ex-JOIN Community Union members. Where the Young Patriots set a bar for revolutionary swagger among already-political poor whites, Rising Up Angry set its sights on reaching the young and disenfranchised across the city, many of whom didn't identify as poor or share the southern heritage that united the Patriots. For radicals seeking new directions, Rising Up Angry provided a way to carry the best of JOIN's politics beyond Uptown. They intended to build an organization rooted in working-class culture and recruited a cadre of working-class radicals that could help see the radical vision of social transformation to fruition. Their first endeavor was a professional-looking newspaper that brought Left politics to the neighborhood level, featuring blurbs about rock concerts, cars and parties bookended by articles about liberation fronts in Africa, the United Farm Workers and, of course, pictures of greaser youth hanging out.

One evening Rising Up Angry founder Mike James approached Wozniak while he was hanging out in nearby Monument Park with some greasers who had a reputation for violence. As James walked toward them one of Wozniak's friends hurled an empty bottle at him, shattering glass everywhere. James walked right over to the kid and retorted, "Hey, that's not cool. Even pigs don't shit in their own beds." James's confidence and bravado made an impression, so when he came back around a few days later Wozniak took a newspaper from him and said he'd try to come to the Federal Building rally. It was *Angry*'s first issue and the cover depicted a woman on the back of a motorcycle holding an M-16. The masthead read,

"Rising Up Angry, To Love We Must Fight." One read through the paper showed Wozniak that there was far more going on with the world than he'd known. He decided it was really his family and neighbors who had lacked common sense.

A few days later Wozniak headed out to the rally. Before leaving his house he painted "Free the Chicago 8" on a four-foot-wide banner made from bed sheets he'd found in his mother's closet. He added the subtitle, "Northwest Side Greasers Support the Conspiracy 8." When he got there he met dozens more Angry members, the Puerto Rican Young Lords, the Young Patriots and, of course, the Panthers. Hampton's fiery oratory roused the crowd, but for Wozniak it was the vision, not just the timbre, Hampton put forth that opened his eyes. Rising Up Angry had turned out almost one hundred people for the rally and when a group of local neo-Nazis showed up across the street, Angry amassed its forces to confront them, successfully chasing them away. Before the rally was over, Wozniak agreed to be a Northwest correspondent for Angry's paper.

When the radio reported Fred Hampton's death on the morning of December 4, 1969, Wozniak sat at his parents' breakfast table in shock. Instinctually he knew it had to be a police murder, but that hardly prepared him for the gruesome images soon plastered across newspapers. When he looked at the broad mocking smiles of the cops in those photos he recognized the "telling criminal smirk" he'd seen time and again on his neighbors' faces as they bragged to their sons about the day's patrols. He contemplated the gravity of the situation. How would people react? Was Chicago on the verge of a race war? Where did that leave him and his newfound comrades?

That morning he tied a black armband around his arm and went to school. His silent memorial didn't go over well and marked the beginning of regular school discipline for his political activities.

The following Saturday he took rapid transit to Hampton's wake on the West Side of Chicago. Almost all of the mourners were Black and Wozniak's panic set in. It was one thing to go to a rally at the Federal Building, but seemed another to arrive at a murdered Panthers' funeral in an all-Black neighborhood knowing emotions were running so high. After he accidentally stepped on the patent leather shoe of a young Panther, Wozniak awkwardly begged forgiveness and braced for retaliation. The tall teenager just looked away.

When Wozniak returned home that afternoon, he found the back door to his parents' housed was locked, something they never did. As the door opened his father came out and started pummeling him, something *he* never did. Small for his age, Wozniak immediately fell to the porch as his mother yelled hysterically, "Where were you? Where were you?" They already knew. A police officer in the neighborhood had scared the elder Wozniak with a phone call asking why his son was at a Black Panther's wake. As the leader of the local Red Squad, the unit of the police dedicated to surveilling and disrupting Left organizations, it was only a matter of time before Wozniak's neighbor knew about his comings and goings. Wozniak was busted. When his radical politics got him kicked out of his Catholic school, he transferred to the local public high school and kept on passing out copies of Angry's newspaper, talking to other students about the Free Huey campaign and what *really* happened to Fred Hampton. Rising Up Angry became his new home.

....

As it had been for new radicals in JOIN Community Union and the Young Patriots, the moral and political demands of Black Liberation supplied the catalyst that called Paul Wozniak to activism. Fred Hampton's murder only proved the brazen lengths the State would go to silence dissenters. Visible and violent police retaliation against the Left only pushed him toward deeper radicalism. It did the same for millions of others who, equally opposed to U.S. military action abroad, felt a revolution was necessary.[1] With people's lives on the line, more and more young leftists realized there could be no neutral stance. Of course there was no universal agreement about how to proceed. For all the outpouring of revolutionary sentiment, fault lines widened on the Left as radicals debated how masses of North Americans could be stirred to action. Even more, serious questions emerged about exactly how white activists should act in solidarity with liberation movements—both movements abroad and those in the U.S. whose leaders faced the imminent threat of jail, infiltration and execution.

The debate about the direction of the U.S. Left had come to a head in June 1969 at the Students for a Democratic Society convention in Chicago. There, in the dingy Chicago Coliseum, the largest student organization in the U.S. broke into factions that disagreed bitterly over interpretations of Marxist-Leninist theory and who exactly would be the leading force in making a revolution. Prior to the convention, competing factions had published arguments and counterarguments in movement publications under bylines that became permanent monikers for their ideological positions. The Revolutionary Youth Movement (RYM, pronounced "rim") argued that SDS should take a militant approach to active solidarity with Third World politics by supporting the self-determination of the Black "internal colony" in the United States and national liberation struggles abroad. RYM then split into two sections: The Weathermen proposed immediate, armed action to confront the machinations of imperialism and racism on U.S. soil; while the newly minted RYM II asserted that a new communist political party could be built by organizing workers in U.S factories. Despite their tactical differences, both RYMs came to the June 1969 convention united against a third faction: the Progressive Labor Party. PL, as it was known, opposed any form of nationalism on the grounds that it divided workers. PL argued that class struggle was the primary struggle, the demands of Black nationalists were divisive and the only place for students in the movement was in an alliance with workers.[2]

With Weather and RYM II on one side and PL on the other, leaders came to the convention ready to battle for control over the future of SDS. Each side wanted the other expelled, and both vied for the votes of SDS's national members—upwards of 100,000 in 1969, about two thousand of whom were at the convention. The threat of expulsions and counter-expulsions were a long time coming, which attracted a fair number of media reporters there to document the conflict, but most SDS members across the country had no idea what these factions were talking about. After an extremely contentious series of debates (and fistfights), RYM activists expelled the Progressive Labor Party. The conference signaled an unfortunate fact: SDS was, in effect, dead, its leaders divided over questions of class, race and strategy.[3]

It was a disorienting moment for the group's rank and file, who failed to see the point of the endless debates. It was even more frustrating for radicals outside the student movement who watched as ideological infighting consumed meetings, drew attention away from local work and slowed movement building. There were important ideological differences to discuss, but for Chicago's working-class radicals it seemed like a lot of middle-class intellectual bullshit. Many former JOIN members felt both remaining factions failed to address the permanent underclass living in neighborhoods like theirs—the greasers, domestic workers, dropouts, welfare recipients, addicts and under-the-table laborers. For them, the choice between organizing in factories and building a radical army left out key terrain: the struggle against racism, poverty and imperialism rooted in their communities. All sides diagnosed imperialism as the disease, but they prescribed vastly different medicine.[4]

In the ashes of SDS the white New Left faced a three-way fork: one path led to direct, armed insurrection; the second toward a national party built from the shop floor; and the third, less-traveled among the era's revolutionaries, veered toward the community. These activists had, in many ways, grown up politically together. Some understood that these leftists were trying to work out strategies for real problems of movement building. Many remained friends as they argued out their tactical differences. Still others, like Uptown's Young Patriots, who never felt part of the student movement anyway, sidestepped the ideological infights by forming their own community organizations and mocking middle-class leftists for excluding the very masses they were arguing about. Of course, there was a thread of reactive anti-intellectualism in this, but for ex-students like Mike James the idea of anti-imperialist neighborhood organizing simply looked like the best path given the headway JOIN made in the preceding years. It wasn't the only path, but for JOIN's seasoned organizers it was an equally important one that few others were willing to try.

Prior to the SDS convention James already sketched out the first issue of *Rising Up Angry*. For him, the political chasms mattered less at the community level where it was usually a mistake to come on too strong with a political line anyway—at least at first. One of James's first new recruits to the project was Steve Tappis, an SDS member who was also one of the original authors of the Weathermen's manifesto. Tappis moved to Chicago in 1968 to work at the national SDS office and organize in a local machinery factory. While his own family enjoyed some class mobility from blue-collar Brooklyn to New York's suburbs, he was different from most SDS members in that he never attended college. After high school, he took a job as a janitor because the pay was good and allowed him to do movement work in his spare time. After moving to Chicago to work with SDS, he was able to live on savings and part-time work.

Tappis's identification with the community, workplace and the militant strains of the student movement gave him a unique vantage point. He supported the thinking that gave rise to the Weathermen, and later the Weather Underground Organization, but by the close of the 1969 SDS convention, Tappis realized something important: Rebellions rarely come when scheduled and often seem farthest away when material conditions would seem most ripe. The revolution they wanted was going to take some time. So, when Mike James proposed an alternative to the RYM II versus Weathermen debate, Tappis decided to focus on neighborhood organizing. Unceremonious as his decision was, it was notable during an era of bombastic fights. Tappis could have walked down any of the paths tunneled from the SDS convention floor. Rather than reject RYM II or the Weathermen, Tappis felt that all three roads needed paving and his best work could be done at the community level.

For the former JOIN leaders Tappis met in Chicago, the question of radical community politics cut especially deep. Together, they had demonstrated, perhaps only to themselves, that the very people the government counted on for consent could be moved to dissent. Dozens of them had accompanied Peggy Terry on her vice presidential tour across the U.S.; others like Diane Fager and Bob Lawson tried to take JOIN's lessons on the road in cities like Detroit and Cincinnati before returning to Chicago. They knew it would not be quick work, but the promise of JOIN's model inspired them to apply the insights of the preceding years without making the same mistakes. The first thing they needed to acknowledge was the role class had played in fracturing JOIN. Rising Up Angry, they decided, should be built from the ground up with folks from working-class communities. Angry's original members included James and Tappis with local activists Mary Driscoll, Stormy Brown and Norie Davis, JOIN alum Pat Sturgis, and Jim and Lisa Cartier. Others soon joined them, including Paul Wozniak, Peter Kuttner, Angry's resident filmmaker, and Aaron Fagen who drew the newspaper's popular comics. After returning from Detroit, Diane Fager and Bob Lawson joined too. Each played a formative role in building an organization where people felt involved and respected. For Mary Driscoll everything about Rising Up Angry was unique because working-class people were the ones organizing other working-class people. "It was the approach of people who have the same needs."

Janet Sampson joined Rising Up Angry because the group validated what she'd always felt in her gut: she and other working-class people were not to blame for their troubles. Sampson had arrived in Chicago at age sixteen after her mother left her father. The experience jarred her and got her asking questions about the world around her. She'd grown up in a large working-class family where the specter of Vietnam and the very real possibility that a relative could be drafted loomed large in her mind. The nightly body count on the news increased her anxiety, and she began to notice the hypocrisy of newscasters and politicians as they declared "progress" when only a few thousand, instead of many thousand, troops died in a given week. She was asking other questions as well. Why was her mother looked down upon by friends and family for leaving her abusive, alcoholic father? Why did some members of her family hold deeply racist views, even though they knew firsthand the injustice of working hard but getting nowhere? "I was told by my mother that if you worked hard you would eventually move up the ladder. But I looked at her and saw this wasn't the case. She worked just as hard as anyone yet never moved up." Rising Up Angry's Norie Davis was the first person to point out to Sampson that this wasn't her fault. Sampson had just moved in with her boyfriend, already a member of Angry, and felt immediately at home among Angry's radical family. Over the course of six months, at a series of "rap sessions," parties and women's meetings, she began to understand many of her problems within the context of imperialism, which, as New Left logic went, carried on two wars: one abroad and the other at home. To Sampson, this explanation and Angry's balance of theory and action clarified her life experience and gave her a way to change things.

....

From its inception, Angry set out to create a culture of radicalism rooted in working-class life. Through his work with JOIN, Mike James developed a knack for seeing where people might go politically. He also grasped the importance of celebrating, instead of condemning, working-class culture. For James, fast cars, rock music and softball games blended easily with the struggle against empire. Rising Up Angry was founded on a serious belief that political transformations were just as likely to begin at a weekend softball game as they were at a meeting or rally. Taking their name from lyrics in a song in the bizarre youth power flick *Wild in the Streets*, Angry canvassed Chicago as a whole searching for the best locations to reach people that the broader Left had ignored: white gang-affiliated youth. In working-class Chicago, almost every corner had a gang, usually named after their particular section of town: Brainerd Park, C & D (Clark and Devon), CORP, the Gaylords, the Simon City Royals, Bel-Airs and the PBC (Paulina Barry Community). Some gangs boasted more menace, but most were simply social. None, though, shied away from a turf battle if provoked.

Angry viewed gang kids and greasers as part of a potentially radical underclass. They adopted the Panther view that the "lumpenproletariat"—the most marginally employed or disenfranchised—would become the vanguard of the revolution. As Left logic went, they needed to cool the infighting and "fight the pigs" instead. Angry's members, as Steve Tappis put it, were "hassled by the pigs, fucked with by [their] bosses, channeled into bullshit jobs, drafted into the Army, lied to by the politicians, and ripped off by the stores and businesses." At least in theory, the rap about unity made sense to kids who distrusted police and policymakers more than they distrusted each other. Still, Rising Up Angry needed a solid opener before greasers would be lining up for political education classes and turf-neutral sports. Following Lenin's maxim that revolutionaries should also publish newspapers, James assembled a team to put together the first issue of *Rising Up Angry,* a semi-weekly paper that showcased local culture interspersed with politics. Steve Tappis ran the printing press and JOIN alums Diane Fager and Bob Lawson signed on to write the content. Angry made its first inroads with greasers by taking their pictures and publishing a neighborhood happenings section. James would travel around snapping photos of the kids on the corner and put them on a page called the "Stone Grease Grapevine." As community members saw their images respected in print they started asking for stacks to pass out around town. Initially, it was more about the small-time fame, but for a growing crowd the paper also became a grassroots university. *Rising Up Angry* placed community concerns in a national and global context, validating people's financial struggles, then agitating them to stand with workers of color. There was no particular political line, but Angry's founders did meet to talk about ideological issues and plan ways to discuss them. They added coverage of Irish nationalists struggling against English rule in order to encourage whites to make the connection to anti-imperialist struggles in the Third World, especially Cuba, Guinea Bissau, China, Vietnam and Puerto Rico.[5]

Grabbing the attention of greaser youth like Paul Wozniak, *Rising Up Angry* articles pointed to Chicago's ghettos as the local trenches in a Global Left war for independence. They asserted freedom from empire building and colonial occupations, from U.S. liberalism and capitalism, from police harassment and job discrimination. When Angry's leaders rapped with neighborhood residents about "the war at home and the war in 'Nam," they took the time to listen to people with respect. Residents could join Angry regardless of whether they were for or against the war. The group knew people's reasons for joining the military were complex. One of Angry's early members, Rich Kroth, knew firsthand that any gang kid hauled before a judge got two choices: join the Army or go to jail. The ultimatum was its own kind of draft, but given what Kroth and his peers dealt with in the neighborhood, the Army didn't seem like such a raw deal. It was a way out. For Kroth, Rising Up Angry was the first Left organization he knew of that validated the realities facing working-class youth.

At the neighborhood level, Angry organizers emphasized that condemning the war did not mean condemning enlistees. As with most issues, Rising Up Angry took the slow road, providing opportunities for returning vets to talk to youth in the neighborhood. As Angry organizer Pat Sturgis put it, "There were some who chose to serve in the military, but were against the war and chose to resist from the inside. There were others who didn't go but were very staunch supporters of those who did." Angry recognized that the decision about whether or not to go to Vietnam was independent of a person's opinion about the war itself and invited veterans to speak about their experiences, the good and the bad. Returning GIs were blunt about the realities of war and the hurdles they faced back home.

One soldier, Fritz Kraly, joined the anti-war movement as soon as he was discharged from the Marine Corps. He took up the cause of a good friend, Al Metzger, who had gone AWOL from the military. By working with the Chicago Area Military Project, Kraly helped to secure Metzger a reasonable deal. Soon after, Kraly joined Rising Up Angry's newly minted volunteer legal team, which regularly counseled AWOL soldiers and draft resisters. When Angry organizers were arrested at Great Lakes Naval Training Center for "entering a military reservation for a purpose prohibited by law" (that is, to invite service members to a Fourth of July picnic), the legal aid team took up their defense. Kraly was impressed with the group and the alternatives they showed young vets, and he quickly decided the group represented the best way for him to help other young soldiers.

By the early 1970s direct resistance by enlistees spiked dramatically. In addition to hundreds of cases of individual desertion, fragging and sabotage, Vietnam Veterans Against the War began organizing veterans and supported the emergence of public actions by soldiers. The Stop Our Ships Movement saw fifty thousand San Diego residents sign a petition to prevent the USS Constellation, docked there, from going to Vietnam. Soldiers made numerous attempts to sabotage the ship's seaworthiness, and white and Black sailors joined together in a sit-in protesting the dishonorable discharge of several Black sailors. The commander of the Constellation returned the ship to San Diego for fear of mutiny at sea. In Oakland, more than half the crew of the USS Coral Sea signed a petition to prevent that ship, too, from sailing to South Asia. Angry supported the action by publishing an open letter to service members railing against the "imperialist military system" and comparing their difficulties to the struggles waged in the "neighborhoods, factories, and schools." Rather than turning enlistees off, Angry's stance on the war appealed to returning vets and the group's newspaper became one of the best sources of news on the GI Movement, so much so that some Vietnam Veterans Against the War chapters distributed it as their own monthly paper.[6]

As the older siblings of Angry's new recruits came home from Vietnam, they joined Angry too. In a sense, this represented a reversal of the fortunes that had diffused SDS's Economic Research Action Project. Where escalation in Vietnam had shifted that group's attention away from community work and projects like JOIN in 1965, Rising Up Angry managed to link the local and the international in a way that made sense to everyday people. In spring 1971, the national anti-war movement launched a "Spring Offensive"—a series of actions supported by former and active service people. Angry's members travelled to a May Day rally in Washington, D.C., taking part in multi-day street actions that resulted in seven thousand arrests. During the protest sympathetic locals organized food and blanket drop-offs for the protestors and guards allowed them to distribute the supplies at makeshift detention centers.

Rising Up Angry also hosted large anti-war events of their own in Chicago neighborhoods. One rally at the Church of the Holy Covenant featured George Smith, a former Green Beret and prisoner of war, as the keynote speaker. Smith claimed that the National Liberation Front had released him as a good faith gesture when Norman Morrison, a Quaker, immolated himself in front of the Pentagon in 1965 to protest the war. Hundreds of community residents attended the rally, signifying to Angry that anti-war dissent had finally reached a visible and sustained fever pitch among working-class communities. Soon enough, vets were bringing their wives, mothers, uncles and neighbors to the rallies. Rising Up Angry also turned out thousands to a Chicago protest against national Armed Forces Day (also dubbed "Armed Farces Day"). According to Angry about three thousand people showed up. Veterans drove in from as far away as Milwaukee. Parents brought young children, and young people brought their parents. In contrast to the popular Sixties profile of protesting students, rock musicians and Yippies, Chicago's early Seventies anti-war movement had become a family affair.

....

Not all of Angry's early recruits were enticed by anti-war rallies, guest speakers and veterans meetings, though. As part of its commitment to cultural work, Angry also organized dances and music performances to bring working-class youth together around something positive—with political overtones of course. While some organizations tried to draw a sharp line between political and cultural activism, Angry members were inspired by Antonio Gramsci's writings on culture and consciousness. They saw culture as both an organizing tactic and a weapon.[7] In fact all their early programs aimed to build a revolutionary counter-culture with its own language, traditions and discipline rooted in the hearts of working-class Chicagoans. Their role was to make radical politics "common sense." Acts such as MC5, Fast Eddy, Aaron's Rod, Weapons of Peace, Taxi and Bran Spankin' performed at Angry's weekend dances. While most of the music itself was apolitical, band members expressed their sympathies by playing fundraisers and using their notoriety to aid the cause. MC5's lead singer Rob Tyner often stopped their sets to urge support of Panther political prisoners and resistance to the Vietnam War.[8] The draw of popular bands also gave Angry added leverage to set some rules for attendance: no gang fights. The dances served as safety zones where rival gangs were expected to leave their beef at the door. It mostly worked, but a citywide gathering of gang-affiliated youth occasionally had its hazards. To quell disruptions, Rising Up Angry's women leaders served as a security force for each event. They decided to use the macho posturing as an opportunity to lay down a rap about building unity and shatter assumptions about women's roles. Diane Fager arrived to one dance to find a line of people winding completely around the block. When a fight broke out, she and the other women in Angry walked right into the middle of the brawl. They physically separated rival members and reminded them they were on "the People's Turf." Shocked by the intervention, the gang members stopped in their tracks.

Beyond turf battles, Rising Up Angry also spent many of its early months quelling racial skirmishes. A few joint events with the Black Panthers and Young Lords showed the possibilities of racial unity, but it was one thing to reject racism in words and another to do so in deeds. When white high school students accused a Black male of attacking a white female, several of Angry's new recruits seemed torn between their new anti-racist beliefs and what they thought it meant to survive in their own neighborhoods. Suddenly, members who had renounced racism were arming themselves for the expected race riot. Sitting in a coffee shop with Steve Tappis, one young member asked, "Hey, can you help me out?" When Tappis asked him what he needed, the kid blurted out, "I need a gun, we are going to fight the nigs." Tappis pointed to the clenched fist button pinned to the kid's jacket and asked what happened to the rap about racial unity. "Oh yeah," the kid replied.

Angry decided it was time for a direct appeal to gang leadership. Organizers knew there was a disconnect for many young folks between their ideals and who they thought they needed to answer to. Even a decade after JOIN tried to seed "an interracial movement of the poor" in Chicago, Angry was challenged to create a culture where it wasn't seen as a weakness to walk away from a racial fight. In reality, no one was really pushing for a race riot, and Angry knew if they could reach enough gang leaders they would each tell their crew to cool it. Angry organizers went block-to-block talking to the more levelheaded guys on the street. A week later, they pulled together a meeting of white gang leaders. It was agreed, "If they don't mess with us, we won't mess with them." Angry spread the news; the fight was off and Angry had garnered some legitimacy as a broker for neighborhood beefs.

Incidents like these illustrated the frailty of diminishing racial tensions. One member, who went by and still only goes by the name Stone Greaser, recalled that Angry's enthusiasm for increasing the peace was well intentioned but sometimes dangerous. While leaders chilled more than one inter-neighborhood fight, they only narrowly averted a few major disasters, like when Angry published a false story about a truce between the Gaylords and the Simon City Royals. According to Stone Greaser, the false information came close to getting people killed.

Rising Up Angry was still finding its way, taking great leaps forward then stumbling a few steps back. One of the most difficult challenges for the group was what to do about the more hardened racists they came across. For a while the group accommodated a tier of members who stuck around for the fun, but resisted the more radical politicking. There were also plenty of people who resisted the group altogether. It wasn't exactly in Angry's interest to attack the people they were trying to organize, but for all the peacemaking Rising Up Angry wasn't opposed to a little street fighting of its own, especially if it meant a scuffle with fascist sympathizers.

Lane Technical High School in Chicago was an all-white school that started to desegregate. Racial tensions ignited. One Angry member, Tom Gilchrist, attended Lane Tech and started receiving near-constant threats for selling Angry's papers at the school. Then, Rising Up Angry members heard that the owner of Lenny's, a nearby snack-shop and school lunchtime hangout, had provided baseball bats to white kids during a racial skirmish to "beat the blacks with." When another Angry member was assaulted by a group of neo-Nazis, Angry decided that it would destroy the organization's credibility if they let the incident go. About twenty members visited Lenny's. Leaflets with swastikas printed on them had been left all over the tables. One Angry member took a leaflet from a neo-Nazi and then immediately hit him in the face. In this moment, all political theory boiled down to the simple fact that their members had been threatened and massive retaliation was in order. Pandemonium bloomed as the factions clashed. Diane Fager was knocked to the ground, boots pelting her sides; Gilchrist singled out the Nazi leader with an old-fashioned challenge, "You and me, outside, one on one."

In the realm of high school fights, it lasted an eternity: three or four minutes. As the sirens approached, Angry members retreated to cars parked around the campus. The incident established that the organization would fight against organized racism, but the fact remained: Angry was physically fighting a part of the community the group saw as its base. The incident was bittersweet. It established street credibility, but also tampered with the group's revolutionary confidence. Reflecting on the incident, Angry's newspaper explained that the group believed most of the folks they fought had simply been caught up in the melee and that only a small group of them were "Right-wing Nazi-type, racist idiots in Lenny's whose fathers and brothers are pigs and they want to become pigs too." Nevertheless, the uncomfortable fact was that uprooting racism among Chicago's working-class white youth might have as many "fight the people" moments as "fight the real enemy" transformations. Ironically, Weather Underground member Bill Ayers was widely criticized for a speech in Cleveland in 1969 in which he suggested "fighting the people" might be necessary. Ayers and Rising Up Angry's organizers may have opted for different paths, but both groups demonstrated they ultimately believed in some level of direct confrontation with racist elements.

Through incidents like these, Angry drew a long, deep line in the sand between its organizing framework and Saul Alinsky's approach, which saw no role for explicit anti-racist confrontation. Instead, Angry treated everyday life as a teachable moment and organizers worked hard to balance their Marxist-Leninist influence with an open culture where residents could come into the organization, get exposed and maybe develop more radical politics over time. One of Angry's best attempts to propagandize against racism appeared in the concept for a film called *Trick Bag*, directed by one of Angry's founding members, Peter Kuttner. Kuttner was a Chicago-born filmmaker who helped found the Newsreel documentary collective (today, Third World Newsreel). As a teenager he had attended a Chicago public high school with sharp class divisions. Every day at school, he watched students and teachers dole out privileges and punishments along class and race lines. The experience taught him more about the world than he ever learned from history or economics textbooks.

Before joining Angry, Kuttner had traveled to New York City to find work as a cameraman under the British Broadcasting Service's Richard Liederman. He tracked the filmmaker down at New York's infamous Chelsea Hotel but arrived just as the film crew left to shoot an anti-war protest at the Pentagon. He headed straight to D.C. It was October 21, 1967, nearing the pinnacle of the radical Sixties, and the protest attracted more than 70,000 people. Kuttner arrived as protestors broke past the military barricades, ascended the Pentagon stairs and occupied the upper terrace. He filmed the whole thing. Following the Pentagon protests, he met up with other filmmakers who agreed to pool their footage. From that point forward, the Newsreel collective made it their mission to document and promote the New Left's activities. With chapters across the country Kuttner was dispatched to his hometown where he joined Rising Up Angry.

Kuttner and James came up with the metaphor of a "trick bag"—a purchase of bad drugs—to explain the raw deal of racial superiority for whites. A mix of cinéma vérité and Studs Terkel's man-on-the-street testimonials, the short film featured working-class Chicagoans talking honestly about the costs racism exacted on their lives. Most everyone believed the United States could erupt into a race war at any time. *Trick Bag* was intended to redirect the white community's blame away from people of color and turn attention toward their own responsibility. As Angry's logic went, racism was as bad a deal for whites as it was for people of color. The message was simple: Don't buy it.

. . . .

With projects like *Trick Bag*, Angry demonstrated its analysis. However, it was another matter to take the dialogue past testimonials and street fights. By the early Seventies, the group had grown far beyond the point of a radical newspaper. Angry's experienced organizers had always wanted to build toward a revolution, but without losing their hard-earned base in the community. They launched a women's discussion group and regular study sessions to engage members in deeper dialogues about the history and dynamics of U.S. empire, women's liberation and class oppression. More importantly, they launched two community service programs that ultimately went the furthest in training neighborhood residents in both the politics and practice of radical self-governance: a legal program tackling housing, crime and veterans' issues, and a community-run health clinic. Involvement in these programs introduced new recruits to the organization's politics and Angry began experimenting with ways to move members toward a broader understanding of political problems and solutions. It was soon resolved: "Rising Up Angry is neither a Leninist party nor a mass organization. We are half of each. The programs are our vehicle for organizing the people and involving the people."

Initially made up of five lawyers under the leadership of a steering committee, the Rising Up Angry legal program trained neighborhood people to perform intakes, write legal briefs, and handle basic "know your rights" counseling on immigration, police brutality, housing rights and the draft. The legal program helped potential draftees with conscientious objector claims, ironed out welfare denials and defended kids who otherwise would have been stuck with a distracted public defender. In its first two years the legal program helped about five hundred people and boasted twenty-five volunteer lawyers. The program complemented almost every aspect of Angry's work; it generated projects new members could get involved with and gave organizers a chance to keep their fingers on the pulse of community issues. The most steady of those issues for working-class Chicagoans was housing rights. While the war and police harassment certainly touched most residents in some way, dilapidated housing, slumlords and urban displacement impacted everyone. With the expansion of the community programs, Angry also returned to one of JOIN's strongest suits: tenant organizing. Organizers converted a donated van into a mobile lead-testing lab after a substantial number of neighborhood children tested positive for lead poisoning. With landlords determined to ignore the problem, Angry decided to embarrass city officials by picketing outside the American Academy of Pediatrics Conference in Chicago. One protester held a sign reading, "Lead in the Ghetto, Napalm in Vietnam." It wasn't totally an exaggeration. Lead poisoning was a dangerous epidemic in low-income neighborhoods.

When half of Margaret Burton's eleven children tested positive for lead poisoning, more than seventy-five people marched to the Chicago Civic Center Housing Court. They carried striking pictures of dozens of housing violations her landlord simply refused to fix, from cracked ceilings to peeling paint, leaking pipes and broken windows. Complaints to the court resulted in eviction proceedings against the Burton family, supposedly so the landlord could begin repairs. Given just three weeks and no financial support to find a new home, Mrs. Burton was accused of turning down housing that had never been offered to her in the first place. A judge reprimanded her stating, "You can't be choosey—you better take what they offer you. It's summertime, you can live in the streets." After withholding her rent until repairs were complete, she was threatened with jail time. Once again Rising Up Angry flooded the courthouse with supporters and succeeded in convincing the judge to let her apply her back rent toward a home of her choice.

To draw publicity to the hundreds of North Chicago homes with conditions like these, Angry hosted a series of "People's Tribunals"—mock trials against notorious slum landlords—bringing out residents and a wide range of community groups during 1972. By deliberately targeting landlords who had buildings across the city, Angry established a common cause among multiracial neighborhood groups. Tenants from the South Side and Lincoln Park testified at the tribunals alongside Uptown's Appalachian, Latino and Native American residents. Together they organized a massive campaign to put notorious slumlords the Gutman brothers on trial after three people died in their dilapidated buildings. A child, Jennifer LaBarge, was decapitated when she poked her head inside an elevator shaft that lacked safety glass. Another child, Eric Roy, was killed when an uncapped radiator turned on for the first time in winter. In another building, tenant Bill Stein died while trying to escape an electrical fire. The rear fire exit had been nailed shut by management to keep out vagrants. City officials never investigated the deaths. An Angry-led investigation uncovered that the Gutmans owned almost one hundred and fifty buildings across Chicago. Home to the city's poorest residents, the buildings were in a universal state of disrepair with falling plaster, inaccessible fire escapes, high levels of lead paint and unchecked infestations of rats and roaches.

The Gutmans didn't take kindly to the charges. When Angry's tenant organizers showed up at the Gutmans' buildings, they were greeted by hired thugs wielding baseball bats, knives and other weapons. Tenants began sneaking organizers into the buildings for meetings and inspections. Nonetheless, two Angry organizers were eventually arrested for trespassing while conducting outreach at a building on Magnolia Street. They later learned that a neighborhood woman who lost most of her belongings in a fire was offered money by the Gutmans on the condition she discourage neighbors from attending the People's Tribunals.

Unsurprisingly, the mock trial convicted the Gutmans, although no actual court of law would hear criminal charges against the brothers. Following the tribunal a barrage of lawsuits and withheld rent payments did motivate the Gutmans to begin a clean-up campaign, but Angry was quick to publicize that most of their repairs amounted to little more than a coat of paint slapped over lead-tainted walls the city had ordered removed. In what seemed like one of the first real citywide victories in years, the Angry-led coalition eventually succeeded in pressuring the City of Chicago to enforce code violations against the Gutman brothers. Soon after, the *Chicago Tribune* ran a six-part exposé on slum housing, which blasted Chicago's temporary villain: "They commute daily from their comfortable Northwest Side homes to oversee their empire. Much of it is like a fortress with heavy, wire-backed doors and lobbies of forbidding cages in which tenant-managers dispense the mail and police the arrival of unwelcome visitors and inspectors." The slumlord made a nice scapegoat for city developers speculating cheap land for urban redevelopment.

....

While Rising Up Angry's original focus had been on young working-class men, the housing activism and other community programs provided women new opportunities to take on a central role in the organization. Initially, women functioned like an auxiliary; they shaped the politics and did the same behind-the-scenes work, but on the streets they usually focused on building relationships with the wives, girlfriends, sisters and mothers of greaser men. They linked young women to family planning and health information, and passed out the first stapled and bound newsprint copies of *Our Bodies, Ourselves* to working-class women across Chicago.[9]

Sharing a practical commitment to women's health concerns, women in Rising Up Angry developed a close collaboration with the abortion counseling service of the Chicago Women's Liberation Union—known as "Jane," the code name women would ask for when calling the hotline. Prior to the 1973 *Roe v. Wade* decision, women seeking abortions relied on a clandestine network of illegal and sometimes mafia-connected clinics. These backroom stalls were often dimly lit, unsanitary and unsafe; even the most competent clinics lacked counseling or a humane atmosphere for patients. It is impossible to know exactly how many abortions Jane's volunteer doctors performed as an underground service. Laura Kaplan's book *The Story of Jane* suggests that thousands of women made the call. "Our society's version of equal opportunity means that lower-class women bear unwanted children or face expensive, illegal and unsafe abortions," Jane's founders wrote, "while well connected middle-class women can frequently get safe and hush-hush 'D and C's' in hospitals."[10]

The affiliation with the women's movement helped reinforce the leadership of women within Angry. Under the leadership of Diane Fager, Norie Davis, Janet Sampson and longtime Chicago residents Stormy Brown, Christine George and Mary Driscoll, Angry evolved a version of feminism uniquely rooted in working-class women's needs. In theory, most of Angry's male leaders were on board, but the deliberate focus on women's issues didn't come easy. What was Angry's role when organizers found out a man was abusing his wife? Would they help a woman who wanted an abortion when her husband forbade it? What would they do about male leaders less eager to share control of the organization? Judith Arcana, a founding member of Jane, worked closely with the women in Angry as they grappled with how much to assert women's liberation politics. In Arcana's opinion, the conflict seemed rooted in the often unspoken "stand by your man" ethos in oppressed groups. Few organizations reached the communities Angry did; and challenging sexism drew accusations from some men that the women were creating another, divisive kind of "fight the people" moment. Both tough and smart, women in Angry pressed the point over a number of years and Arcana watched as the women got stronger and more insistent on adding sex and gender as central tenets of the group's analysis. It was simple: A working-class people's organization needed to address and reflect working-class women as well as men. Standing by your man meant struggling with him.

In an era when some feminists started to advocate separatism, women in Rising Up Angry made a conscious choice to stay in a mixed-gender organization. To them, separating made no sense in the context of neighborhood organizing. Like the Black feminism that emerged from within the Panthers years earlier, they pointed out that the revolution they wanted involved the liberation of every-one and was not truly revolutionary unless women's equality was won. Over several years they pushed for women's issues to be more than an "add on" to the work with local men, and pushed men to participate in the health and housing work. Naturally, they argued, men in Angry should become feminists—or at least walk the talk. When a friend from one of Angry's sister organizations in Philadel-phia came to visit, the women put him to work in the health clinic by day and took him out spray painting "Fuck the Patriarchy" on buildings at night. Angry's women leaders made a huge impression on him. He returned home ready to support women in his own group, October 4th Organization, who were starting a women's committee.

Rising Up Angry's commitment to co-ed organization also meant they could reach working-class women who felt invisible in the broader feminist movement. Angry's community health clinic represented the best of the group's feminist politics, Panther-inspired service provision and community education. Mary Driscoll was one of the Angry leaders who helped establish the clinic in the Lakeview–Lincoln Park neighborhood. Today, that neighbor-hood is the heart of gentrified Chicago, but in the late Sixties and early Seventies it was solidly working-class white and Puerto Ri-can. Driscoll grew up in a working-class family of staunch Chicago Democrats. While away at college, she was radicalized by the anti-war sit-ins against napalm manufacturer Dow Chemical Company. Like many other first-generation college students who got involved with the movement, radical politics clarified Driscoll's childhood experiences around class and focused her outrage about the war, racism and economic injustice.

In Lakeview–Lincoln Park, many residents depended on local hospitals providing free and reduced-cost services. This was before

Planned Parenthood and before community health centers for the uninsured. Residents without health care had nowhere to go but the emergency room. This became a shell game, as it was common for hospitals to abruptly announce they had reached their quota of indigent care. One hospital, Augustana, announced that it would no longer accept any patients who were on public aid or who were otherwise unable to pay the full fees. In response, a group of neighborhood residents staged an impromptu demonstration and Angry members rushed down to support the action. Sitting down in the front lobby, they demanded that all free services be continued. The campaign proved successful; the hospital agreed to fund a community clinic in the basement of a local church. The Fritzi Englestein Free Health Clinic, named for a member of the congregation who helped establish the clinic, became an integral part of neighborhood life as volunteer doctors and nurses trained community volunteers to perform medical intakes, take pulses and serve as nurses' assistants. The clinic offered three main services: pediatrics, venereal disease testing and gynecology.

Beyond helping community members get proper diagnoses and medical attention, the clinic also provided clients with emotional support, documentation needed to get time off work and urgent care. Neighborhood resident Soledad Rodriguez was instrumental in getting the clinic started. Her husband, José, had a full-time job as an auto mechanic and Sole worked on and off outside of her home to help make ends meet for their six children. The Rodriguez family members were among the most active neighborhood residents in the service programs. The older Rodriguez kids worked in the lab, and José did fix-it jobs around the clinic while volunteering with Angry's legal program. Sole devoted her days and nights to keep the clinic going.

When a woman who lived two blocks from the health clinic was denied insurance coverage for basic tests and medication, Rising Up Angry's all-volunteer staff, including doctors from the county hospital, were able to help her. It turned out she had cancer. She was taking care of her ailing mother and was terrified about what would happen to both of them. With the help of clinic doctors acting as advocates, Angry got her into Cook County Hospital for treatment. A few months later she was in remission. The Fritzi Englestein clinic expanded from two nights a week to a full-time program that took the model of the Black Panthers' "survival programs" a step further.

. . . .

As Angry's service programs expanded to meet the needs of women and families, the group became less one note. At a time when many radicals argued whether gender, race or class was the "primary contradiction," Angry had integrated all three into the fabric of their activism. When it came to the group's longevity and impact, Angry's embrace of feminism, and subsequent expansion into community programs, became one of its greatest strengths. The participation of families, especially organizers' own children, hastened this culture shift. Angry organizer Stormy Brown, a single mother of two, met Mike James through a friend while working at the 3 Penny Cinema in Lincoln Park. The couple began dating and soon had a child. Mary Driscoll and Peter Kuttner along with Janet Sampson and Rich Kroth had children soon after. As the Angry family expanded, more neighborhood families joined the organization and organizers invited their parents and extended families to events.

When Angry hosted a Mother's Day luncheon honoring more than a hundred women from the health and legal clinics, Rising Up Angry's Christine George decided she would bring her aunts with her. It was a first. Born in Chicago to a working-class Greek family, Christine George spent the majority of her youth in the Austin neighborhood on the Far West Side. Her family was apolitical but leaned conservative, so it wasn't until a classmate's father introduced to her to radical politics that she started to grapple with her own positions. Her friend's father was active in the unsuccessful fight to save Italian and Greek neighborhoods from University of Illinois expansion. Entering into the University of Wisconsin in 1964, George originally saw herself becoming a diplomat, but a campaign to prevent the university from turning over information to draft boards drew her into campus activism. Later that year, she was elected secretary of SDS.

Like many first-generation college students who joined the movement, she was teasing out the impact of race, class, ethnicity and gender on her own life. While her parents were conservative, her own upbringing inspired her commitment to organizing in working-class communities. In Rising Up Angry she found a Left project where her white ethnic identity, radical politics and commitment to reaching working-class community members weren't in conflict. When George brought her family members to Angry's events, she knew women like her aunts still didn't see leftists as normal, but for George the family-friendly and truly working-class culture in Angry provided a necessary bridge between the excesses of the Sixties and the practical politics of the Seventies.

With all the changes, the organization had broadened from a cadre structure to an elected leadership, which brought in significantly more community members, but only for a short time. As the war in Vietnam wound down, so did many movement organizations. The war and the draft had been a focal point for recruiting. Its enormity and brutality, along with the fact it had lasted through both Democratic and Republican administrations, had given credence to the idea that war was part of a larger system of imperialism.

Without the war, organizations failed to grow at the same pace.

Rising Up Angry wasn't the only organization finding it hard to adapt. Like other Left formations of the sixties and seventies, Angry had asked core members to become full-time revolutionaries. This model made sense to those who expected a socialist revolution in the United States before 1970. But such a victory seemed all but impossible by the mid-seventies. Many organizers, some in the struggle for nearly two decades, started thinking about building careers and devoting more time to their families. Steve Tappis moved on after Angry's first few years. Bob Lawson and Norie Davis went to work on SDS founder Tom Hayden's senatorial campaign, and then to support the United Farm Workers. Mike James remained involved, but no longer in leadership.

Despite its steady base in the community, the organization's focus waned by the mid-seventies. In 1976, Diane Fager and others started a process of bringing Angry to an end. Fager was painfully aware of how other radical organizations were parting in acrimony and she wanted better for her friends. She had heard about groups that ended in fistfights and bitter accusations. Together, Angry's leaders decided to hold a series of meetings for the community members involved in the programs to decide next steps and possible dissolution. Following months of discussions, the group came to consensus that Rising Up Angry should end with its reputation intact.

After seven years, Rising Up Angry's organizers concluded that there were many places they could continue to work for social change. Members went on to organize in the labor movement, and work in social and health services, universities, the National Lawyers Guild and the environmental movement. José and Sole's daughter used her training at the health clinic to get into medical school. Fager began working for Chicago's Department of Education. Mike James opened Chicago's Heartland Café and weekly radio show.

More so than the Patriots or even JOIN, Rising Up Angry's members remain a close-knit family supporting each other in ongoing work for social justice. In 2009 they came together for a forty-year reunion and art exhibit showcasing hundreds of photos and more than one hundred issues of the *Rising Up Angry* newspaper.

Undoubtedly, Angry's connection to the community was a predictor of its endurance during a period when other New Left organizations either went underground or died out. Angry's insistence on putting down roots in working-class communities and its fights around housing and health care reflect the better strands of the American populist project. While their work did not transform the nation or end imperialism, Rising Up Angry represents a unique and important moment in the history of the North American Left. They espoused a version of socialism as much rooted in U.S. working-class experience as in the inspiration of Third World revolutions. Part of their strength was their commitment to apply radical ideas in new and flexible ways. Leaders read Mao's *Little Red Book* and were deeply influenced by the writings of SNCC organizer James Forman and Guinea Bissau's Amilcar Cabral, whose own organizational practice prioritized culture, literacy projects and grassroots community campaigns. But Angry also existed as a living experiment in how an organization can address various concerns without dogmatism.

This maturity can only come when radicals learn how to listen to people's needs. Angry, at its very best, knew how to listen: to the boys-on-the-block, young mothers, servicemen, kids hanging out in pool halls, the unemployed and the overworked. They practiced popular education long before the term became widespread on the Left. Through their journey, they discovered two important truths: Revolutions are elusive even in a nation's most tumultuous decades, and yet the pillars of oppression are not immovable. With little more than a dedicated cadre rooted in working-class Chicago, some of these pillars shifted and many even crumbled. They accomplished their work by taking a long-term approach—the kind of organizing that cultivates radical families as much as it cultivates radical change. "That was one of the things about Rising Up Angry," Mary Driscoll recalls. "We were part of the community we were organizing."

CHAPTER 4

• • • • • • • • • • • •

Lightning on the Eastern Seaboard:
October 4th Organization and White Lightning

Working class communities have been slow to anger, but we're angry now. . . . We've been slow to take to the streets, but we're learning from our Black sisters and brothers. Kensington [Philadelphia] today is like a time bomb. And if you refuse to hear the ticking, you'll have to hear the explosion.

—October 4th Organization, Philadelphia, 1972

The Sixties were a shockingly violent decade for activists in the United States, yet it was the Seventies that ushered in a deeper systematic retaliation against civil rights and social justice. It was a sobering decade. Twenty-five years after World War II boosted the nation's economy, the post-war decline of manufacturing jobs coupled with urban planning disasters and depopulation, blighted northern cities. Urban centers experienced a spiral of disinvestment as suburban sprawl continued drawing wealth away from the city. Businesses buckled and northern factories scurried south in search of cheaper labor. In 1973 the rising cost of oil spiked the U.S. trade deficit and consumer prices rose to the highest point since the end of the Korean War. By 1974 more than 7 percent of the nation's workforce was unemployed. Black workers were hardest hit with unemployment levels surging to 15 percent. Even workers who had enjoyed a degree of security in the past were in an unfamiliar position—uncertain where the next paycheck would come from and in danger of losing their homes. Once comfortably blue collar neighborhoods like Chicago's Southwest Side, Philadelphia's Kensington, and New York's Mott Haven section of the Bronx started to show more obvious signs of decline: adults milling around at midday, boarded up row homes and tenements, shuttered factories, mysterious fires and block after block of abandoned cars. It was exactly the economic crisis Students for a Democratic Society had predicted when it founded Jobs or Income Now; it just peaked ten years behind schedule. Just as SDS leaders Tom Hayden and Carl Whitman warned in "An Interracial Movement of the Poor," the document laying out the vision for projects like JOIN, it would take strong, permanent bases of unity among white workers and workers of color to curb rising fear that racial equity came at their own expense.

Progressive organizers faced a different terrain than the one they had seen in the radical Sixties. It was shaped, among other things, by severe economic recession, the splintering of New Left community organizations and mounting right-wing backlash. An overall job shortage combined with white workers' perception of favoritism toward workers of color created the conditions for resentment. In 1971 new affirmative action policies fueled this fire as Nixon's Labor Department passed legislation to correct the "underutilization" of minorities in federal contracting.[1] Politicians looking to fortify a conservative "law and order" agenda fomented white chauvinism for their own gain by exploiting people's fear of economic insecurity. They were part of a New Right taking shape in the United States. Broadly defined this movement included traditional Republicans, libertarians and conservative Democrats among its foot soldiers.[2]

The New Right's ascendance began in the final days of the McCarthy Era as politicians and pundits saw new ways to consolidate right-wing political influence in the United States. At first the movement argued for an alternative to economically conservative, but socially liberal, northern Republicanism by returning to the fervent states' rights and anti-interventionist foreign policy outlook once found in the Grand Old Party. At a glance, this movement resembled a discordant collection of organizations with little else in common. Soon, the emerging New Right made sense of its patchwork by articulating a cogent criticism of New Deal-era social welfare, government bureaucracy, communism and civil rights. The New Right fostered an ethnocentric nationalism and began harnessing social anxieties about the emerging countercultures of beatniks, student leftists and organized people of color.[3]

In the late Fifties, economic conservatives such as William F. Buckley and the intellectuals surrounding the *National Review* magazine vocally embraced racism, arguing that white southerners had the right to forcibly resist integration because whites represented the era's advanced race (though Buckley later changed his tune). As the movement grew, Barry Goldwater's 1964 campaign for president pushed a platform of states' rights and shrinking federal government. He and other New Right politicians rejected Lyndon Johnson's Great Society and any efforts to expand social welfare. When Goldwater lost, his supporters turned inward and spent the better part of a decade perfecting their strategies. At the end of the Sixties the spinal column of the Democratic Party was forcefully realigned as the Dixiecrats fled the party and joined the Republicans. By the start of the Seventies, the U.S. looked more conservative than the post-war social order Sixties activists had rebelled against.

On the East Coast, two groups inspired by Chicago's Rising Up Angry emerged to harness the era's revolutionary aspirations and address the unique conditions of their working-class neighborhoods. Philadelphia's October 4th Organization (O4O) and New York's

White Lightning each played David to the Goliath of organized political backlash and economic decline. In Philadelphia, Goliath was cop-turned-mayor Frank Rizzo, who harvested the anxieties of Italian, Irish, Polish and Greek communities to secure his throne at City Hall. "Tough on crime" barely described a mayor wielding the police force as shock troops against neighborhoods of color and the Left. For Rizzo the mounting financial crisis provided an opportunity for fearmongering, but industrial collapse and a widening wealth gap proved a Goliath of its own for Philadelphia residents.

In the Bronx, White Lightning faced off against the behemoth of New York's Rockefeller Drug Laws, named after then-Governor Nelson Rockefeller. Among other changes, the laws spelled major prison sentences for minor possession. Rockefeller's "mandatory minimums" marked a decisive early battle in the War on Drugs. The state spent more than $76 million locking people up for drug offenses between 1973 and 1976 alone, ignoring the fact that hard drug use actually increased during the same period. Blacks and Latinos composed more than 90 percent of drug convictions over the next two decades and incarceration rates soared to record levels. As New York went, so went the nation. State after state echoed Rockefeller's harsh punishments for nonviolent offenses and the U.S. prison population more than doubled by 1980. Over the ensuing two decades it quadrupled.[4] Implicit in White Lightning's fight against harsh drug penalties, though, was another Goliath at work in their communities: addiction.

O4O and White Lightning had chosen formidable targets. Rizzo and Rockefeller emerged as just two figures providing tempo for the New Right's dance to power. They did so with support from both sides of the political aisle. Rizzo, a right-wing Democrat, refined the language of white ethnic resentment and acted out his special hatred for the radical Left. Rockefeller, although considered a liberal by GOP standards, drafted the blueprint for the wholesale warehousing of the poor, especially Black and Brown nonviolent drug users. And yet O4O and White Lightning emerged not to weaken a particular opponent, but from the best impulses of the revolutionary moment: the belief that social transformation was not only necessary, but also possible. For the better part of the Seventies, October 4th Organization and White Lightning built on the progressive traditions in Kensington and the Bronx. Like JOIN, the Young Patriots and Rising Up Angry, they built a small but notable cadre of white radicals by providing direct community services and organizing against racist policy, the "war on the poor" and the seemingly endless war in Vietnam.

....

Founded in 1971 by a small group of working-class radicals and ex-students, October 4th Organization took its name from an uprising during the American War of Independence. On October 4, 1779, a throng of Philadelphians stormed the warehouses of merchants and businessmen that hoarded food and clothing in order to inflate prices. The original O4Oers seized supplies and redistributed them to the hungry.[5] The new O4O took this example as an inspiration. With an aim to "unite the people against big businessmen, merchants and politicians," the group's program reflected a spirited progressive populism and the "rising dynamism" of the revolutionary moment.[6] In this moment few organizations felt like a lone David facing off against Goliath. They had the power of numbers, moral purpose and optimism on their side.

Founding member Marilyn Buggey had grown up poor in Philly's Germantown neighborhood. As a teenager, her father would remove the light bulb from her room so that she couldn't study, insisting she work rather than go to school. The family needed the money, but she eventually got herself into Temple University and left home. Her fiancé, Jack Whalen, drove a cab for a living. In a short amount of time he had gone from a quiet adolescence in Union, New Jersey, to become a student activist at La Salle University. He might have preferred to stick with his original interests—baseball, girls and playing drums in a rock band—but politics found him. La Salle required students to complete Army ROTC coursework in order to graduate. With a moderately sized anti-war contingent, campus activists protested the requirements and won. Tame compared to the demonstrations that year at Columbia University, the La Salle campaign nonetheless garnered two thousand signatures on a petition and culminated with a 250-person sit-in, which ended compulsory ROTC. Their victory opened a floodgate for on-campus political activity.[7] Yet Buggey and Whalen grew frustrated with the insularity of campus activism. Both dropped out of college and moved to the Kensington neighborhood to live near the headquarters of the *Free Press* movement newspaper. There they met Robert Barrow,[8] Dan Sidorick, Chris Robinson and several others who became the nucleus of O4O. The organization provided a refuge for radicals alienated from the middle-class student movement. O4O activists shared the belief that a large portion of the student Left was divorced from the realities of U.S. workers.

At Goldman Paper Company in the Kensington neighborhood of Philadelphia these harsh realities were visible everywhere. Deindustrialization had taken a heavy toll in Kensington. Dozens of mill workers were laid off with just three days' notice. Company owners threatened remaining workers with termination if they took sick days and harassed them into surrendering vacation time to avoid further layoffs. Instructed to operate large sheet-cutting machines alone, workers were told to ignore the dangerous labor shortage. The United Paperworkers International Union proved only marginally helpful, so Goldman workers like Dan Sidorick began organizing Kensington's at-risk and unemployed workers under the banner of October 4th Organization. They heard the same story from everyone. Out-of-work men were being redirected to local Navy recruiters. Up until the Vietnam War ended in April 1975 the military remained the best bet for a steady job—that is, if they hadn't already been drafted. Women were told to find domestic work or low-wage clerical jobs, as if the pay and insecurity of those jobs made up for the lost factory work some had done for decades. In response workers rallied outside the unemployment office at 5th and Olney just about every week demanding, as JOIN had, "Jobs or Income Now."

With this early action, O4O set itself apart from other Left organizations by uniquely combining labor activism and community-based organizing. In Kensington there was no separating the two. Originally founded as an industrial township, outside the original borders of Philadelphia, Kensington was first settled by English, German, Irish and Scots immigrants. The population expanded during the twentieth century with new arrivals from Poland, Italy and Eastern Europe, including a substantial number of ethnic Jews. Journalist Peter Binzen's description of the neighborhood in 1970 reads a lot like *Harper's* sensational portrait of Uptown. "Kensington's air is polluted, its streets and sidewalks are filthy, its juvenile crime rate rising, its industry languishing," he wrote.[9] According to Binzen, bars and dingy row houses provided the backdrop for idle youths hanging out on street corners, ready for trouble. Fabric mills and machine factories spanned the skyline. Many were boarded up. While an accurate description of some blocks, most were lined with small, tidy row houses with postage-stamp front yards, well kept by renters or owners who had been there for generations.

When it came to the city elite's portrayal of the neighborhood, Binzen's choice of chapter title in his book *Whitetown USA* captured the sentiment: "Kensington Against the World." In reality, neighborhood politics were more complex and O4O's founders knew that the real Kensington belied simplified media reports of a downtrodden neighborhood filled with proud and hardened racists. The right-wing hoodlums, cops and a few reactionary groups were always there and racial conflicts did occur, but O4O's work proved many more residents opposed these extremists than supported them. When a group of neighborhood troublemakers broke into a Puerto Rican family's home and started trashing it, dozens of neighbors filed into the house and stopped the assault. The cops drove by while it was happening, yet did nothing to intervene. It was practically policy for police to let such racial skirmishes play themselves out.

Beyond a local neo-Nazi and some diehard George Wallace supporters, it was Frank Rizzo who served as the city's most visible architect of this racial antagonism. The Philadelphia police followed Rizzo's lead and Rizzo made no secret of his support for white ethnics "protecting" their neighborhoods. Rizzo wasn't brilliant or even that charismatic, but his control over the city showed a skilled hand in machine politics. Rizzo was born in an Italian enclave of South Philadelphia and joined the police force in the Forties. For decades the city's Italian American workers held some of the lowest paying jobs the city had to offer. Italian immigration to Philadelphia picked up in the late 1800s when Congress passed laws allowing the importation of cheap labor, mostly into the country's low-wage manufacturing sector. To survive, most new Italian immigrants relied on padrones in order to find work and housing—an arrangement resembling part indentured servitude and part ward politics. The padrone system fit Rizzo's style of governance perfectly and helped secure his tenure in the police department. Granting favors and exacting tributes, Rizzo projected the image of a strong father figure who had pulled himself up by his own Italian bootstraps. His campaign messages evoked stories of European immigrants who arrived with little and, through the virtues of hard work and discipline, built a well-earned stability.

The New Right found an unlikely partner in the Democrat Rizzo, but he proved himself a worthy tribune for the cause. As a Democrat he resembled more the total-domination style of machine politics embodied by Louisiana Governor Huey Long than the simple fear-based racism of George Wallace. In 1959 Rizzo led a series of raids on Philadelphia's growing bohemian coffeehouse scene. While the department pointed the finger at beatniks, many believed the raids were a pretext for anti-gay harassment. Police justified one raid by saying that a young girl told them she went to the café to meet lesbians. As one journalist put it, "Creeps, kooks, liberals, phonies, fags, ultraliberals, lefties and bums—Rizzo's morality dictates that he must save his city from the shaggy perverts whose politics or culture spread like dandruff."[10]

It was clear he planned to disembowel the Left and stir whites' fears about civil rights and the city's growing Black population. In 1967 he was promoted to police commissioner, a last stop on his way to City Hall. As an Italian-American, his promotion was a kind of coup at a time when Philadelphia's Irishmen dominated the department and anti-Italian bigotry ran high. Rizzo was undeterred though, and political events provided plenty of fodder for a tough Italian policeman looking to bolster his reputation. In November 1967 Philadelphia police beat up and arrested dozens of Black high school students during a demonstration calling for Black history classes and school improvements. The cops were following Commissioner Rizzo's direct orders after he shouted, "Get their black asses!"

The following year, in the wake of Martin Luther King Jr.'s assassination, riots erupted in a hundred U.S. cities, burning some blocks to the ground. Philadelphia escaped substantial damage, attributed by many to Rizzo's use of mobile buses to quickly deploy hundreds of officers to trouble spots. Only four years earlier, North Philly had erupted into an infamous riot after police arrested a Black couple for illegal parking. Damages were estimated at $2 million. This time, however, Rizzo was in charge. Large showings of police force shored up Rizzo's image as a man who could keep the rabble in line. Rizzo was also skilled at conflating the Black communities' spontaneous outrage with organized civil rights actions. He laid the groundwork for his mayoral campaign by convincing white voters that the civil rights movement's real goals were specious and violent. Rizzo even had a group of hardcore Black supporters who he bonded with over their mutual hatred of radical dissidents (and a well-known policy of generous patronage). By the time he captured the mayoral seat, however, he minced few words about his plans for rebels, anti-police demonstrators and Blacks. In one of his more notorious statements, he bragged to a reporter, "I'm going to make Attila the Hun look like a faggot."[11]

As a new generation of rebels came of age in the City of Brotherly Love, Rizzo became notorious for his crackdowns on the Black Power movement and the New Left. In September 1969 police raided the Black Panthers' North Philly headquarters under the pretense of a fugitive search. A few months later, several Panthers were arrested on firearms charges, all of which were later dropped. In August of that year, Rizzo directed another raid on the Panther offices after unidentified Black men allegedly shot two police officers. He forced the Panthers to strip naked and invited the press to photograph them.[12] With the Panther leaders in jail, police gutted their offices seizing furniture, clothing, records and equipment. Word of Rizzo's brute force spread quickly in the Black community and across Philadelphia's Left. His efforts at intimidation backfired as hundreds of North Philly residents showed up to join the Panthers and rebuild their office before arrested leaders even got out of jail. In each incident Rizzo sharpened his use of the media to drive home the message that liberal dissidents would be punished. He revealed in graphic detail what he thought the government should do with the Panthers. "I don't know why we let idiots like them survive. Maybe the laws have to be changed. . . . These creeps lurk in the dark. They should be strung up. . . . I mean within the law."[13]

By all accounts Rizzo relished his shock value. Apparently, so did some voters. In 1971, Rizzo became the first Italian-American mayor of Philadelphia. He was voted in by white working-class residents in South Philly, Kensington, Fishtown, Frankford and Port Richmond. An estimated 20,000 Republican voters switched their affiliation to the Democrats in order to vote for Rizzo in the primary, helping him win the mayoral seat by a 50,000-vote margin. His victory reflected the ambitions of many white ethnic workers who faced some of the toughest times seen since the Depression. It also symbolized the apex of a decades-long process of Italian-American assimilation into the city's power structure.

Assimilation or not, Rizzo capitalized on the fact that many white ethnic groups who had arrived in a melting pot of indistinguishable whiteness were eager to reclaim their immigrant roots and traditions. Groups like O4O and White Lightning recognized the importance of these identities, as well, and encouraged members to explore the cultural traditions and progressive histories of their ancestors. However, Rizzo fortified a conservative brand of white ethnic chauvinism and deployed it toward a fine-tuned politics of resentment and discrimination. As the economy buckled under severe recession, white workers and immigrants who had ascended from poverty to a semblance of security felt in a precarious position. The real Philadelphia, Rizzo claimed, was threatened by civil rights, intermarriage and suburbanization. The noble working-class who had built the city (by which he meant only European immigrants) needed to shore up "defenses." Philadelphia's population had fallen below two million people as middle-class whites moved to the suburbs. Those who remained were anxious about scarcity and job competition with the factories closing down. Their presumed competition came from Black workers who had moved North looking for work and, to a smaller extent, new communities of Puerto Ricans, Chinese and Cambodian immigrants. As middle-class whites left for Bucks, Chester and Montgomery Counties during the Fifties and Sixties, the Black population in Philadelphia more than doubled. With it grew resentment from the city's remaining white elite and some white working-class residents who couldn't afford the train to the suburbs.

Despite the relative insularity of the neighborhood, many of O4O's members already had close relationships with Black and Latino Philadelphians. In some cases they went to school together and often they worked together. O4O member Sue Milligan[14] got a job in an insurance firm after high school where she worked with many Black women. She related to these women as friends and coworkers, hanging out after work and partying together along with several of her friends from Kensington. Before Milligan ever heard about O4O, those relationships catalyzed her political awareness. One of her good friends had recently gotten involved with the Black Muslim movement and admired Malcolm X. Milligan had only ever heard about Malcolm X's "white devils" comments, so she worried what this might mean for their friendship. Malcolm had changed his thinking, her friend explained. He opened to the possibility of working with whites and in 1965 he had outlined a model for multiracial alliances similar to the one SNCC and the Panthers adopted. This inspired Milligan. Malcolm X had seen the same deep connections between race and class oppression that she was starting to see. Milligan began reading more and having discussions with her Black friends about institutionalized racism. She didn't join O4O immediately but once she did Milligan joined the Women's Committee and started attending the group's education sessions. Like most other radical groups at the time, O4O members read and discussed Marx, Engels, Mao, Che, emerging feminist theory and literature from the era's current political movements. In practice, both Milligan's personal relationships and O4O played equally important roles in her political education. Each helped her develop the deeper values that turned her into a lifelong organizer.

O4O's unique labor–community organizing model spoke to Milligan as well. O4O organized in both workplaces and the surrounding neighborhood from its inception. While some leftists debated whether workplaces made better sites for mass mobilization than neighborhoods, which usually lack a single unifying issue, O4O "didn't have the luxury of choosing one or the other," as Milligan put it. In neighborhoods like Kensington where machine shops and factories sat interspersed with narrow row homes, the workplace and the community were inseparable. In contrast to other neighborhood-focused groups like JOIN and Rising Up Angry, or even the Revolutionary Youth Movement II, which grew out of SDS and focused solely on factory organizing, O4O carved out a unique position by organizing where they lived *and* where they worked.

O4O's Chris Robinson grew up in the then working-class and semi-rural Fox Chase section of Philadelphia. After a stint in SDS he joined Revolutionary Youth Movement II in order to organize workers, but through O4O he found Kensington to be the best of both worlds. O4O activists made sure their neighbors remembered the city's history of multiracial women's organizing among Jewish, Italian and Black garment workers in the 1920s. They set a practical and moral pole for Kensington to continue in that tradition and hundreds joined the cause, as neighbors and workers. Class was always the group's starting point, and addressing racism was simply part and parcel of fighting capitalism. For O4O's Dan Sidorick this approach meant organizing his coworkers at Goldman Paper Company against layoffs and dangerous working conditions by day and his neighbors against police brutality, the war and big business by night.

. . . .

During its early days O4O's leaders looked around for an issue that could jump-start the organization, expose Rizzo and unite people. Rizzo's regime had well-known outposts in the neighborhood, including social service providers like the Lighthouse Settlement. These outposts provided both obstacle and opportunity for O4O. Founded in 1893 to provide social services to the neighborhood's mill workers, the Lighthouse of the Seventies provided recreational and social services to the majority-white neighborhoods of Kensington and Fishtown despite sitting within arm's reach of North Philadelphia's Black and Puerto Rican communities. When the Black Panthers and Young Lords campaigned to start a free breakfast program at the Lighthouse, a powerful group of white residents called the Committee of 11 rallied to stop the program and the distribution of leftist newspapers like the *Free Press*, which Rizzo had declared "even more dangerous than the Panthers." Several members of the board expressed interest in change but none wanted to anger Rizzo or alienate those white residents who were protesting loudly about racial mixing in the neighborhood. The board decided to create a separate division to "service" Black and Puerto Rican residents, which meant de facto segregation from the other programs. The group decided to go on the offensive with a campaign to democratize the Lighthouse Settlement.

After surveying residents, O4O found that a good number of people opposed the racial bias of their more vocal neighbors. However, most feared losing their jobs or facing other retaliation if they spoke up. They also weren't too pleased that the Lighthouse barred young women from joining sports leagues. Working with local activists of color, O4O issued a set of demands to the Lighthouse that included ending discrimination, diversifying its board and creating a sports program for girls. They kept up pressure as well to set up community-sponsored events like free concerts in Lighthouse Field. When their demands were denied, they placed a band and a generator on a flatbed truck and led a march through Kensington. Three hundred residents joined them in the pouring rain. The action yielded no immediate changes, but it gave O4O a chance to test its mettle and identify neighbors sympathetic to their cause. With its base of support secure O4O started both a jobs project and a community school, but it was in confronting police brutality that the group really earned its street credentials.

Throughout surrounding neighborhoods O4O started distributing pocket-sized cards for the People's Bail Project including information about individuals' rights during arrest, booking and trial. Leaders recognized the effort as critical to build unity among working-class neighborhoods across the city. The cards provided an opportunity to talk directly with white residents, reminding them that police harassment was something all working-class residents had in common. On an individual basis, this undermined the mayor's basic tactic. Rizzo was relying on fear and the magnetism of overly simple explanations: crime in Philadelphia was up and so too was the city's Black population.[15] White residents were left to draw easy conclusions about cause and effect. Rizzo made his solution clear: Control the rising Black population, show them who's boss, lock them up and throw away the key. Such logic asked white communities to assume if people of color went to jail they must have deserved it. O4O worked to point out the fallacy of such assumptions.

Police behavior in white neighborhoods made this argument easy for them. According to O4O community surveys, police seemed to do anything they wanted to poor white residents in Kensington and nearby Fishtown. One incident in the neighborhood drove the point home. In September 1970 Philadelphia police shot and killed Paul Frankenhauser, a young Fishtown resident. When the cops responsible were let off with no penalty, Frankenhauser's family contacted O4O for help. The following April the group planned a protest demanding that the city reopen the investigation into his death.[16] Community members, including Frankenhauser's wife Joann, decided to disrupt one of Rizzo's rallies in the heart of the Fishtown neighborhood. The police anticipated the protest and members of its Civil Disobedience Squad were already on the scene.[17] The Frankenhausers and O4O demanded an audience with Rizzo, at which point the police attacked the unarmed residents shattering the skull of O4O co-founder Robert Barrow. When Whalen pulled up in his taxi, it immediately doubled as an ambulance and a getaway car. A lawsuit against Rizzo for Robert Barrow's beating resulted in a $5,000 settlement.

Over the next few years, O4O expanded its programs to address just about every issue likely to build community power and improve conditions. At one point the entire leadership of O4O participated in setting up community self-help centers and planned a "Community Health Fair" at the McPherson Square Library that drew people from surrounding neighborhoods to get free testing for diabetes, glaucoma, anemia and lead poisoning. Hundreds of city residents showed up to talk to volunteer health providers, get tests they hadn't been able to afford and lend their voices to O4O's demand for universal health care.

....

With a growing membership, O4O also started raising questions about the bigger context, nationally and internationally. Radical organizations in the late Sixties and early Seventies, especially those focused on neighborhood work, were always on the search for ways to "bring the war home." O4O knew that protests and preaching about the ills of U.S. foreign policy would just push residents farther away. With hundreds of locals fighting in Vietnam, the war was already right at home for them. O4O's Sue Milligan had seen dozens of friends drafted. Some never came back. Others came home badly injured and psychologically wounded. The local high school her brothers attended had the highest Vietnam War casualty rate for a student body in the entire country; fifty-four Thomas Edison High School students lost their lives in the war. Illustrating the broader problems with the war meant finding a different approach from the student movement's mass rallies. During a pair of carpet-bombings just before Christmas 1972, B-52 bombers unleashed thirty bombs over heavily populated sections of Haiphong and Hanoi in North Vietnam. Timed just days after the breakdown of the Paris peace talks between Henry Kissinger and Le Duc Tho, the "Christmas bombings" destroyed thirty multi-unit residential buildings in the Kham Thien area and leveled the 900-bed Bach Mai Hospital, killing twenty-five doctors. Pentagon spokesperson Jerry Friedman described the destruction as "some limited, accidental damage."[18] Columbia University professor and retired general Telford Taylor, who was in Hanoi at the time, vividly described a very different scene in the *New York Times:* "Hospital grounds were torn by huge fresh craters and the buildings that escaped hits were shattered by blasts . . . with rescue workers carrying patients piggyback, cranes and bulldozers and people using only their hands desperately clearing debris to reach victims said to be still buried in the rubble, and the frantic hospital director running from one building to another."[19]

Although the war was never short on atrocities, the bombing became a powerful symbol for the anti-war movement and spread dissent far beyond radical circles. In New York, the cast members of seventeen Broadway plays gave up their pay on Richard Nixon's Inauguration Day and contributed the money to the hospital's reconstruction. Public repulsion was so widespread that the Internal Revenue Service took the unprecedented step of officially disallowing tax-deductions for any contributions to the Bach Mai Emergency Relief Fund.[20] O4O came up with their own way to help. They launched a blood drive, walking door-to-door in Kensington and Fishtown to recruit donors. The organization wanted to show the world that the workers of Philadelphia were opposed to the war. At house after house they found supporters. Hundreds of willing participants joined the effort. Many donated money. The rest showed up at the blood bank the following Saturday. Even among Kensington's more conservative residents, nobody agreed with bombing a hospital.

The blood drive also provided an opportunity to talk about the costs of war. Many residents had already made the connection. Their own local hospitals were in dangerously poor shape and low-income women regularly received shoddy treatment when seeking health care, especially for reproductive health issues. Health care and women's issues also emerged as a natural place to build strong coalitions with activists of color. Through their friends at the Third World Women's Alliance, O4O members learned, for the first time, about the U.S. government's practice of forcibly sterilizing Native American and Puerto Rican women, as well as Black women and women prisoners. The Third World Women's Alliance published a newspaper called *Triple Jeopardy* dealing with the impacts of racism, poverty and sexism on the lives of low-income women of color. After inviting *Triple Jeopardy* to a meeting to discuss how they could support each other, O4O women formed a multiracial coalition with the Puerto Rican Socialist Party to tackle issues with particular impact on women's lives.[21] Their major campaign drew in a broader cross-section of women's groups focused on improving patient treatment at St. Joseph's hospital in North Philly.

Over the next several years O4O's women's group emerged as an anchor point for the group's community work. Like Rising Up Angry, women in O4O never considered splitting off into a separate women's group. Instead the group resolved to struggle together around sexism in the same way they struggled within the organization around class and within their community around racism. At one point a couple of male members of the steering committee were suspended for sexism, but O4O's overall approach was to educate, discuss and learn together. The O4O women's group started organizing regular educational forums for both men and women on issues like equal pay and reproductive freedom. The forums also provided a space to uproot sexist attitudes among members and reinforced the idea—which needed pointing out at the time—that women are and have always been strong leaders.

With the forums as a model O4O used ongoing popular education methods to deepen conversations with residents on a range of issues from city corruption to foreign policy. During one session, O4O bused Kensington residents to the Main Line suburbs to see how the rich lived. They made special stops at the homes of nineteen individuals O4O believed directly oppressed and exploited the neighborhood, especially landlords and elite industrialists.[22] This simple geographic tour of the city's political economy focused people's anger. O4O understood that in a community the strong arm of "the boss" isn't always as visible as in the workplace. The tour showed there were real people reaping real benefits from O4O members' cycle of poverty. By showing where these landlords and corporate elites profited in nearby poor Black and Puerto Rican neighborhoods, the tours also helped residents see common cause across racial lines. A special issue of the local *Kensington News Bulletin* provided background information on the nineteen targets, which the *Philadelphia Daily News* dubbed, "A handy tabloid-size directory of Who's Who and Where He Got His."

Knowing where he got his, or how he kept it, mattered like never before among families devastated by unemployment, record inflation and the city's disregard. It also helped O4O choose its targets. In one campaign the organization took a page from the unemployed workers' movements of the Thirties using direct action "office visits" to challenge Philadelphia Energy and Gas Company for cutting off electricity to families behind in their bills. Twelve O4O members accompanied one mother to the utility offices to demand her electricity be restored. The single mother of two had paid her back debt but couldn't make the extra $25 reinstallation charge. As a result of the action, PECO restored her service.[23] In another incident, city inspectors failed to hold anyone accountable for a massive sewage backup in the home of a young Kensington family. The city's property licensing department claimed they didn't know who owned the house. After two months and hours spent scooping the sewage out with buckets, the family called O4O for legal help. A volunteer lawyer uncovered a chain of previous owners and missing city records that could have been replaced within days, not weeks. O4O planned a sit-in to demand the city repair the broken pipe and locate the owner. The day before the action a plumber appeared at the home to clean up the waste and fix the sewer line.

With interventions like these, O4O did its best to improve

people's daily reality. Each action earned them new supporters. About sixty people served in the organization's core leadership at some point, and about five hundred participated as regular members over the years. Unfortunately, not every action succeeded and rising unemployment only made things harder for the region. Philadelphia lost 40,000 jobs between 1971 and 1974, most in the manufacturing trades and private construction. When the city announced almost three hundred jobs would open up in September 1974, ten thousand workers stood outside in the rain to apply. It was a waste of time. Mayor Frank Rizzo had already filled the positions with his supporters and their friends. Many people in Kensington always disliked the mayor and the city's machine politics, but Rizzo had a big enough base to aim for reelection that year. After all, backdoor promotions to civil service positions were just one of the perks offered to his loyal supporters.

In the lead-up to his 1974 reelection, Rizzo returned to his old tricks trying to divide residents in North Philly and Kensington along racial lines by dedicating himself to blocking the relocation of Thomas Edison High School. The Vietnam War had devastated the student body, but the school itself looked like its own kind of war zone. The school building at 8th and Lehigh—then named Northeast High School—was declared a fire hazard in 1956. At the time, city officials responded by redistricting. They opened a new school in the far Northeast to serve the city's remaining middle-class families, but they kept the old building open. The city just gave it a new name and filed in poorer Black, Puerto Rican and white students from North Philly and Kensington. Because Edison was the only boys' public school in the area, neighborhood boys had no choice but to attend Edison High, unless they were fortunate enough to attend Catholic school. The campaign to rebuild the high school in a new location near Lighthouse Field forced the issue of neighborhood unification. Rizzo seized the opportunity to remind white residents that the new locale would bring Black and Puerto Rican students closer to the heart of Kensington. O4O naturally joined parents and students in pressing for the new school site. When Rizzo's forces asked people in Kensington to call the governor to voice their concerns about the relocation, three times as many people called to vote for the new site.

During his second-term campaign Rizzo had to work twice as hard for Kensington's votes. Many in the neighborhood were fed up with the regime. In the months preceding the election, police harassment of local kids had reached new levels. Cops swept through the area around Westmoreland and Mascher Streets arresting almost every young person in sight, seemingly without provocation. According to a witness quoted in O4O's newspaper, "They got a paperboy who was collecting on his route, a boy walking his mother to bingo, kids on errands for their parents, several people sitting on their front steps, and people hanging in the schoolyard—forty-seven in all." At one point the cops crammed twenty-one kids into a single paddy wagon. Kensington residents reacted instinctively; two hundred parents spontaneously blocked an intersection at Front and Allegheny to prevent further raids. Police had illustrated, once again, that the department's brutality problem lived on both sides of the color line. Protests against the police department increased and so did Rizzo's tough-guy rhetoric. His divisive tactics had failed at Edison, but he wasn't finished. In 1975 Frank Rizzo was reelected as mayor, once again drawing his support from white ethnic communities in the Northeast, South Philly, Richmond and to a lesser extent Kensington. He won, but he spent $1.2 million to do so—three times more than his opponents.[24]

Frank Rizzo hadn't changed, but some minds in Kensington and Fishtown had. O4O built a sense of possibility among workers and residents, breaking through the fears they learned during decades of scarcity and red baiting. Their challenges and successes, however small, showed an innovative approach to organizing white communities during a decade of political and economic fallout. Their workplace-plus-community approach was unique at the time, and helped demonstrate their message of working-class unity in practical ways. They supported local workers when they went on strike and used their newspaper to share dispatches from national groups, such as the United Farm Workers of America. They celebrated the historic campaign of Mother Jones to support textile workers and stop child labor and they highlighted Philadelphia's history of progressive populism. In the end, people in O4O felt like they were a part of something bigger, which is precisely what kept many of them in the movement far beyond the group's lifetime.

Part of this broader connection came from their collaboration with Rising Up Angry in Chicago and White Lightning in the Bronx. Rising Up Angry's Steve Tappis played the biggest role in uniting the three groups. Tappis spent time in both Philly and the Bronx working to set up a formal alliance. At the time there were fewer national forums for neighborhood organizers to share lessons or collaborate so his attempt was more difficult than it would have been a few years earlier. The formal alliance never amounted to much more than moral support, information sharing and reprinting articles from each other's papers, but the groups' shared analysis did bolster their sense of purpose.

．．．．．．．．．．．．．．．．．．．．．．．．．．．．．．

At the time, White Lightning was gearing up to take on its own Goliaths in New York. The campaign against Nelson Rockefeller's draconian drug laws was only one side of the coin. On the other,

White Lightning was fighting to loosen the grip of heroin on poor communities. Like their friends in North Chicago and Kensington, White Lightning members in the Bronx saw their work as part of a broader revolutionary project of long-term neighborhood organizing. They intended to build a permanent base of radicalism among ethnic whites and recovering addicts in close collaboration with the Black and Puerto Rican communities in the South Bronx and Harlem.

Only a few years earlier, White Lightning founder Gil Fagiani was just a face in the crowd at the 1968 Democratic National Convention. Like many in attendance his politics were catalyzed by the moral cause of civil rights and opposition to the war in Vietnam. Through the chaos of demonstrations, counter-demonstrations, police riots and mass arrests unfolding in front of him, Fagiani arrived at a much more personal realization. He could no longer deny he was addicted to heroin. He had traveled to the convention with his fiancée by bus to be part of what he expected would be a defining moment of his generation. He packed a small amount of heroin for the journey, but his supply quickly diminished. While his comrades faced off with police in a highly publicized street battle, Fagiani fought a far more private battle as the turmoil of withdrawal wracked his body.

Fagiani's internal struggle with his upbringing fueled both his politicization and his addiction. Like many Italian immigrants his family had followed a path from the city to the suburbs. Originally raised in the Villa Avenue section of the North Bronx, he moved to a suburban development in Connecticut when his family received a Veterans Administration loan. There he first observed the extent to which European descendents—many of whom were moving away from the working-class—were obsessed with race. This preoccupation intensified the status anxiety of Italian Americans, who had long been regarded as the least educated, darkest people in town. He learned quickly that past discrimination against Italians didn't necessarily translate into empathy for groups facing the same or worse. While Fagiani gravitated toward his mother's sympathy for the civil rights movement, he began to feel deeply alienated from his community. He wanted out.

Hoping to find a career path and some focus, Fagiani enrolled in Pennsylvania Military College. During summer break following his junior year, he joined a Cornell University student project working with the East Harlem Tenants Council. While serving the Puerto Rican community in a day camp, he attended his first anti-war demonstration, started reading progressive political literature and became outraged with the slum conditions he saw firsthand. In the Thirties, East Harlem had been a bastion of support for the "Red Congressman" Vito Marcantonio whose seven terms in the House of Representatives made him the most successful radical politician in U.S. history. Between 1934 and 1950 Marcantonio led a multiracial coalition of Blacks, Puerto Ricans and Italians, while championing anti-imperialism abroad and housing rights for Harlem residents. By the Sixties, however, most of New York's Italian-American leaders were staunchly conservative.

East Harlem, too, had changed. The neighborhood shifted to a Puerto Rican majority after construction began for some of the first public housing in the city. On the face of it, New York was finally doing what generations of reformers had demanded: clearing slums to build modern housing. New public housing brought new faces to the neighborhood, but as people of color moved in most of the remaining Italian Americans fled, and the legacy of Marcantonio's coalition politics dissolved—at least for a while.[25] For Fagiani, the exodus and the increasingly conservative tilt of New York's Italian-American population reinforced his estrangement. On one hand, he was developing a keen political eye and a sense of outrage. On the other, becoming more alienated from his culture intensified his heroin addiction. In 1967, at the end of his senior year, Fagiani moved back to East Harlem. He worked for a while with the East Harlem Tenants Council, participated sporadically in left-wing political activities, and cut ties with his friends and family as he became more and more deeply involved with street drugs. A cousin intervened and attempted to enroll him in a treatment program, but Fagiani was placed on a waiting list.[26]

In November 1969 Fagiani entered Logos, a residential drug treatment program in the Bronx. Logos, and the recovering addicts Fagiani met there, became the backbone for a new radical community organization: White Lightning. In the U.S. the drug trade and, by extension, recovery programs had become some of the few places where people of various races and classes regularly mixed. This was especially true at Logos. Its multiracial residents included Blacks, Latinos and whites, many of whom were fed up with the program's rigid hierarchy. Employing the "Therapeutic Community" model, Logos emphasized intense, confrontational group sessions geared to help residents move each other toward sobriety.

In 1970 residents saw warning signs that Logos was becoming something like a cult. The group's director decided to eliminate community reintegration as a final phase of the program. Embracing the "Synanon" model, he wanted to convert Logos from a treatment program to a lifelong utopian community.[27] Fagiani and other participants formed a protest caucus called the Spirit of Logos. In their first campaign they attempted to convince New York City's Board of Estimate (the credentialing body at the time) that Spirit of Logos was, in fact, the real program that should receive city funding, not Logos. Their initial campaign demanded Logos administrators end the blacklisting of ex-residents for jobs, welfare and parole, and called for Logos residents to have a part in organizational decision-making.

Dr. Michael Smith, who worked at Logos through Lincoln Hospital, had strong left-wing sympathies and was impressed with Fagiani's initiative. He recruited Fagiani into Think Lincoln, an organization working to reform the notoriously dilapidated hospital. Lincoln served the predominantly Puerto Rican and Black communities of the South Bronx. The area was one of the poorest in the entire metropolitan area, with the average household income under $3,000. The hospital's five buildings had been condemned in 1961, but there'd been no progress on a new facility. With its dismal survival rates and archaic equipment, Lincoln was dubbed "the butcher shop." Patients and staff at Lincoln in the late Sixties described human excrement backed up in toilets, lead paint and plaster peeling from the walls, and one floor where the pediatric patients shared a room with the dysentery ward. The neighborhood's infant mortality rate was thirty per one thousand live births—double the national average.[28]

The hospital quickly became a flashpoint for community and radical organizations. In 1968 hospital mental health workers, including hundreds of Black and Latino residents hired to provide non-medical services like translation, revolted over administrators' broken promises, working conditions and the quality of patient care. During a three-day sit-in they ran the hospital themselves and won the termination of three dictatorial administrators. Forming the Health Revolutionary Unity Movement (HRUM), they demanded immediate changes, as did the New York Black Panther Party, Think Lincoln, the Republic of New Afrika and the local Young Lords Party. Beyond the practical concerns of letting a horrible hospital serve a poor neighborhood, the fight to change Lincoln also had symbolic significance. Lincoln Hospital was built in

1839 as "The Home for the Colored Aged," a nursing home for elderly runaway slaves. To many in the neighborhood, the city's failure to address conditions at Lincoln was just proof that the same centuries-old racism was alive and well in the North.

The Panthers organized at Lincoln until April 1969 when police arrested the entire New York leadership for allegedly plotting to blow up public sites in Manhattan. Though all were later acquitted, severe government repression mounted against leaders of color. Soon after, most Black and Latino activists left Think Lincoln and Spirit of Logos to join HRUM. The exodus mirrored the racial division of labor in the Left overall. In this case, however, breaking into separate organizations didn't foster alliance or camaraderie. The Third World section of Spirit of Logos ended up dissolving quickly, which left Spirit's white members without a compass. Fagiani and fellow Logos resident Willie Everich regrouped, forming White Lightning to organize ethnic whites in the Bronx.

In the wake of Think Lincoln's dissolution, the Young Lords Party took the lead on the Lincoln campaign, with White Lightning and an array of left-wing groups joining in support. The New York Young Lords formed in June 1969 with the blessing of Cha-Cha Jiménez and the original Chicago chapter. Led by youth barely out of their teens, the New York Lords quickly made a name for itself by using creative, militant direct action to draw attention to the city's utter neglect of basic neighborhood services. In Harlem garbage would pile up for weeks, a putrid insult added to the injury of the ghetto. Residents of El Barrio regularly watched as garbage trucks drove through their neighborhood en route to service more affluent ones. The Lords' first public action was to sweep the waste into the street using large brooms appropriated from the Department of Sanitation. When a few trucks arrived, most of the garbage had blown back to the sidewalks. The next day the Lords returned the garbage to the streets—this time creating a five-foot wall in the middle of 3rd Avenue. The "garbage offensive" provided a burst of conviction in New York's Puerto Rican community, which also made up 70 percent of the area surrounding Lincoln.[29] The Lords understood the hospital's "brutal neglect" of the community as its own kind of garbage.

The Lincoln campaign reached a crescendo in the summer of 1970. On July 14, one hundred fifty people invaded the hospital. Commandeering an entire floor for a detoxification program, they demanded, as one flyer put it, "total self-determination of all health services through a Community-Worker Board to operate Lincoln Hospital." While the takeover itself lasted just twelve hours, the Lords, HRUM and a nascent White Lightning continued to work closely with staff for months afterward. Community organizers set up guerilla programs that employed dozens of neighborhood residents and helped hundreds of addicts. In the detox unit, political education became a central part of the therapeutic process with classes and discussions challenging the gospel of drug addiction as a personal pathology.

The community organizers were aided by a significant number of Lincoln's doctors. Unknown to the takeover orchestrators, Lincoln physician Charlotte Phillips had been recruiting progressive medical professionals to the hospital for months.[30] When the activists stormed the facility, they were actually welcomed by much of the staff. Any medical personnel sitting on the fence got a substantial push to choose sides when the hospital's pattern of neglect made even bigger headlines. One day after the takeover, Carmen Rodriguez, a resident of Logos and friend of Fagiani's, died at Lincoln due to gross malpractice during an abortion. Disgusted, Dr. Mike Smith, who later became a member of White Lightning, displayed her medical charts to the local press in an act of medical disobedience. The charts revealed that doctors failed to record Rodriguez's pre-existing heart condition. She had died of cardiac arrest.

For a few years, it seemed as if almost all the borough's radical activity was linked back to Lincoln in some way. "It was the closest thing I could see in the United States to what socialism might actually look like," Fagiani recalled. Thanks to the takeover and steady community pressure, a new Lincoln Hospital opened in 1976.

. . . .

For the newly minted White Lightning it only made sense to continue addressing the health needs of the community. At first, drugs were Lightning's singular issue. Even their name was a dual nod to their mission of organizing whites and to one of heroin's many street names. According to member John Duffy, White Lightning was primarily a group of ex-drug addicts committed as much to getting people off drugs as they were to revolutionary programs and politics. This attitude was uncommon in the Sixties and Seventies when groups such as Abbie Hoffman's Yippies and the Weather Underground (at least for a period of time) viewed narcotics as a tool for personal liberation, part of pummeling bourgeois socialization out of the mindscape.[31] In other radical circles, like some chapters of the Panthers, drug use was grounds for expulsion. White Lightning staked out another position. Its base included people in various stages of recovery. To expel members for drug use was out of the question, so White Lightning focused its policy on confronting the politics of the drug trade and the criminalization of addicts.

Strongly influenced by the pamphlet "Capitalism Plus Dope Equals Genocide" written by New York Black Panther Michael Tabor, Lightning saw drugs as a deliberate attempt to destabilize ghetto communities for corporate profit. Tabor's pamphlet criticized the popular concern that Sixties counterculture had made drug use fashionable in white middle-class communities. He argued it was the drug epidemic in poor communities, especially communities of color, which presented the real danger. Tabor also attacked the Therapeutic Community model for denying the socio-economic origins of drug addiction. "These programs were never intended to cure Black addicts," Tabor asserted. "They can't even cure the White addicts they were designed for."[32]

In a creative re-interpretation of Marxist theory, Lightning's take on the political economy of dope framed the addicted pusher as an exploited worker, not a perpetrator. For them, the real criminals were drug companies that overproduced for the illegal market, along with the cops and organized crime factions that profited from trafficking. Adopting a Panther-like political program, Lightning demanded an end to the flood of drugs in working-class communities and adamantly opposed legal addictive drugs such as methadone. To Lightning, both prescription and illicit drugs were forms of chemical fascism, effective in neutralizing and controlling poor communities through a nearly guaranteed path to prison or the morgue. Though it took more than thirty years for published reports of crack-cocaine trafficking by intelligence agencies to surface, Lightning and the Panthers always suspected government culpability in the growing drug epidemic. Through its newspaper, Lightning accused the New York Police Department and federal government of complicity in the drug trade. They alleged that dealers and users alike were arrested for the sole purpose of reselling contraband. When New York Police Commissioner Patrick Murphy reported that four hundred pounds of heroin and cocaine had mysteriously disappeared from police evidence lockers, Lightning seized the opportunity to publish their "Cops Push Dope" tract accusing police and intelligence agencies of funneling the drugs to poor neighborhoods.[33]

In one of its most defining campaigns White Lightning attempted to defeat the first wave of Rockefeller Laws. In 1973 New York Governor Nelson Rockefeller, a liberal Republican and potential presidential candidate, was looking for a way onto the national stage. By targeting drug users he fortified his tough-on-crime image. In an address to the state legislature, he warned, "The crime, the muggings, the robberies, the murders associated with addiction continue to spread a reign of terror. Whole neighborhoods have been as effectively destroyed by addicts as by an invading army. This has to stop."[34] Rockefeller proposed a new set of laws ordering mandatory minimum sentences for drug possession. Holding more than one ounce of marijuana would result in a fifteen-year prison term. Heroin and cocaine possession, in any amount, could mean lifetime residency behind bars. The concept of mandatory minimum sentencing would soon be copied in multiple states and incorporated into federal sentencing guidelines—sending hundreds of thousands of nonviolent drug offenders to prisons.[35] To craft his hard-line legislation, Rockefeller borrowed heavily from the federal 1951 Boggs Act, which made little distinction between drug dealers and users for purposes of sentencing. Affluent families often found competent legal counsel for members charged with possession, while working-class families relied on the over-burdened public defender's office. These families watched their loved ones disappear to Attica, Sing-Sing and a dozen other facilities in the state.

Lightning saw the drug crackdown the same way it saw the military draft: as an opportunity and a threat. While the laws threatened to lock up their base, such obviously punitive legislation also had the potential to broaden dissent. In 1973 Lightning joined United Parents Who Care (UPWC), a grassroots movement that reached far beyond traditional leftist circles. UPWC was mostly made up of white working-class parents whose children had drug problems. Building the coalition was a challenge for the group because the families tended to be fairly conservative. Most were only drawn to activism because their own children were facing prison time. Often they struggled against any talk of broader social reforms. White Lightning tried to turn this tide. Inspired by the way Black and Latino radicals had used their histories of resistance to build pride and solidarity across racial divisions, Lightning studied the history of European immigrant groups and tried to infuse lessons about their struggles into their community work. Examining the 1891 lynching of eleven Sicilians in New Orleans, the group connected the history of lynching to the current impact of drug laws on poor communities. They asked members to explore their ancestors' participation in radical unions such as the Industrial Workers of the World or the many progressive parties European immigrants had formed, especially European Jews. Some UPWC members were happy to claim these histories and situate their troubles in a broader context, but many were not.

Lightning struggled to move even those white immigrants who came from socialist countries. Life in the United States was hard. The McCarthy era taught them to keep their heads down and American capitalism made alluring promises. Some of the families in United Parents Who Care had even established a moderate degree of security as small shop owners or foremen. Lightning's platform started to seem a bit too radical for people who just wanted to help their kids. It didn't help that Lyndon La Rouche's National Caucus of Labor Committees made a habit of crashing community meetings and spouting accusations about White Lightning's "counter-revolutionary" leaders. Adding a nail to UPWC's coffin,

New York authorities were quick to exploit the political gulf. One father, with whom Fagiani worked closely, received a call from the police demanding, "Did you know this guy Gil you work with is a Communist?" Fed up with the perceived dogma of the Left, parents began to drift away.

Adding to their troubles, the New Left's general ambivalence toward poor and working-class whites had cemented White Lightning's estrangement from the broader student movement. Lightning's organizers started to feel like they were on an island all their own, save for their connection to Angry and O4O. Fagiani recalls common remarks from some student radicals deriding Lightning's base as "racist rednecks" and hopeless reactionaries. He felt constrained by what he perceived to be an overarching rigidity in the larger movement around methods to undermine white supremacy. His approach was to connect positive stories of white ethnic history to current struggles among people of color. He authored a pamphlet comparing the trial of Panthers Bobby Seale and Ericka Huggins to the persecution of Italian-American anarchists Nicola Sacco and Bartolemo Vanzetti, drawing useful parallels. However, he suppressed his own work, feeling that any positive portrayal of European identity would be denounced as racist. Recalling a time when he attended an Italian feast with a leftist who commented that she was eager for the day when such "reactionary" cultural and religious celebrations were abolished, Fagiani feared that White Lightning and its sister groups might forever be out of step with the rest of the movement. The gulf between professed radicals and ordinary people sympathetic to the cause seemed impossible to bridge.

....

Alienated from the white Left, White Lightning relied implicitly on their preexisting relationships with radicals of color, but as

these groups atomized—either around ideas of cultural nationalism or simply under the weight of growing state repression—White
Lightning's leaders had to confront difficult questions about what
they could really accomplish. Perhaps more than any other white
working-class organization of the era, Lightning's members struggled the hardest with the racial division of political labor. The model
implicitly relied on having others to work alongside, but Lightning's
closest allies—the Panthers, Lords and HRUM—had begun to
fragment, leaving the group without a strong multiracial alliance. By
1971 Lightning had to decide how they could emulate the programs
of Third World liberation groups without formal coalition.

Key leaders in Lightning also struggled to focus just on white
residents' problems in a region like the Bronx where even they
grew up in racially mixed neighborhoods. Terry Doyle, Willie Everich and John Duffy all grew up in the Bronx as white minorities
within neighborhoods of color. For them, cultural nationalism and
strict solidarity politics made little sense. Throughout the life of
the organization all three remained intensely uncomfortable with
organizing in ethnically seperate groups. Duffy's parents were Irish
immigrants. His father worked in a meat factory and his mother
was a domestic worker. After the death of his father, Duffy's mother
raised him and his brother on a meager combination of social security and veteran's benefits. As a kid, Duffy witnessed the Mott Haven neighborhood shift from Italian, Jewish and Irish to a majority
Puerto Rican and Black. One of the few white families that stayed
in the neighborhood, Duffy and his brother quickly assimilated
into Black and Puerto Rican culture. Duffy dropped out of school
at fifteen but was schooled, as he remembers it, by "the brightest
youth in the ghetto"—the Black Panthers, the Young Lords and
the Nation of Islam. For Duffy, Spirit of Logos and Think Lincoln evolved organically the same way his childhood friendships

did—people were united by their common experience. Building unity across race was practical, not ideological. It wasn't that members like Duffy rejected solidarity models of organizing whites in support of people of color's demands, it was just that some of White Lightning's members simply knew no white community to call "their own." Given the mandate of the time, they tried. "It was what it was," Duffy says now. But many of Lightning's members later wondered whether the separation of forces diffused any longer-term impacts for their work.

....

Lightning members did their best to develop their own approach given the conditions of the time. Once the Rockefeller Laws passed, Lightning took a page from Rising Up Angry and O4O by providing legal aid and addressing other community issues. They provided advice and advocacy for those arrested for possession, conducted radically minded drug recovery groups and launched their own series of Serve the People programs including a legal aid service. Taking a page from Rising Up Angry's legal defense program, Lightning started providing free clinics for women on issues like how to obtain a divorce. New member Kirsten Andersen was one of several women in Lightning to join the group's broader efforts and see a natural fit for women's programs. Andersen moved to New York from rural New Jersey and joined White Lightning after a period of searching for movement groups where she could do practical work with everyday people. She was at once impressed by and struggled with the group's emphasis on discipline, theory and focus. As part of her initiation, Fagiani administered an oral test of her political orientation. His verdict was, "Great on class and race, but a little weak on women's issues." More so than Rising Up Angry or O4O, Lightning's leadership was mostly male, so she was obviously upset by the ruling. She joked later though that Fagiani was probably right. She, like all young movement leaders, had just as much personal growing to do as the people they were trying to organize. Andersen found that White Lightning, contradictions and all, provided the chance she was looking for to develop political projects that tackled class, race and gender in tandem. During her first few months she helped build a women's caucus called Women Hold Up Half the Sky, a name taken from Mao's writings on women's equality.

One of White Lightning's busiest legal programs was its housing clinic. The group evolved to tackle poor housing conditions both out of necessity and strategy. Besides drug addiction, slum housing created one of the biggest health hazards in the neighborhood. Some apartment windows were painted shut, lead paint flaked from walls, staircases lacked railings and landlords rarely followed through on fixes. These poor conditions had been intensified by white flight. Beginning in the 1950s nearly 100,000 people, mostly white families, left the Bronx for neighborhoods in Queens, Staten Island and Connecticut. With white flight, New York City disinvested in the Bronx and absentee landlords stopped making improvements on a deteriorating housing stock. It wasn't that the properties were vacant, though. More than 100,000 new residents, nearly all Black and Latino, moved into the Bronx during the same period.[86]

Soon, both newcomers and old-timers faced a common enemy: redlining. Bank lenders simply refused to give loans or mortgages to individuals in neighborhoods they deemed deteriorating. Looking around the Bronx, anyone could see the bombed-out tenements, shops and vacant lots as landlords and investors abandoned properties. Some still hoped to cash out though. In Mott Haven, arsons reached epic proportions. In the mid-Seventies a rash of suspicious fires tore through blocks designated for redevelopment, including the Fordham area dividing the South and North Bronx. An estimated seven thousand fires plagued the region over a two-year period. *Time* magazine counted the Bronx fires as part of a national trend in poor neighborhoods where 40 percent were ignited to collect insurance money.[37] One fire on Christmas Eve destroyed the Lightning storefront at 109 East 184th Street and two others gutted a nearby residence and restaurant. The fires left most residents unable to rebuild. As a result, landlord abandonment soon peaked and a second round of arsons gripped the neighborhood. Landlords and city developers assumed residents would just move on without a fuss. For the area's poorest residents, moving on was no more an option in 1975 than it had been when white flight started two decades earlier.

Adopting the legal aid model of Rising Up Angry, Lightning members Terry Doyle, Willie Everich and Bill Whalen became experts on New York housing law. They alternated between organizing rent strikes and representing tenants in court. In most cases, victories came from their do-it-yourself approach to housing court. Lightning received housing law training from the Metropolitan Council and El Comité, a militant Puerto Rican group active in combating gentrification. These trainings provided members with the legal and practical skills needed to help residents navigate housing court.[38] Soon enough, Everich was helping residents collectivize their own buildings. New York City rent control laws at the time made this tactic viable, but landlords and their lawyers regularly threatened to sue the activists for practicing law without a license. Lightning's legal team replied, "Go ahead! You can't get money out of a turnip." In one case, Lightning halted the displacement of tenants being evicted by a local branch of the Seventh Day Adventist Church. Lightning disrupted church services by leafleting the congregation about the pastor's real estate dealings.

Even as the group expanded to address other community concerns, White Lightning never strayed far from its anti-drug roots. When Fagiani and others spent time visiting Rising Up Angry and touring college campuses to talk about their work, they decided to make an important stop in Ohio, the home of the Eli Lilly Corporation. Lilly was responsible for manufacturing the majority of methadone consumed in the U.S. at the time. The drug was developed during World War II as a substitute for addictive drugs and administered to lessen the pain of soldiers maimed in battle. Lightning objected to the use of any drug meant to prolong and enable addiction—methadone use just substituted state-sanctioned dependency for an illegal high. Even as early as 1960 patients reported nasty consequences from the drug including difficulty breathing, heart troubles, insomnia and confusion. Lightning's Ohio protest was small but it also garnered them a new recruit. For Gene Bild, whose brother Steve was active in Rising Up Angry, the focus on the drug epidemic resonated as did the group's criticism of therapeutic community models for addiction treatment. Bild was active in the Panther Defense Committee before Fred Hampton was killed and found in White Lightning a place to combine solidarity work with direct organizing on the issues he cared about.

....

Through the legal clinic and drug recovery programs, Lightning did some of its best work. Organizers helped people kick drugs, stopped evictions and won building improvements. Yet, the wins were arguably small in the scheme of their revolutionary goals. Questions about the real effectiveness of their strategies created a steady backdrop and, at times, a huge obstacle. In the Sixties white radicals were driven by the moral vision of civil rights, the radical program of the Panthers and the intellectual leadership of SDS. The

Vietnam War, too, had created a focal point for dissent that unified people from all corners. Now, leaders found themselves lacking direction. By the mid-Seventies, the recession, factory off-shoring and urban depopulation flipped familiar terrains of Left organizing on their sides. Even the most profound reform victories seemed temporary in the face of severe recession and growing conservatism. Politicians like Rizzo sharpened the perceived victimization of whites through a language of resentment and a baseless rhetoric of "reverse racism." This language continues to build political careers to this day. The movement was right where the government wanted it to be: in a state of exhaustion following years of assassinations, trials, disruptions and uphill work.

Before the stone hit the pond this trajectory was clear to organizers. They faced yet another fork in the road. In 1975 Lightning's Bill Whalen left to work at the Alinsky-inspired Northwest Bronx Community and Clergy Coalition, which organized Black, Puerto Rican and white residents together around neighborhood issues. Many of his comrades in Lightning disagreed with this choice, citing the coalition's lack of revolutionary outlook. Whalen, however, saw building a broad neighborhood coalition as a hands-on attempt to challenge racism. The interracial coalition served the whole neighborhood, giving it the latitude to address the complex issues raised by gentrification and neighborhood integration. Pushed out by urban renewal in Harlem and the Lower East Side, many of the Blacks and Latinos moving into the Bronx were leaving worse-off areas. "It could have been a recipe for jealousy as people of color often rented the buildings with elevators while whites had the walk-ups they had lived in forever," Whalen points out. "The presence of a coalition, putting forth ways for people to work in common, was a powerful example." His brother, O4O's Jack Whalen, also took a job in a settlement house where Philly residents came together around common issues rather than racial identity. While the Whalen brothers' aims were always revolutionary, many of their peers disagreed that any real revolutionary work could happen in these venues.

Frustrated with the slow progress of neighborhood organizing, by the mid-1970s other Left leaders turned to party-building and Maoist-influenced Marxist-Leninism as a framework for revolution. An ideology that promised a break from the one step forward, two steps back pattern seemed like a logical and necessary next step given the state of the movement. A New Communist Movement emerged in the 1970s to build national political parties that could, at least theoretically, lead the working class to power. Veteran leaders attracted to these politics attempted to stitch together Left organizations vying for the title of vanguard by forming new parties independent of existing socialist and communist organizations.[39] This strategy was simultaneously a mark of maturity and a fatal trap. On the one hand, it forced hundreds of activists to further grapple with the limits of reform and pushed a movement born of the U.S. civil rights struggle to connect the political dots rippling across the globe with the expansion of neoliberalism.

Party building took a substantial number of movement organizers away from day-to-day work in the community and neighborhood projects suffered. Leftists looking to build revolutionary political parties recruited the "best and the brightest" from the ranks of community organizations. Groups such as the Revolutionary Union, which later morphed into the Revolutionary Communist Party, and the October League (Marxist-Leninist) recruited members from existing labor and community organizations. White Lightning's John Duffy joined the October League, and several members of O4O joined the newly formed Revolutionary Union. For years these organizers grappled with the limits of neighborhood politics. They saw it become increasingly difficult to translate local reforms to more than citywide importance even in cities as large and influential as New York, Chicago and Philadelphia. Most movement leaders agreed that the fragments of the Left would eventually have to unite in a single party or broad-based organization, but the push toward party-building steamrolled the hard-won gains of community organizations. At the time it seemed for the greater good. Those organizers who joined Left parties in the 1970s hoped to get past incremental change and reach thousands rather than dozens of people.

Just as it was for the Young Patriots Organization when leaders split over the party question, White Lightning and O4O didn't survive the splits. Duffy saw White Lightning's move from a neighborhood group to a vanguard organization as something that destroyed its credibility with the very people it intended to organize. O4O's Sue Milligan agreed. It wasn't the right time for a party, she felt. "Most of those organizations had no real base in the working class—you can't create a real movement on theory alone." That theory and Left politics continued to guide her activism; she just wasn't convinced to adopt a party line. For Dan Sidorick, the New Communist Movement had both benefits and drawbacks. "There was a real need to think beyond the neighborhood and analyze how we might change the course of the nation."

Inspired by the history-changing global events of the Sixties, they were right to, at least, attempt that new course. Their search for a "right way" mirrors the crisis of formation that faces almost every social movement. Once organizations emerge to coordinate spontaneous uprisings, new democratic experiments become necessary. White Lightning and O4O's radical community organizing showed important gains, but finally hit simultaneous roadblocks. By 1976 both O4O and White Lightning quietly dissolved. With

the memory of the government's counterintelligence program loom-
ing large, O4O members decided to destroy nearly all the organization's archives.[40] Bill Whalen remained at the Northwest Bronx
Community and Clergy Coalition as Executive Director. Marilyn
Buggey and Jack Whalen took time away to deal with health and
family crises, returning later to community work outside the Left
party structure. Doyle stayed connected to progressive politics and
is today a gardener in Central Park. Everich is a respected percus-
sionist in New York City's Latin Jazz scene. Following Lightning's
dissolution, Duffy worked in faith-based community organizing
before becoming a Hollywood line producer. Fagiani is a social
work administrator and poet still active in the Left.

....

Before shuttering its doors October 4th Organization did recon-
vene for one last campaign. In 1978, a broad coalition of Philadelphians finally defeated Frank Rizzo, albeit unceremoniously.
According to the city charter, Rizzo could not run for a third term.
Stepping down was the last thing on his agenda, so against the
advice of top aides, he authored a ballot measure that would remove
mayoral term restrictions. The Stop Rizzo Campaign amassed its
own rainbow coalition, bringing the kind of unity to Philadelphia's Left created only by a strong enemy and years of alliance
building. According to Michael Simmons, a Black member of the
Philadelphia Workers Organizing Committee, the backbone of the
campaign came from Puerto Rican and Black activists. The Black
United Front Against Charter Change coalesced nationalists, Baptist churches and assorted radicals. The Philadelphia branches of the
Young Lords and El Comité anchored work in the Latino community, while white radicals carried their own weight with members of
O4O going door-to-door in Kensington and Fishtown to mobilize

voters. Even the city's middle-class liberals created the Committee to Protect the Charter and businessmen miffed at a gigantic rise in taxes under Rizzo contributed more than $200,000 to oppose the initiative. At a rally near the end of Rizzo's term, Black radicals marched under the banner "Hey Rizzo, have you heard? Philly ain't Johannesburg!" Rizzo always maintained he was free of racism and shrugged off the comparison. In his campaign message, though, he simply urged his supporters, "Vote White."

Aware of the mass anti-Rizzo upswell, the mayor's cronies did their own part to swing the results. Election observers documented several instances of polling places in anti-Rizzo precincts being moved far out of the neighborhoods to deter voters. Witnesses also reported violent harassment of Stop Rizzo activists. Their efforts to protect their patriarch failed. More than 170,000 new voters registered so they could weigh in on the battle—most were Black voters united in their opposition to Rizzo's politics. The mayor's attempt at a third term was defeated by nearly two-to-one.[41] More than 36 percent of Kensington voted against Rizzo. Despite his obvious defeat, the former mayor—who always insisted he wasn't a racist—told the press he would move on to create a national "white rights" organization if not allowed a third run. "I am now going to defend the people, the people of this city that I believe have been kicked around too long. . . . I'm going to defend the rights of American citizens who happen to be ethnics. The whites have to join hands to get equal treatment."[42] Rizzo maintained that the white working class needed a defender who would help keep minority rights in check. The *Philadelphia Daily News* opined that he was grooming himself to be "a kind of Northern replacement for George Wallace." Rizzo's white rights organization never materialized, but it didn't have to. The backlash to civil rights was quickly moving from the margins to the mainstream of electoral politics. Over the next decade both Republicans and Democrats would come to reflect a similarly paternalistic politic, making major strides with Ronald Reagan's election in 1980.

Throughout history there have been times—like in Chicago, Philadelphia and New York—that demonstrate how these rainbow coalitions changed both lives and conditions. Unlike David facing his Goliath, they faced theirs with more than just luck. Like their Chicago counterparts, White Lightning and O4O measured their greatest successes in the sense of power and purpose they built for hundreds of working-class people over the years. They drew on the long history of progressive populism in their neighborhoods and immigrant traditions, and in doing so aided others to begin the kind of personal–political transformations that ultimately sustain people as lifelong radicals even in times of austerity and defeat. Like JOIN, the Patriots and Rising Up Angry, they found that fighting together for a better world—in whatever form or era—is what changes lives and sustains our hope when we need it most

Epilogue
10TH ANNIVERSARY REVISED
AND EXPANDED EDITION

"We know that there is no help for us but from one another, that no hand will save us if we do not reach out our hand. And the hand that you reach out is empty, as mine is. You have nothing. You possess nothing. You own nothing. You are free. All you have is what you are, and what you give."

—Ursula K. Le Guin, *The Dispossessed*

A decade has passed since the publication of *Hillbilly Nationalists*. Two decades have passed since we, the authors, started searching for anyone who could tell us more about the poor white radicals mentioned in the footnotes of books about the Black Panthers, the New Left, and the other great upheavals of the Sixties and Seventies. We set out to educate ourselves about the ways multiracial coalitions are built and destroyed. We wanted to understand, in depth, a moment in U.S. history when the Black Freedom Movement inspired and coincided with Indigenous and Third World liberation, women's and queer liberation, and movements uniting the poor across race and geography. We recognized this lineage as our own. As young white organizers, our work and solidarity politics stem from the inspiration of these alliances and an understanding that "systems of oppression are interlocking." This concept, articulated in 1977 by Black feminists in the Combahee River Collective, speaks in profound terms to the triumphs and tensions of this defining era, when radicals evolved analysis and strategies to address what Keeanga-Yamahtta Taylor named the "intertwined malignancies of capitalism—racism, sexism, and poverty."[1] These movements and their radical imagination shaped our own generation. We are indebted to their vision.

The first edition of this book arrived from the printer in 2011, the same week the Occupy Movement focused national attention on capitalism's excesses and intensifying economic disparity. We fondly remember our editors emailing us to say they had walked through Zuccotti Park, giving out free copies of the book, which hadn't even reached our doorsteps yet. We soon set out on a book tour, visiting Occupy encampments in dozens of cities and giving away more free copies. We hoped the story of these alliances might remind activists of the liberating potential of "intercommunalism" defined by Huey P. Newton, and the necessity of addressing racialized capitalism. Even in those early weeks of Occupy, the pitfalls of racism and single-issue politics were evident, signaled most clearly in the misguided call for an occupation on occupied territory. We spoke alongside community organizers in each city, reinforcing the need for movements that unite the dispossessed while reckoning explicitly with present-day impacts of conquest, segregation, and violence.

Over the last ten years, we've made more than ninety appearances for this book across the United States, Canada, and the U.K. On the road, we heard from brave immigrant rights organizers and veterans of the sanctuary movement in Tucson, activists in rural

West Virginia, leaders of a rebooted Poor People's Campaign, a new generation of organizers in Chicago and Philadelphia, and white radicals counter-organizing at gun shows in Oregon. We've had the pleasure of hearing how activists continue to be inspired by this history as they search for answers and forge coalitions of their own. Rather than offer prescriptive answers, we encouraged audiences to explore: *What do you see in these historic Rainbow Coalitions that can help you confront racial capitalism to build a politics of solidarity today?*

This question has never been more timely. During the last decade, a new wave of Black freedom movements has emerged with an explicitly intersectional analysis. So, too, have prolific movements for immigrant rights, Indigenous sovereignty, climate justice, feminist and queer/trans dignity and safety, disability justice, and an end to xenophobia, Islamophobia, anti-Asian racism, and war. Inspired by these movements—and confronted with a continuous feed of stark racial violence—thousands of white people are waking up or recommitting to the cause of racial justice. Organizations across North America are mobilizing to define a contemporary solidarity politics, while challenged by the task of confronting violent white nationalism and far-right extremism long left unchecked. The ferocity of backlash against the #BlackLivesMatter movement is a project of national gaslighting writ large. And, as reactionary politicians and media disinformation undermine safety and voter protection, minimize Standing Rock, outlaw trans life, or leave immigrant children in cages, we see again the need for mutual solidarity built on long-term organizing and deep attention to relationships. As in 1968, building a praxis of solidarity is just as critical today—just as necessary for producing the change we need, and just as critical for self-defense. The global rise of fascism today demands the rise of a united global Left. We cannot afford to make the mistakes of the past or forget that similar threats exist today.

So, what can we learn from these original Rainbow Coalitions, and the white working-class radicals within them? Working under the model of "rainbow politics," the five groups we profiled in this book formed alliances with Black and Third World liberation struggles to forge an innovative class politics that directly confronted America's legacy of racism and colonization. With little more than a dedicated cadre of organizers, JOIN Community Union, the Young Patriots, Rising Up Angry, October 4th Organization, and White Lightning demanded the Sixties Left take working-class whites seriously as a force for change. From Chicago to Philadelphia and New York, these organizations dedicated themselves to cultivating the radical potential of poor and working-class white communities, even as the architects of neo-conservatism targeted these same communities to stoke racial anxiety and malign the aims of feminism. In response, these New Left organizers worked together to interrupt these messages every way they could. They published newspapers, held rock concerts and picnics infused with leftist politics, organized rent strikes and anti-police brutality marches, wrote poetry and sang labor songs alongside country and blues. They even ran their own candidate for president in 1968, when they ran Peggy Terry for vice president alongside Eldridge Cleaver for president, to counter Richard Nixon and segregationist George Wallace.

They found that separating struggles into single issues was a luxury they could not afford. In poor neighborhoods, people's survival meant juggling multiple concerns at once: unsafe housing conditions, late welfare checks, police brutality, the draft, domestic violence and women's oppression, labor grievances and unemployment, childcare, drug addiction, factory closures, and racism. The programs they created—in the tradition of participatory organizing and, over time, the Black Panthers' Serve the People model—engaged neighborhood residents in a kind of radical self-governance that transformed self and society. In doing so, they laid the groundwork for multiracial alliances with communities facing similar conditions. And because members took part in a broader movement, their visions went beyond immediate reforms. While JOIN's march to the Summerdale police station in 1966 demanded the dismissal of a particular cop, their chants demanded something much more radical: community control of the police. In other words, they demanded systemic change in poor communities from Uptown to southside Chicago. When Rising Up Angry rallied against the war, they did not sing, "Stop this War," they sounded an S.O.S.—Save Our Sailors—and veteran marines marched with them en masse. They recognized that people's sense of power is born when they act to change their own conditions and also ask for something larger— an end to all forms of oppression. The job of community organizers, they showed, is to direct power toward justice and solidarity.

They took seriously the need for ongoing political education among community members, drawing inspiration from Paolo Freire and Miles Horton, developing regular classes on local and international issues, and sending numerous leaders to the Highlander Folk School in Tennessee, which remains a powerful home base for today's social justice movements. Their approach stands in stark contrast to the legions of well-paid diversity trainers we see running workshops now. These organizations studied deeply together and held transformative conversations at the kitchen table, the health clinic, and the pool hall. They set out to nurture the innate abilities of working people. They got people thinking deeply about the root causes of the miseries they faced and developed political discipline alongside programs that met people's immediate needs. Because they married politics with music, poetry, food, theater, and even sports, they created a culture where former gang members and single mothers came to see their experiences in the context of imperialism and their freedom tied to its undoing.

Because they studied history, the leaders of these groups also understood the role racism had played in fracturing prior U.S. movements. Therefore, leaders listened when activists of color called on white radicals to address racism at its source and "organize their own." In proposing a racial division of labor, Black Power leaders aimed to curb white racism within the civil rights movement and to point out the obvious: racism could not be overcome by ignoring white communities, nor mobilizing white communities in a race-neutral way. In different ways, each group experimented with a new organizing model within white communities that was unequivocal in tackling racism. They balanced the need to meet people "where they were at" while demonstrating solidarity and common cause on issues that united neighbors across racial lines.

Until then, Saul Alinsky's model of organizing through the Industrial Areas Foundation (IAF) remained the gold standard, centered on self-interest and the sanctity of the single issue to unite individuals against a common target. The first community in Chicago organized by the IAF was a white ethnic community, known as the Back-of-the-Yards, where residents later deployed many of their organizing skills to uphold segregation. Over time Alinsky acknowledged the limits of IAF's model, which made few demands on its members to challenge white supremacy. "Last time I was in Back-of-the-Yards, a good number of the cars were plastered with [George] Wallace stickers; I could have puked," Alinsky later said. Without addressing racial disparity or prioritizing the kind of principled political education needed to uproot racism, the inevitable occurred. "Like so many onetime revolutionaries, they've traded in their birthright for property and prosperity. This is why I've seriously thought of moving back into the area and organizing a new movement to overthrow the one I built twenty-five years ago."[2]

Alinsky looked to the Rainbow Coalition for inspiration. He was well aware that the Panthers had evolved a different set of "rules for radicals," introducing an internationalist approach and inspiring dozens of organizations to adopt a race-conscious solidarity rooted in community service. In the aftermath of Fred Hampton's assassination, Alinsky asked Panther Bob Lee to visit his office. As Lee told us, "Alinsky thought that the Rainbow Coalition was something close to what he had always wanted to see in Chicago, but could never pull off . . . He had an organizing school and wanted me to be a part of it. That's like meeting Moses! Moses was one bad motherfucker. The book of Exodus—all it is about is organizing, gaining power. He was raised in the Pharaoh's house, knew the Pharaoh's ways and knew how to take down the Pharaoh . . . He had selected six of us to come to the Industrial Areas Foundation. We heard so many speakers—Stoughton Lynd, many journalists. I still think there are three people who have influenced me the most: my father who ran numbers from his nightclub, Saul Alinsky, and Mao."[3]

This new alliance between Lee and Alinsky never developed much further. Alinsky died in 1972 and Lee returned to Texas shortly thereafter. However, it suggests another way of considering the legacy of the original Rainbow Coalitions. While Alinsky originally focused on the mobilizing potential of individual self interests, the practice of rainbow politics rested on the development of solidarity between oppressed groups, combining common cause issues with a political commitment to the idea that each group's liberation was interconnected. They demonstrated that there can be a journey from self-interest to solidarity only if there is a disciplined praxis to make it real.

The groups profiled in this book grappled with ways to fulfill this commitment, as each went through several formulations of what it meant to work under or alongside leaders of color. Rising Up Angry came to understand their work primarily in terms of solidarity with "Third World" radicals at home and abroad, while they developed a decisively feminist approach and an anti-imperialist program that embraced veterans alongside war resisters. The Young Patriots adopted the Black Panthers' revolutionary nationalism and discipline as a political party, including an eleven-point platform. White Lightning emerged in direct alliance with radicals of color addressing drug addiction and poor healthcare in their communities. October 4th Organization uniquely combined both factory and neighborhood organizing in the industrial area of Kensington, Philadelphia, centering a socialist class politics that saw dismantling racism and sexism as a necessary part of any working-class movement. In fits and starts, their work revealed there were ready radicals in blue-collar neighborhoods, white ethnic enclaves, northern "slums," and industrial centers. In doing so, these groups demonstrated the possibility of a revitalized multiracial, working-class movement in the United States and beyond.

....

Over the past fifty years, racial politics in the United States have certainly changed, and the backlash has been predictably severe. The engineers of the American conservative movement have slyly manipulated white anxieties to dismantle civil rights and secure their road to dominion. The brazen white nationalism and far-right extremism we see today is not new, but it is emboldened and amplified in a largely unregulated digital landscape. Disinformation now reaches further than ever before—a radicalizing force we are just beginning to reckon with. Too often, progressives still blame the rise of the far right on poor and working-class whites. Simple facts disprove this. In both the 2016 and 2020 elections, the majority of

Trump's supporters were better off than most Americans—about a third earned more than $100,000 annually.[4] More recently, *The Atlantic* described the class backgrounds of 193 arrestees in the January 6 Capitol insurrection as "middle-class and, in many cases, middle-aged people without obvious ties to the far right—[who] joined with extremists in an attempt to overturn a presidential election."[5] We must not fail to discern the power behind digital disinformation campaigns, and the truth that wealth and profit-seeking provide the most durable scaffolding for white supremacy.

White organizers today should not overlook the difficult work to be done even as more white people speak the language of ally-ship. Whether urban or rural, poor or upper class, the Black Power Movement's call to "organize your own" should not become a relic of the past. We're not referring to a narrow identity politics, we're talking about a praxis of mutual interest that is rooted revolution-ary internationalism and collective liberation. If we learn just one thing from these Rainbow Coalitions, it's that people learn to be in solidarity through consistent organizing and political education that is both immediately relevant and deliberately collectivist. These activists proved, again and again, that revolutionaries are made, not born. And that organizing, when sustained, transforms both lives and possibilities.

To cite the advice that Rising Up Angry's Mike James offered his peers in 1968, serious organizers need to "get off the Inter-state" and connect to the progressive potential of the heartland.[6] Many of those we interviewed for this book believe the white Left's failure to mobilize masses of white workers and poor white Ameri-cans alongside students in the Sixties was a "fatal flaw." Doing so might just have changed the course of the New Left then and our terrain now. For JOIN Community Union, the tension between the student movement and locals proved instructive even as it was challenging. Both student organizers and community leaders recall invaluable personal and political lessons from their collaboration. As Peggy Terry put it, they needed each other. "Those kids stopped a war and . . . if anybody has failed, it's the system and not them." Still, beyond the organizations we have profiled and a handful of others, the white New Left missed many chances to reach "forgotten Americans," and conservatives were only too quick to court those communities with promises of security, order, and individual rights, thus ushering in decades of neoliberal policy and consolidated power.

Among the five groups we profile here, participants tell us how profoundly their lives were changed by their personal relationships with activists of color and New Left radicals, by their exposure to international social movements, and by the radical community they created. These organizations disproved the mythology that poor and working-class whites clung more firmly to racism than politicians, corporate liberals or the middle class, even as they were honest that they had sometimes failed to reach their own neighbors.

White organizers today must get even more serious about organizing in our own backyards.[7] Rural organizers have the opportunity to bring the white working class into alliance with Asian and African refugees and Latinx immigrants. Feminists have the opportunity to honor the vision of the Combahee River Collective and remember the pitfalls of single issues—building instead a truly multiracial, trans- and queer-inclusive feminist movement. We have an opportunity and obligation to reach disaffected young men who are being targeted by the alt-right and men's rights movement online. Even wildfires, hurricanes, and drought give us the opportunity to reach impacted poor white communities outside of cities, and bring these populations into a global climate justice movement rooted in mutual aid and kinship—connecting Indigenous peoples from the

Arctic to the Kalahari, uniting Puerto Rico and the Philippines, Miami and Paradise, California.

The people who have shared their stories for this book did so out of a steadfast belief that remembering our past might embolden today's dreamers and justice seekers. Their heartland, not necessarily a single place on the map, was the home of possibilities—for a nation reimagined by everyday people who were no longer willing to settle for anything less than a truly great society. And today? Where is the heartland today, and where is the Left within it? What do you see in these historic Rainbow Coalitions that can help you build a politics of active solidarity?

If it weren't for the millstone of government repression, the original Rainbow Coalition might have guided these organizations and the broader New Left through changing times. Instead, it's the inspiration of their experiments and missteps, their theory and practice, that guides us today. However imperfect, these coalitions defined a solidarity politics that—for a short time—bridged the gaps that have historically weakened social movements. Bob Lee told us that the "Rainbow Coalition was just a code word for class struggle." It is our hope that this book contributes to a future where we no longer speak in code and instead build even more enduring freedom movements for our times.

—Amy Sonnie and James Tracy, March 2021

Acknowledgments

The fact that you hold this book in your hands is the result of a collective leap of faith. Since very little scholarship has been done on these organizations, we depended largely on interviews with movement participants and, in many cases, their personal archives. At least initially, these individuals received a phone call from complete strangers who were infants when this history took place. Their willingness to build relationships with us is testament to their shared vision of political community and faith in a new generation of activists who believe a better world is possible.

Steve Tappis and Gil Fagiani were the first to accept our invitation. Their generosity and political insight provided threads that hold this text together. Diane Fager and Mike James also went above and beyond providing feedback and archival material for this project. Early on Dan Sidorick and Sue Milligan sent copies of rare October 4th Organization materials, few of which remain; without these we would know little about that group's unique history. We have also benefited greatly from their insight and ongoing feedback, along with that of Jack Whalen, Bob Lawson and Carol Tappis. Our deepest thank you goes to Margi Devoe for inviting us into her home and sharing her mother, Peggy Terry, so graciously. Without Peggy Terry's extensive personal archives much of this book would not have been possible. We also extend our sincerest thanks to Dennis Winters for the invaluable interviews he conducted with Peggy in the late 1990s and to Jonathan Nelson at Wisconsin Historical Society for archiving Peggy's collection.

It goes without saying that we are indebted to all those we interviewed, often more than once, who additionally shared stories and materials. A list of those individuals appears below. Additionally, archival research for this book was conducted at Temple University's Urban Archives, Tamiment Library and Robert F. Wagner Labor Archives at New York University, San Francisco Public Library, Oakland Public Library, Wisconsin Historical Society's Social Action Archive, University of California Berkeley, and the Council of the Southern Mountains archive at Berea College in Kentucky. Thanks also to Bolerium Books in San Francisco for providing volumes of precious materials at a discount.

Finally, to our network of supporters for their love and insight. To Melville House and Kelly Burdick, thank you for believing in the importance of these stories. To Malik Rahim and Sharon Martinas who inspired us to pursue this research, and Josh Warren-White who connected us. To Hy Thurman who vastly deepened our understanding of this history, and to close friends who provided substantive feedback: Dan Berger, Malkia Cyril, Roxanne Dunbar-Ortiz, Diane Fager, Harmony Goldberg, Mike James, Paige Kruza, Sue Milligan, Dan Sidorick, Jen Soriano, Emily Thuma, and most especially, Chris Dixon. And to our respective friends and families for sustaining us through the (very) long process of research and writing, we say thank you to: Kat Aaron, Kirsten Andersen, Micah Bazant, Gene Bild, Paul Boden, Ingrid Chapman, Max Elbaum, Ananda Esteva, the Gabriel Family, Emma Gerould, Harjit Singh

Gill, Matt Gonzales, Mike Gray, Sam Green, R. Kumasi Hampton, Rahula Janowski, Jennifer Kirby, Chelsea Kirkland, Amanda Klonsky, Left Turn crew, Lynn Lewis, Allison Lum, Kari Lydersen, Jamie McCallum, Sam Miller, Leroy Moore, Peter Plate, Jean Rice, Aaron Sarver, Madigan Shive, Sarah Shourd, the Sonnie Family, Lisa Sousa, Shannon Stewart, Juliette Torrez, the Tracy Family, Daniel Tucker and *AREA* magazine, and Tom Ward.

Interviews

We could not have uncovered this essential history without the first-person stories of dozens of individuals, many of whom we spoke to numerous times over the years. Their insights shaped our understanding and writing in countless ways.

Andy Keniston, February 2008
Al Metzger, August 2009
Bill Whalen, February 2008 and April 2008
Bob Lawson, December 2007, June 2011 and ongoing via email
Bob Lee, September 2006 and September 2007
Bob Simpson, August 2006
Burton Steck, January 2008
Carol Coronado, March 2009
Carl Davidson, August 2006
Cathy Wilkerson, April 2010
Chris Robinson, March 2007
Christine George, December 2007
Chuck Armsbury, March 2007
Dan Sidorick, May 2007, May 2011 and June 2011
Diane Fager, August 2006 and ongoing via email
Earl Billheimer, April 2009

Estelle Carol, August 2006

Fran Ansley, January 2008

Fritz Kraly, March 2008

Gene Bild, November 2007

Gil Fagiani, October 2006, July 2008 and ongoing
 via email/phone

Hy Thurman, December 2015 and March 2021

Jack Whalen, December 2007

Jaja Nkruma, May 2006

Janet Sampson, December 2007

Jean Tepperman, December 2007

Jim Redden, April 2007

Jimmy Curry, August 2006

John Duffy, February 2007

John Sinclair, April 2008

Jose "Cha-Cha" Jimenez, February 2008 and July 2011

Judith Arcana, April 2008

Kirsten Anderson, May 2008 and June 2008

Margi Devoe, March 2008 and ongoing via email/phone

Marilyn Katz, July 2007

Mark Rudd, July 2008 and June 2011

Mary Driscoll, August 2007

Mary Hockenberry, March 2008

Melody James, September 2006

Michael Simmons, March 2010

Mike James, August 2006, March 2008 and ongoing
 via email/phone

Mike Klonsky, December 2007

Mike Laly, December 2007

Dr. Mike Smith, April 2008

Paul Finamore, February 2007

Paul Wozniak, April 2010, May 2010 and June 2011

Pat Sturgis, May 2007

Peter Kuttner, March 2008

Rennie Davis, July 2008

Rich "Pipe" Kroth, December 2007

Robert Barrow, October 2005

Steve Goldsmith, July 2008 and August 2008

Steve Max, December 2010

Steve Tappis, September 2005, June 2006 and ongoing
    via email/phone

Stone Greaser, October 2007

Sue Milligan, June 2007, May 2011 and June 2011

Terry Doyle, November 2006

Tom Hayden, January 2006

Willie Everich, July 2007

Revolutionary Hillbilly:
An Interview with the Young Patriots' Hy Thurman
BY JAMES TRACY AND AMY SONNIE

Authors' note March 2021: Hy Thurman is one of the original members of the Young Patriots. While photos and ephemera of the Young Patriots sparked our initial research for this book, we had the hardest time finding the group's founders. As Hy puts it now, "Many of us didn't want to be found." Hy sought us out after this book was published in 2011. He's telling his story now and deepening his lifelong commitment to multiracial poor people's movements.

AUTHORS: How did you come to be a part of the Young Patriots Organization and what did YPO hope to accomplish?

HT: My brother Tex was a leader in the Peacemakers, a street gang that morphed into the Goodfellows and eventually became the Young Patriots Organization. We organized the Young Patriots in 1968 in Chicago's Uptown neighborhood to help alleviate the oppressive conditions that residents faced on a daily basis and to give the poor a voice to fight Mayor Richard J. Daley's oppressive machine of class hatred and racism.

Between 1966 and the later months of 1968 was a hellish

environment on the Uptown streets. Many of the original Peace-makers and Goodfellows were either forced to leave Chicago by the cops, killed, or drafted into the Vietnam War. There were only a few Goodfellows left. Bobby McGinnis, Junebug Boykin, and I assumed the leadership positions and began recruiting other members. We also decided to change the name to the Young Patriots because we felt that Patriots protected and fought for their people. Due to our continuous growing knowledge of socialism we wanted a name that would be recognized and easily explained and distanced from the Goodfellow name that was associated with crime—although, we still liked being associated with the badass part [of] the Goodfellows.

In addition to police brutality, housing discrimination and urban renewal all played a major role in me getting involved to organize in Uptown. Parts of Uptown was a slum and that part was where the poor were forced to live under the oppressive powers of absentee landlords who collected rent but refused to make any improvements to their properties. Uptown was designated as a renewal area and a city college was to be built where the majority of the southern whites lived. The city had no plans to relocate any of the residents. Mayor Daley hand-picked the committee, made up of landowners and business owners, to oversee all urban renewal plans and did not include any poor residents. Sixteen poor men, women, children and the physically handicapped were murdered by being burned to death when slum landlords hired people to set fire to the buildings to force residents out. No charges or prosecutions were brought against anyone.

AUTHORS: It might surprise some readers that police brutality was so prevalent in a white neighborhood.

HT: Daley would use the police as his personal gang, and they were allowed to use their own interpretation of the law while performing their jobs as police officers. It seemed that any cop that was determined to have behaviors of a psychopath or couldn't fit in the city's middle-class neighborhoods were assigned to Uptown, South and West Side, and poor Latino or other poor neighborhoods in Chicago. They would not give it a second thought to shoot, torture, or beat you.

Women and young girls were not exempt from their perverted behavior either. [One time] myself and three other Goodfellows, including a woman, were stopped by a three-man Chicago police car and were ordered out of our car. After checking our identification and not searching the car, the driver, Bobby McGinnis, was ordered to sit in the backseat of the patrol car while the rest of us were ordered to stand out in the cold where we could be watched. The cops said that they found a bag of illegal pills in our car. They told Bobby that they were going to "fuck the girl" or we were going to jail for possession of illegal drugs and that the car would be impounded as evidence. We made the decision that we were going to try to outrun the cops and go to an area of Uptown where other Goodfellows were known to hang out and prepare for a confrontation. This time we were successful. The cops passed us as we entered a local hangout restaurant with other neighborhood guys and gals.

These and other incidents with the fascist cops led the Peacemakers, JOIN, and other groups to organize a march on the Summerdale Police station against brutality and murder. Two days after the march, a brother of a Peacemaker was murdered by the cops and the JOIN office was raided and drugs were planted, which led to the arrest of two Students for a Democratic Society students [who were organizers in Uptown]. This was when the Peacemakers changed their name to the Goodfellows and started serving the community.

AUTHORS: Doesn't this go against the common perception that things were pretty good for white working-class people in the post World War II labor order?

HT: According to a book written by Roger Guy titled *From Diversity to Unity,* the unemployment rate in Uptown in the late 1960s was 47 percent. And the southern migrant population exceeded the number of stable jobs in Chicago. Those that could get work usually worked for day labor agencies. Day labor agencies were private agencies that worked similar to temp agencies—the difference being that day labor agencies did not offer the opportunity for full-time employment and were paying below the minimum wage. I worked day labor a few times. I was always assigned to the most menial jobs. Sweeping floors and jobs that were at a high risk of injury. Back-breaking jobs, such as loading and unloading cargo from trucks, were usually what we were assigned to. On the evening of my second day when I returned to the day labor office, an employee of the agency asked me into his office. He said that since I was new I did not know the procedure for how they paid the laborers. He said I was responsible for paying for the transportation to and from the job site. Twenty percent of my earnings were going to be deducted from my earnings. He said that they were doing us a favor by choosing us to work and we should be grateful. There was no one for me to complain to so I decided to discontinue my association with them and seek other means of earning a living. He still took 20 percent of my earnings for the two days worked.

This kept many in perpetual poverty. Many were driven to selling blood. In Uptown and many poor neighborhoods, blood banks or stores were located very near the day labor agencies. When individuals and families could not find employment or would need to supplement their employment or welfare they would have no other choice but to sell their blood, turn to crime, prostitution, or other illegal means. Still for those who had arrived from the South with disease such as black lung, brown lung, tuberculosis, and lead poisoning and any number of physical illnesses this was not an option and they were too sick to work and had to rely on the government for assistance which wasn't much. I had to swallow my pride several times and resort to selling my blood to survive.

AUTHORS: Your organizing led to an alliance with the Black Panthers and Young Lords, the original Rainbow Coalition. Tell us what you recall about this evolution.

HT: To my recollection, the Black Panthers were aware of our commitment to the movement of racial equality due to the Goodfellows and other poor organizations participating in the Eldridge Cleaver-Peggy Terry Presidential Campaign in [1968]. Peggy Terry, a poor white woman and organizer living in Uptown, was chosen to run as Eldridge Cleaver's vice-presidential partner on the Peace and Freedom Campaign ticket running against Alabama's governor due to his racist and white supremacist beliefs. That campaign also wanted to show that poor blacks and whites could unite in solidarity. About six months later Black Panther Bobby Lee came to meet with us to propose a formal alliance. This meeting was actually captured in the film *American Revolution II*.

On April 4, 1969, which was also the first anniversary of the assassination of Dr. Martin Luther King, Fred Hampton, Bobby Rush and Bobby Lee of the Illinois Black Panther Party invited the Young Patriots to join with them and the Young Lords—a former Puerto Rican street gang—to announce the original Rainbow

Coalition of revolutionary solidarity. The three would make a statement that in the most segregated city in the United States that it was possible for all races to work together. As we were forming, it was agreed by the groups that neither organization would control the coalition. Each organization would control their community and fight for self-determination. We would come together in solidarity to support each other's programs and challenge the Daley administration, unite in demonstrations and stand side-by-side to defeat racism and fascism. We agreed to serve with their security detail by standing shoulder to shoulder at many functions.

AUTHORS: As a consequence of your work in the original Rainbow Coalition, you were harassed for many years by the government. Why did the coalition scare the powers that be so badly?

HT: I think a lot of the fear was generated by how the federal and local governments view the Black Panthers and us stepping out of our assigned roles in society. The day after we cemented our solidarity of revolutionary brotherhood, the FBI and their illegal COINTELPRO began surveillance of the Young Patriots . . . FBI documents that had been sealed after the Chicago police and the FBI clearly state that the Black Panthers were the number one threat to national security and that the BPP had recruited other like-minded organizations. The memo from the FBI in Chicago to J. Edgar Hoover identifies the two dangerous organizations as the Young Lords and the Young Patriots. Hoover stated in a separate memo that there was a rising messiah in Chicago that had to be eliminated. Everyone in the coalition believed [they were talking about] Fred Hampton.

I believe that if the original Rainbow Coalition continued that it would have been a major force in Chicago by uniting thousands of poor people who usually fought against or avoided each other—and a model to organize and gain power in Chicago and the rest of the country. Daley and Hoover were not about to let that happen . . . [P]oor communities uniting, especially poor whites uniting with other racial and minority groups preaching revolutionary change and socialism, was a major threat. The coalition either had to be controlled or destroyed. I strongly believe that the Rainbow model can be used today if it is effectively organized.

AUTHORS: What were you guys thinking when choosing the Confederate flag as a symbol? Would you ever recommend trying to "reclaim it" in the spirit of multiracial rebellion?

HT: As we grew politically and respected the Black Panthers and the Young Lords, we determined that there was no place in the movement or the world for the Confederate flag. It symbolizes a period of time when our Black brothers and sisters were mere property to be sold or destroyed at the white man's convenience. The Confederate flag was created to serve as a symbol of plantation owners to perpetuate slavocracy. I would not recommend its use by any group for anyone or any purpose and believe that it should be destroyed as a tribute to those who suffered pain and anguish in a great dark period of our history.

We originally used the flag, and I don't recommend this now, as a symbol of rebellion and to get people talking . . . Southerners then as well as now associate the flag with being a rebel. So, we wanted to talk to poor whites about living conditions in Uptown and try to get them involved in the Young Patriots to improve their living conditions. When we would wear the rebel flag, we would place a Free Huey button, Black Panther button, and a rainbow button surrounding the flag. Some had the flag embroidered on the back of their vests and some on berets. It did invoke much conversation. Not so much the flag as the other buttons. We would explain the Young Patriots goals and that all poor people have the same poverty and the poor Blacks, Latinos, American Indians, and Asians are all being exploited and kept in poverty by the capitalist system. Once we broke the ice we were able to identify their needs and get them help. Many were surprised to hear that the Black Panther Party played a major role in getting medical personnel and equipment for the Young Patriot health clinic and provided food for kids before they went to school.

AUTHORS: Recently, political commentators who should know better have mischaracterized the Young Patriots as being white supremacist. They are using this distortion to urge the left to work with the racist right. What do you have to say about this?

HT: First of all, the Young Patriots were against racism. That went to the core of what we believed. I want to be very suspicious of any right-wing organizations that would want to unite with the left. You know, they have to see what their motives are because I don't think their motives are the same as ours. The Young Patriots knew that fighting racism was in the true interest of poor white people. Why would the racist right want to unite with groups like ours? I don't understand that at all . . . And if you look at what's happening today with Proud Boys and many other organizations, these are white right-wing. These people are not in any way concerned about the little guy. They're only concerned about conspiracy theories and that will destroy our movement if we let it in. The Young Patriots and the Rainbow Coalition were destroyed by the right. They are going to try to destroy any movement that's fighting fascism.

AUTHORS: You have remained in the movement to this day, most recently, as a co-founder of the Northern Alabama School for Organizers (NASO). Tell us about your work?

HHT: NASO came about as a way to help movements last, to help everyone develop their own skills and analysis. I'm in Alabama and getting involved in several organizations here but . . . there seemed to be a major problem with attrition in organizations. So [when] we put together the North Alabama School for Organizers, we wanted to create an environment for new organizers so they could have a creative learning and educational environment to help build a movement that will last. We started out with classes in organizing and our first class was very successful. Our school also offers classes on Native American history and culture. We even had a class about the politics of Jesus where some local pastors in the area spoke about how Jesus was an organizer and how he was basically a socialist. That continued into a class about the teachings of Martin Luther King and his seven steps of nonviolent protest. You know, we talked about labor unions, we talked about the Poor People's Campaigns, past and present.

AUTHORS: It sounds like you bring a lot of the lessons from the original Rainbow Coalition with you into this work.

HT: The old Survival Pending Revolution programs have stuck with me for sure. We are developing services that people might need like, healthcare, transportation, food. [Like] some of the old programs that we used to have. There will soon be an automotive free clinic that will teach people how to work on their cars. That's a survival program for a lot of people, especially in areas where there's no public transportation and here there's not very much transportation. We have to make sure that they can keep their cars, you know, running so they can get to where they need to go or to their jobs. NASO has had a hand in a homeless construction coalition that builds small shelters with our unhoused neighbors. We're getting into collective land buying now where we'll be working with the Cherokee Nation. The goal of all this is to educate people to have control of their own communities, and we're already starting to work on making that local.

AUTHORS: Why do you think it's important to study and prioritize political education when building coalitions that confront racism and other forms of oppression?

HT: When I started organizing back in the Sixties, and we didn't have a lot of resources, as far as you know, for education—be that regular education or political education. So, we had to reach out and look at, you know, Third World countries and what was going on [in those movements], and to the Black Panthers and other organizations to try to get political information. In the end, if anyone goes out and tries to organize they need to be educated. They need to learn as much as they can about whoever it is that they're trying to organize. We don't need people thinking that they are there to save people, that they are the answer to the problem. Solutions have to come from the ground up and people have to learn how to solve their own problems. I think that's a part of organizing right there when you talk the language of the people that you're trying to organize. This is what we learned from the Highlander Folk School, the Panthers, and other groups about political education.

AUTHORS: Since Hillbilly Nationalists was first published in

2011, two films have come out featuring the Rainbow Coalition: the Hollywood film *Judas and the Black Messiah* and the documentary *The First Rainbow Coalition* on PBS. What do these films contribute to the conversation?

HT: I think Ray Santisteban's documentary is one of the best I have ever seen, besides *American Revolution II,* that actually shows the first meeting between the Patriots and the Panthers. It tells the story of how we came together and why we came together, as you know, as people of different colors and working together.

I think that *Judas and the Black Messiah* is a Hollywood film. It doesn't give the entire story. I know it's trying to go through William O'Neil's story, showing the dark side of what went down. I'm afraid that shows a fictional dark side of Fred Hampton, too, which wasn't really there. It shows him as being extremely angry. There was also a scene where Fred Hampton comes to Uptown and meets with [a Young Patriot named] Preacherman. First of all, Hampton didn't come to meet with the Patriots in Uptown. That was Bob Lee, the field secretary of the Panthers. The film shows someone from Uptown standing up and yelling at the Panthers. That just didn't happen. It just isn't true. The Panthers were treated with respect at every meeting in Uptown that the Patriots invited them to. They chose to focus on the informant and chose not to show the Survival Programs.

I'm kind of reluctant to talk about this, because I think this, it's up to the Black Panthers and the black community to say how this film should be judged. Hollywood is always going to change the details of history. A few years back, a miniseries on the Rainbow Coalition was pitched to ABC by a well-known writer. They told him that they would [only] do it if they could show a gunfight between the Patriots and Panthers. That's how these people think.

We said there was no way that we would ever allow our history to be told like that, so the film never happened.

AUTHORS: You just recently published your own memoir, *Revolutionary Hillbilly: Notes from the Struggle on the Edge of the Rainbow*. What was it like telling your own story?

HT: It was probably one of the hardest things I ever did. I got to a certain point, you know, memories and everything started flooding back and I got set back by PTSD. And I actually had to take a break from writing. It was very difficult. I would get on a subject, and all of a sudden, I would start remembering, you know, some of the atrocities and brutality and just oppression, you know, that people were going through. It wasn't until I got, I guess, a third of the book that I started feeling good about it. I wanted to publish a book that an eighth grader could read but could also be used in a college. It needed to be very straightforward because I remember the days, you know, before I could read well. When I went to Chicago as a teenager, I was reading on the third-grade level. [Since it was published], I've gotten some reports back from people who are still in high school who love it. Some professors that I know have said they can use it in their classes as well. I'm glad that the two of you pushed me to get it done.

Read Hy Thurman's memoir, *Revolutionary Hillbilly: Notes from the Struggle on the Edge of the Rainbow* (Regent Press, 2020).

List of Abbreviations

BYNC	Back-of-the-Yards Neighborhood Council
CFM	Chicago Freedom Movement
COINTELPRO	Counterintelligence Program [of the FBI]
CORE	Congress of Racial Equality
ERAP	Economic Research and Action Project
HRUM	Health Revolutionary Unity Movement
JOIN	Jobs or Income Now
LID	League for Industrial Democracy
NAACP	National Association for the Advancement of Colored People
NWBCCC	Northwest Bronx Community and Clergy Coalition
NWRO	National Welfare Rights Organization
O4O	October 4th Organization
PFP	Peace and Freedom Party
PL	Progressive Labor [Party]
RYM / RYM II	Revolutionary Youth Movement
SCEF	Southern Conference Educational Fund
SCLC	Southern Christian Leadership Conference
SDS	Students for a Democratic Society
SNCC	Student Nonviolent Coordinating Committee
UPWC	United Parents Who Care

Notes

Documents unattributed to a particular archive come from the personal collection of the authors.

Many items cited from Peggy Terry's personal collection can now be found at Wisconsin Historical Society under the "Peggy Terry Papers, 1937–2004," call numbers Mss 1055; PH 6582; Audio 1460A; VHA 898-903. We are honored to have played a part in documenting her collection.

Foreword

1. Catherine Fosl, *Subversive Southerner: Anne Braden and the Struggle for Racial Justice in the Cold War South* (New York: Palgrave Macmillan, 2002), 304.
2. U.S. Bureau of the Census, *Historical Statistics of the United States: Colonial Times to 1970* (Cambridge, MA: Cambridge University Press, 1976).

Introduction

1. Author George Katsiaficas defines the New Left as a "world-historical movement" in the post-World War II era, which sought the wholesale remaking of economic and political systems. For the purposes of this book we agree with this broad definition, but in dealing with U.S.-based organizations we use the term more specifically to refer to those interrelated social uprisings in North America between 1956 and 1975, including the civil rights, student, national liberation, feminist, gay liberation, countercultural, anti-war, progressive labor, and new communist movements. All of these uprisings made a defined break from the Old Left's platform and terrain, though some drew stronger lessons from the old. All were interlinked to varying degrees, and shaped by the leading influence of civil rights organizers in the United States and Third World Liberation movements globally. Notable European Left movements also shaped activists'

understanding of the world social order during this period. Where differentiation is needed, we refer specifically to the Black Liberation, student Left, labor or other movements. See George Katsiaficas, *The Imagination of the New Left* (Boston: South End Press, 1987), 17–28.

2. Speech by Preacherman (William Fesperman), July 19, 1969, Oakland, CA. Recording available from Pacifica Radio Archives, United Front Against Fascism Series, No. 5-9. Other details about the United Front Against Fascism Conference are drawn from interviews and "Gathering of the Clans," *Newsweek*, August 4, 1969.

3. While the term "Third World" may seem outdated today it was commonly used at the time to refer to those nations, mostly in the Global South, struggling to gain independence from foreign rulers or suffering the long-term impacts of colonial occupation. To better understand the concept of "Third World" politics and liberation in the context of this era, we recommend Malcolm X's historic speech, "Message to the Grassroots" (1963), widely available online; the essay "What is the Third World?" from the Third World Women's Alliance newspaper, *Triple Jeopardy*, 1969–70; and the article "Strike Over But Struggle Goes On," in *The Movement* 5:4, May 1969, 14–17, which includes first person interviews with the Third World Liberation Front activists in San Francisco. See also, Jason Ferreira, *All Power to the People: A Comparative Study of Third World Radicalism in San Francisco, 1968-1974* (PhD diss., University of California Berkeley, 2004); Laura Pulido, *Black, Brown, Yellow and Left: Radical Activism in Los Angeles* (Berkeley: University of California Press, 2006); and George Katsiaficas, *The Imagination of the New Left,* cited above.

4. James Miller, *Democracy is in the Streets: From Port Huron to the Siege of Chicago* (New York: Simon and Schuster, 1987), 195–196.

5. While some of these organizations have been discussed briefly in other works, JOIN Community Union is the only organization that has been investigated thoroughly, and only insofar as JOIN was part of Students for a Democratic Society's Economic Research and Action Project. Most accounts of JOIN's work and influence end in 1965–66 with ERAP's dissolution, a full two years before JOIN alums created the Young Patriots and Rising Up Angry. Some good starting points on JOIN's work include, Kirkpatrick Sale, *SDS* (New York: Vintage, 1972); and Jennifer Frost, An *Interracial Movement of the Poor: Community Organizing and the New Left in the 1960s* (New York: New York University Press, 2001). In addition to this book, new films, writing and archival exhibits on the Rainbow Coalition and related groups are just starting to emerge, and we hope to see more in the years to come.

6. While all of these organizations focused on reaching working-class whites, JOIN and Rising Up Angry never had exclusively white memberships. The changing landscape of their neighborhoods along with their

commitment to "rainbow politics" made it imperative to serve their entire community. In JOIN this included the important leadership of two Black Uptown residents, Dovie Thurman and Dovie Coleman, and in Rising Up Angry this included several leaders of color, including Soledad and José Rodriguez.

7. Michael Harrington, *The Other America: Poverty in the United States* (New York: Pelican Books, 1971), 14.

Chapter 1: The Common Cause is Freedom

1. The prior year CORE helped organize a massive push for federal enforcement of interstate transit desegregation. It had been more than fifteen years since the NAACP won a 6–1 Supreme Court ruling on the issue in *Morgan v. Commonwealth of Virginia* (1946). The high court's decision was, of course, never enforced. During the summer of 1961, CORE assembled nearly five hundred individuals, Black and white, to board interstate buses in a direct challenge to local jurisdictions. Facing arsons, beatings and threats on their lives, they became known as the "Freedom Riders." See Raymond Arsenault, *Freedom Riders: 1961 and the Struggle for Racial Justice* (New York: Oxford University Press, 2006).

2. Biographical details about Peggy Terry in this book are drawn from a variety of sources including Terry's personal archives, her journals, published interviews with friend and journalist Studs Terkel, unpublished transcripts from biographer Dennis Winters and interviews with her family members. All quotes without citations are drawn from these sources and reprinted with the permission of her daughter, Margi Devoe.

3. See Tom Johnson, "The Mechanics of the Bus Boycott," *The Montgomery Advertiser*, January 10, 1956. See also, Mary Fair Burks, "Women in the Montgomery Bus Boycott," in *Women in the Civil Rights Movement: Trailblazers and Torchbearers 1941-1965*, Vicki L. Crawford, Jacqueline Anne Rouse and Barbara Woods, eds. (Bloomington: Indiana University Press, 1993), 71–83.

4. Estimate taken from a pamphlet by the Coordinating Council of Community Organizations, *Why We March*, circa 1965. Retrieved from Peggy Terry's personal collection.

5. Arthur M. Brazier, *Black Self-Determination: The Story of the Woodlawn Organization* (Grand Rapids, MI: William B. Eerdmans Publishing, 1969), 47–48.

6. See Chad Berry, *Southern Migrants, Northern Exiles* (Urbana: University of Illinois Press, 2000); and Jack Temple Kirby, "The Southern Exodus, 1910-1960: A Primer for Historians," in *The Journal of Southern History* 49:4, November 1983, 585–600.

7. Other great migrations from the region include the forced removal of the Cherokee in the 1830s, and two major periods of African-American migration from central and southern Appalachia between 1865–1900 and 1916–1925. See James N. Gregory, *The Southern Diaspora: How the Great Migrations of Black and White Southerners Transformed America* (Chapel Hill: University of North Carolina Press, 2005); Theda Perdue and Michael D. Green, "The Trail of Tears," in *The Cherokee Removal: A Brief History with Documents* (Boston: Bedford Books, 1995), 160–173; Joe William Trotter Jr., "Introduction to Black Migration in Historical Perspective," in *The Great Migration in Historical Perspective*, Joe William Trotter Jr., ed. (Bloomington: Indiana University Press, 1991), 1–21; Jack Temple Kirby, "The Southern Exodus, 1910-1960: A Primer for Historians," in *The Journal of Southern History* 49:4, November 1983, 585–600; and Isabel Wilkerson's incredible narrative history of Black migration in *The Warmth of Other Suns: The Epic Story of America's Great Migration* (New York: Vintage, 2011).

8. Uptown also included a small population of Blacks and Native Americans, and a growing number of Latinos and Japanese Americans. In 1960 these communities totaled about 6 percent of the neighborhood. By the 1970 census the population showed significant changes as Black, Latino, Native American and Asian populations grew to 23 percent. Uptown's Black population alone increased eightfold, and the Latino population, largely Puerto Rican, grew to 13 percent. See, Elizabeth Warren, *Chicago's Uptown: Public Policy, Neighborhood Decay and Citizen Action in an Urban Community* (Chicago: Loyola University, 1979), 105–109.

9. See, Chad Berry, "Southerners," *Encyclopedia of Chicago*, Web site (accessed January 4, 2008); and Chad Berry, *Southern Migrants, Northern Exiles* (Urbana: University of Illinois Press, 2000).

10. Albert N. Votaw, "The Hillbillies Invade Chicago," *Harper's* magazine, February 1958, 64.

11. Gene Klinger, "What's the Toughest Neighborhood in America?," *True* magazine, October 1971, 27–34.

12. Jon Rice, "The World of the Illinois Panthers," in *Freedom North: Black Freedom Struggles Outside the South 1940-1980*, Jeanne Theoharis and Komozi Woodard, eds. (New York: Palgrave Macmillan, 2003), 41–42.

13. Mike Royko, *Boss: Richard J. Daley of Chicago* (New York: Dutton, 1971), 28.

14. *Chicago Tribune*, as cited in Chad Berry, *Southern Migrants, Northern Exiles*, 186.

15. Campbell Gibson and Kay Jung, *Historical Census Statistics on Population Totals by Race, 1790 to 1990, and by Hispanic Origin, 1790 to 1990, for Large Cities and Other Urban Places in the United States*, Working Paper No. 76 (Washington, DC: U.S. Census Bureau, 2005).

16. Phillip J. Obermiller and Thomas E. Wagner, "Hands-Across-the-Ohio: The Urban Initiatives of the Council of the Southern Mountains, 1954-1971," in *Appalachian Odyssey: Historical Perspectives on the Great Migration*, Phillip J. Obermiller, Thomas E. Wagner and E. Bruce Tucker, eds. (Westport, CT: Praeger, 2000), 134.

17. While not the largest student organization in U.S. history, SDS is by far the most renowned with ongoing influence in 21st century politics. The student group grew out of one of the few socialist federations to survive the Red Scare, the League for Industrial Democracy. The group resurrected its youth wing as growing numbers of young intellectuals, fed up with Cold War ideology, started to coalesce around pacifism, civil rights and their distrust of the powerful. They quickly began to question the limits of their parent organization's model as well. They saw "new insurgencies" brewing in America, in new locations, requiring new strategies. For the definitive history on SDS see Kirkpatrick Sale, *SDS* (New York: Vintage, 1972).

18. Kirkpatrick Sale, *SDS*, 98.

19. Despite its radical tenor, SDS's early vision resided only a little farther to the left than the New Deal of its parent generation. Early SDS documents flatly rejected Soviet-style communism, while noting that virulent American anti-communism was equally corrosive of democratic values. The *Port Huron Statement* dubbed America's lazy form of representative democracy a "politics without publics." In its place, SDS suggested a completely horizontal form of democratic assembly, a "democracy of individual participation." Directly inspired by the southern civil rights movement, they envisioned a society built on fraternity, economic self-determination and a fully participatory democracy. In their early days, they reasoned that the university, rather than the Old Left relic of the Party, represented the most democratic place to develop an intellectually grounded merger of liberalism and socialism for the new era. With ERAP's launch SDS embraced community organizing as a necessary vehicle to complement or even replace the group's campus work. See, Kirkpatrick Sale, *SDS*, cited above.

20. Rothstein, "ERAP and How It Grew," page 3 of unnumbered pamphlet from the author's personal collection.

21. Carl Wittman and Thomas Hayden, "An Interracial Movement of the Poor," in *The New Student Left*, Mitchell Cohen and Dennis Hale, eds. (Boston: Beacon Press, 1967), 204.

22. While Stokely Carmichael is best known for asking whites to "organize their own," civil rights leaders Bayard Rustin, Ella Baker and Anne Braden began encouraging white volunteers to live and organize in white communities as early as 1960. For examples see Clayborne Carson, *In Struggle: SNCC and the Black Awakening of the 1960s* (Cambridge, MA: Harvard University Press, 1981), 101–103; and Becky Thompson, *A*

Promise and a Way of Life: White Antiracist Activism (Minneapolis: University of Minnesota Press, 2001), 51.

23. Despite the growing troubles with white volunteers, Black civil rights leaders did collaborate with several important organizations of white southerners during this period. SNCC's first white staff organizer, Bob Zellner, worked with Carl and Anne Braden of the Southern Conference Education Fund (SCEF) and the Southern Mountain Project to organize white students and poor whites in tandem with the civil rights movement. As SNCC began turning white volunteers away, many more white volunteers swelled SCEF's ranks. Many of them, especially those from middle and upper class families, often lacked sensitivity to poor white southerners. As Anne Braden put it, white volunteers had a reentry problem after leaving integrated civil rights groups where they'd come to see "every white face [as an] enemy." The Bradens have since become icons of the era, and Zellner went on to found Grassroots Organizing Work, or GROW, in the Mississippi Delta in 1967. For more on these important efforts see Catherine Fosl, *Subversive Southerner: Anne Braden and the Struggle for Racial Justice in the Cold War South* (New York: Palgrave MacMillan, 2002), 304; and Bob Zellner, *The Wrong Side of Murder Creek: A White Southerner in the Freedom Movement* (Montgomery, AL: New South Books, 2008).

24. For more on Sherrod's story see Ronald Fraser, *1968: A Student Generation in Revolt* (New York: Pantheon Books, 1988), 52.

25. Richie Rothstein, "ERAP and How It Grew," page 6 of unnumbered pamphlet.

26. In the end, only ERAP's Chicago and Hazard, Kentucky, chapters actually reached majority white communities. The project in Hazard was also pivotal as it illustrated how the rural coal-mining crisis propelled southern migration to northern cities. In Hazard, jobless miners organized for a federal jobs program and compensation from the coal companies. Berman Gibson, president of the unemployed miners' Appalachian Committee for Full Employment, and Hamish Sinclair, secretary of the Committee for Miners, visited college campuses in 1963 hoping to bring student activist support to Appalachia. Campus committees in support of the miners sprouted from a belief that "their work with predominantly white unemployed workers would enable the students to become an active bridge for a new kind of populist alliance, on the grounds of job discrimination against all workers black and white in an automated age." See Hamish Sinclair, "Hazard, Kentucky: Document of the Struggle," *Radical America* 2:1, January–February 1968, 1. Retrieved from Tamiment Library and Robert F. Wagner Labor Archives at New York University.

27. JOIN's first action in May 1964 didn't go over as well as they planned. Chabot and volunteer Max decided they would sell apples in Chicago's

Downtown Loop. The action was intended to evoke the Great Depression when unemployed workers sold apples on city streets as a matter of survival. The apple selling failed to rouse much support. For more on JOIN's early work see, Richard Flacks, *Chicago: Organizing the Unemployed* (Ann Arbor, MI: Economic Research Action Project/Students for a Democratic Society, April 7, 1964). Report retrieved from Tamiment Library and Robert F. Wagner Labor Archives at New York University.

28. Kirkpatrick Sale, *SDS* (New York: Vintage, 1972), 103. The other ERAP chapters fumbled as well. Organizers in Cleveland, Newark and elsewhere spent their first six to twelve months working in local hang-out spots and trying to build relationships. A 1964 headline in *The Michigan Daily* summed up the reality: "ERAP Inches Toward Helping Nation's Poor."

29. For one of the internal arguments cautioning SDS to temper its wholesale shift to community organizing among the poorest of the poor, see Douglas Ireland and Steve Max, *For a New Coalition* (New York: Students for a Democratic Society Political Education Project, December 25, 1964). For a deeper look at this debate, see also Jennifer Frost, *An Interracial Movement of the Poor*; and Kirkpatrick Sale, *SDS*, both cited above.

30. In the Thirties and Forties, the group shaped how New Deal relief money was spent in the neighborhood, creating an infant wellness clinic, a recreation center and a hot-lunch program for unemployed workers. A council offshoot, the Packinghouse Workers Organizing Committee pressured the Armour Company to accept the workers' demands for a union. The BYNC also pioneered what would be known decades later as an "alternatives to incarceration" approach to juvenile crime. Chicago police turned first-time offenders under the age of sixteen to BYNC's delinquency program. If family income was determined to be a factor, BYNC secured employment for the parents and the youth. See, Kathryn Close, "Back of the Yards: Packingtown's Latest Drama: Civic Unity," Survey Graphic, *Magazine of Social Interpretation*, December 1, 1940. Last accessed July 4, 2011 at newdeal. feri.org/survey/40c22.htm; and Sanford D. Horwitt, *Let Them Call Me Rebel: Saul Alinsky: His Life and Legacy* (New York: Vintage, 1989).

31. The tension between the ideologically based community organizing of the Communist Party USA and the progressive-populist version associated with Saul Alinsky is best described in Robert Fisher, *Let the People Decide: Neighborhood Organizing in America* (Boston: Twayne Publishers, 1984). Though he had vocal critics, Alinsky deserves credit for inspiring The Woodlawn Organization, influencing key leaders in the Black Panthers, and even providing the rhetorical—if not political—inspiration for the "community union" concept that JOIN adopted. Also under his tutelage, the Industrial Areas Foundation pressured the Kodak Eastman Corporation to hire Blacks and protested banks and businesses to end redlining in loan practices to communities of color. His *Rules for Radicals* remains

one of the best-selling book on radicalism in the U.S. and Alinsky is still widely respected for developing a model that places full individual participation and local solutions at the center of neighborhood organizing.

32. See Sanford D. Horwitt, *Let Them Call Me Rebel*, cited above, 525. The two sides would clash again years later, but this time it was JOIN's neighborhood leaders who confronted Alinsky, in part over competition for funding. When talk began that Alinsky might start a project in Uptown, JOIN responded, "We are alarmed at this possibility as we are mindful of the results of Alinsky's organizing techniques in the Back of the Yards area of Chicago. It is our deep belief that in organizing poor whites one must deal honestly and openly with the problem of racism in our people." See Peggy Terry, "JOIN Community Union: Funding Grant by SCLC to Realize the Goals of the 1968 Poor Peoples' Campaign in the Uptown Community of Chicago," date unknown.

33. John A. Andrew, *Lyndon Johnson and the Great Society* (Chicago: Ivan R. Dee, 1998).

34. Jon Rice, "The World of the Illinois Panthers," in *Freedom North: Black Freedom Struggles Outside the South 1940-1980*, Jeanne Theoharis and Komozi Woodard, eds. (New York: Palgrave Macmillan, 2003), 43. This article may be the single most succinct account of the power politics of Chicago during the 1960s and how they contributed to the rise of the radical Left.

35. Todd Gitlin and Nanci Hollander, *Uptown: Poor Whites in Chicago* (New York: Harper and Row, 1970), 423–424. Gitlin and Hollander both spent time as organizers with JOIN and have meticulously documented its history and the lives of key Uptown residents. As authors we are indebted to them for capturing this history as they were living it.

36. Richie Rothstein, "Evolution of ERAP Organizers," in *The New Left: A Collection of Essays*, Priscilla Long, ed. (Boston: Extending Horizons Books, 1969), 282.

37. Ruth Moore, "Tenant Union Signs Building Contract Believed City's First," *Chicago Sun-Times,* May 26, 1966.

38. Michael Harrington, *The Other America: Poverty in the United States* (New York: Pelican Books, 1971), 147.

39. The Chicago Freedom Movement's list demanded an end to the northern brand of Jim Crow segregation and the ghettoization that resulted from discriminatory city and business practices. The list also called for the revocation of contracts with firms failing to uphold fair employment practices, citizen review boards to govern the police and increased public services in slum areas. See, *The Eyes on the Prize Civil Rights Reader: Documents, Speeches, and Firsthand Accounts from the Black Freedom Struggle 1954-1990,* Clayborne Carson, ed. (New York: Penguin Books, 1990); and James R. Ralph Jr., *Northern Protest: Martin Luther King, Jr., Chicago*

and the Civil Rights Movement (Boston: Harvard University, 1993).

40. In 1951 Cicero had garnered worldwide headlines when more than three thousand whites rioted under the banner "White Power" to protest the "black slum invasion" of the neighborhood.

41. The chorus included the refrain, *"Well, we're gonna romp, and we're gonna stomp, and we're gonna have us a time. We're gonna get, what the poor ain't got yet. Gonna keep on the Firing Line."*

42. See Bob Lawson and Mike James, "Poor White Response to Black Rebellion," *The Movement*, August 1967, 4; and Peggy Terry, "Poor Whites Must Decide," *The Movement*, August 1967, 4.

43. Details of these events are drawn from personal interviews, with quotes from Todd Gitlin and Nanci Hollander, *Uptown: Poor Whites in Chicago*; and Joseph Morang, "Arrest 5, Seize Dope in Raids on Civic Units," *Chicago Tribune*, September 2, 1966.

44. While on the FBI's payroll, Mosher joined the Young Patriots Organization, a successor of JOIN Community Union, and helped to coordinate the Black Panthers' 1969 United Front Against Fascism conference in Oakland, California. Mosher briefly returned to Stanford to complete his economics degree in 1968 and it was then he says the federal government asked him to start keeping tabs on movement leaders. According to Mosher's reports to federal authorities he considered himself a part of the New Left until a trip to Cuba where a group of young radicals met representatives of the National Liberation Front of South Vietnam who encouraged Americans to take up armed struggle, including bombing draft boards. Upon returning to the United States, Mosher claimed he visited SDS leader Mark Rudd outside of Boulder, Colorado, and that Rudd's support for revolutionary violence cemented Mosher's decision to work as an FBI infiltrator. Rudd recalls no such conversation with Mosher ever took place. He doubts Mosher's story about his Cuba trip as well. For Mosher's own account see T. Edward Mosher, "Inside the Revolutionary Left," *Reader's Digest*, September 1971; and "Testimony of Thomas Edward Mosher," Hearings before the Subcommittee to Investigate the Administration of the Internal Security Act and Other Internal Security Laws, Committee on the Judiciary United States Senate, 92nd Congress, First Session, Part 1, February 11–12 and March 19, 1971. Retrieved through a Freedom of Information Act request by the authors.

45. Martin Luther King Jr., *Where Do We Go From Here: Chaos or Community?* (Boston: Beacon Press, 2010), 26.

46. For more on issues of gender within SNCC and SDS see Sara Evans, *Personal Politics: The Roots of Women's Liberation in the Civil Rights Movement and the New Left* (New York: Alfred A. Knopf, 1979).

47. Numerous other accounts of this moment exist including Clayborne Carson, *In Struggle*, cited above; and Stokely Carmichael and Ekwueme

Michael Thelwell, *Ready for Revolution: The Life and Struggles of Stokely Carmichael* (New York: Scribner, 2005).

48. First published in 1966. Reprinted two years later as Michael James, *Getting Ready for the Firing Line* (Chicago: JOIN Community Union, 1968).

49. Mike James, Diane Fager, Bob Lawson, Junebug Boykin, Tom Livingston, Tom Malear, Bobby McGinnis, Virgil Reed, Mike Sharon, and Youngblood, "Take a Step Into America," *Don't Mourn—Organize!* (San Francisco: The Movement Press, December 1967). Also reprinted in Loren Bartz, *The American Left: Radical Political Thought in the Twentieth Century* (New York: Basic Books, 1971), 406–417.

50. Peggy Terry, "Tellin' It Like It Is," speech to SDS Convention, December 27, 1967. Reprinted in *The Firing Line* newspaper, January 16, 1968.

51. Peggy Terry and Doug Youngblood, "JOIN: A New Outlook for the Movement," date unknown.

52. Martin Luther King Jr., Western Union Telegram to Peggy Terry, March 6, 1968.

53. Peggy Terry's personal journal from the day Dr. Martin Luther King Jr. was shot, April 4, 1968.

54. Fran Ansley, personal letter to Peggy Terry, April 10, 1968.

55. Peggy Terry, "Solidarity Day Speech at Lincoln Memorial," June 19, 1968. Typewritten transcript. Other details drawn from Hoke Norris, "Vanguard of the Poor in D.C. Rally," *Chicago Sun-Times*, May 13, 1968.

56. Interethnic tensions did erupt in Resurrection City as Latino and Native American leaders challenged the Black-white paradigm of race relations in the U.S. and in the civil rights movement. The conversations that began in May–June 1968 represent the beginnings of a more defined revolutionary nationalism for many Black, Latino, Native and Asian organizations. For a more nuanced exploration of the Poor People's Campaign's importance for multiethnic politics, see James R. Ralph Jr., *Northern Protest: Martin Luther King Jr., Chicago and the Civil Rights Movement*, cited above; and Gordan Keith Mantler, *Black, Brown and Poor: Martin Luther King Jr., the Poor People's Campaign and Its Legacies* (PhD Diss., Duke University, 2008).

57. Doug Youngblood, "Letter from Youngblood," *The Movement*, September 1968.

58. Paul Alkebulan, *Survival Pending Revolution: The History of the Black Panther Party* (Tuscaloosa, AL: University of Alabama Press, 2007).

59. "A Letter from Eldridge Cleaver," policy statement, printed by the Radical Caucus of Peace and Freedom Party, Alameda County, August 17, 1968; and "Cleaver for President" flyer, Peace and Freedom Party, date unknown.

60. In his career as a judge and a Democratic delegate, Wallace was originally a liberal on racial issues. The NAACP even endorsed him during the primary in his first bid for governor. Wallace lost to an opponent who had

the endorsement of the Ku Klux Klan. Vowing to "never be outniggered again," Wallace turned coat and secured himself a landslide victory in the next election. Asa Carter, editor of the ardently racist *Southerner* magazine, wrote Wallace's 1962 inauguration speech where he declared, "Segregation now! Segregation tomorrow! Segregation forever!" Playing to whites' racial anxieties, the speech held out the deaths of white settlers in the Belgian Congo as evidence of things to come in the American South. See Stephen Lesher, *George Wallace: American Populist* (Cambridge, MA: Perseus Publishing, 1994), 122–127; and Dan T. Carter, *From George Wallace to Newt Gingrich: Race in the Conservative Counterrevolution 1963–1994* (Baton Rouge: Louisiana State University, 1996), 122.

61. Lesher, *George Wallace*, 104.
62. National Organizing Committee, press release, October 1, 1968; and National Organizing Committee/Peace and Freedom Party, "Statement to the Press," October 2, 1968.
63. *Courier-Journal*, "Youths Cool to 4th Party Candidate," date unknown.
64. Doug Youngblood, "You've Got the Right String But the Wrong Yo-Yo, Georgie Baby," National Community Union paper, circa Fall 1968.
65. California Secretary of State, Statement of Vote General Election, November 5, 1968 (Sacramento: State of California, 1968). See also, Richard Rodda, "Big Southern Counties Deliver 220,000 Votes for Nixon Win," *The Fresno Bee*, November 6, 1968; and Jerry Rankin, "Voting Last Week Shows Minor Party Difficulties," *Red Bluff Daily News*, November 11, 1968.
66. See Guida West, *The National Welfare Rights Movement: The Social Protest of Poor Women* (New York: Praeger, 1981); and Mark Toney, "Revisiting the National Welfare Rights Organization," *Colorlines* magazine, Fall 2000.

Chapter 2: The Fire Next Time

1. Informally, the coalition counted other collaborators as well, including Rising Up Angry, another project descended from JOIN, and radical Third World groups like the Chicano Brown Berets.
2. Letter from an anonymous "Dislocated Hillbilly," reprinted in Bruce Franklin, *From the Movement Toward Revolution* (New York: Van Nostrand Reinhold, 1971), 111.
3. Historical studies of the Panthers tell slightly different accounts of their founding. Good starting points on this history include, David Hilliard and Lewis Cole, *This Side of Glory: The Autobiography of David Hilliard and the Story of the Black Panther Party* (Boston: Little, Brown, 1993); and Elaine Brown, *A Taste of Power: A Black Woman's Story* (New York:

Pantheon Books, 1992).

4. Seale and Newton modeled their survival programs on the literacy schools and wealth redistribution programs established decades earlier by populist Louisiana Governor Huey P. Long, whom Huey P. Newton was named after, the San Francisco Diggers and Irish-American labor radicals in Virginia, the Molly McGuires.

5. For more on the history of the Young Lords Organization in Chicago and the Young Lords Party in New York, see Miguel Melendez, *We Took the Streets: Fighting for Latino Rights with the Young Lords* (New York: St. Martin's Press, 2003); Andrés Torres and José E. Velázquez, eds., *The Puerto Rican Movement: Voices from the Diaspora* (Philadelphia: Temple University Press, 1998); and Darrel Enck-Wanzer, *The Young Lords: A Reader* (New York: NYU Press, 2010).

6. This idea was expressed concretely through the Communist International in 1928 and influenced the Communist Party's support of southern Black sharecroppers and Black industrial workers in the North in the 1930s. For more on this fascinating history, see Robin D.G. Kelley, *Race Rebels: Culture, Politics and the Black Working Class* (New York: Free Press, 1996); as well as Kelley's *Freedom Dreams: The Black Radical Imagination* (Boston: Beacon Press, 2002). The idea was resurrected by Sixties Black radicals and popularized in the 1967 edition of Stokely Carmichael and Charles V. Hamilton, *Black Power: The Politics of Liberation* (New York: Vintage, 1992); and Robert Allen's 1969 release of *Black Awakening in Capitalist America* (Trenton, NJ: Africa World Press, 1990).

7. In the simplest terms, this concept of a nation was different from that of a country or state and mostly defied the imposition of borders. Under this definition, influenced by Stalin, nations were made up of people who share a common culture, language, history and consciousness, and may or may not determine their own right to secede from the imperialist country by claiming an independent land base. For a far more nuanced discussion of the Third World Left than we have space for here, see Laura Pulido, "Ideologies of Nation, Class and Race in the Third World Left," *Black, Brown, Yellow and Left: Radical Activism in Los Angeles* (Berkeley: University of California Press, 2006), 123–152; as well as Jason Ferreira, *All Power to the People: A Comparative Study of Third World Radicalism in San Francisco, 1968-1974* (PhD diss., University of California Berkeley, 2004). For more on the global uprisings from which they drew inspiration, see Max Elbaum, *Revolution in the Air: Sixties Radicals Turn to Lenin, Mao and Che* (London: Verso, 2002); and George Katsiaficas, *The Imagination of the New Left*, cited above.

8. The Patriot Party, "The Patriot Party Speaks to the Movement," in *The Black Panther Party Speaks*, Philip S. Foner, ed. (Cambridge, MA: Da Capo Press, 2002), 239–243.

9. Clarus Backes, "Poor People's Power in Uptown," *Chicago Tribune,* September 29, 1968.

10. Keniston had been living in Kentucky and planned to work with the ongoing coal miners' campaign in Hazard. There, he had met two men affiliated with the Southern Conference Educational Fund (SCEF), a pioneering organization founded in the 1950s to bring white people into the struggle against segregation. SCEF was ahead of its time owing much to the incredible leadership of Carl and Anne Braden, who had faced an infamous sedition trial in the 1950s for covertly helping a Black family buy a home in a white neighborhood. Keniston planned to stay, but the organization hit a wall that year when local prosecutors once again charged the Bradens, and other organizers, with sedition for their racial justice and anti-poverty work. The organization was consumed by the legal battle and Keniston realized other political work there would have to wait. He and his wife, Mary Ellen Graham, moved to Fairborne, Ohio, to find work and it was there that he first met Mike James.

11. This speech was transcribed in FBI surveillance files on William Fesperman, from an appearance at University of North Carolina, Raleigh, September 1969. Retrieved from the personal collection of Bob Simpson.

12. Other New Left organizations also tried to capture the flag away from its racist connotations. The Southern Student Organizing Committee (dubbed by some as the "SDS of the South") experimented with a similar emblem featuring black and white hands shaking over a Confederate Flag. Claude Weaver, a Black Harvard student active with SNCC, created the symbol. See Gregg Michel, *Struggle for a Better South: The Southern Student Organizing Committee, 1964–1969* (New York: Palgrave Macmillan, 2004), 50. To gain a deeper understanding of the history of Southern progressive organizing, see archival issues of *Southern Exposure* and 1960s issues of the Southern Conference Education Fund's newspaper, *The Southern Patriot.*

13. Mike Gray, "Chicago: August 28, 1968," liner notes for *American Revolution II,* DVD, dir. Mike Gray (Chicago: Facets Video, 1969; re-released 2007).

14. Chuck Geary was one of the few local organizers who hadn't actually come up through JOIN Community Union. Geary emigrated to Uptown from Jugville, Kentucky, for the same reason everyone else did: a job. After JOIN's demise Geary decided to start a new program called the Uptown Coalition to focus on defeating urban renewal and fixing up dilapidated buildings. With seasoned organizers like Peggy Terry on the group's steering committee, the group conducted door-to-door surveys counting as many as four thousand residents who would be displaced by plans for a new city college. There is very little scholarship about the considerable contributions of Charles Geary to Uptown's progressive,

anti-racist politics. What little exists tends to confuse Geary's Uptown Coalition with the Rainbow Coalition. While Geary supported its formation, the Rainbow Coalition was formally only an alliance between Panthers, Patriots and Lords. See Charles Geary, *What I'm About Is People* (Chicago: Children's Press, 1970).

15. Untitled article, *Chicago Tribune*, Jul 12, 1970, L17–20.

16. "Young Patriots," leaflet, date unknown. From Peggy Terry's personal collection.

17. Jeffrey Ogbar, *Black Power: Radical Politics and African American Identity,* (Baltimore: Johns Hopkins University Press, 2004), 179.

18. This Poor People's Coalition was unrelated to the national Poor People's Campaign started by Martin Luther King Jr. before his death.

19. Barbara Joyce, "Young Patriots," in *The Movement Toward a New America,* ed. Mitchell Goodman (New York: Knopf, 1970), 546–548.

20. Ward Churchill and Jim Vander Wall, *The COINTELPRO Papers: Documents from the FBI's Secret Wars Against Dissent in the United States* (Boston: South End Press, 1990), 123.

21. See Brian Glick, *War at Home: Covert Action Against U.S. Activists and What We Can Do About It* (Boston: South End Press, 1989), 11. See also the documentary *COINTELPRO 101,* dir. Freedom Archives (Oakland, CA: PM Press, 2011).

22. One of the best historical sources on this tragedy exists in the firsthand footage compiled in *The Murder of Fred Hampton,* dir. Mike Gray and Howard Alk (Chicago: Facets Video, 1971; re-released 2007). See also: Jeffrey Haas, *The Assassination of Fred Hampton: How the FBI and the Chicago Police Murdered a Black Panther* (Chicago: Lawrence Hill Books, 2010).

23. African People's Socialist Party, "Interview with Akua Njere (Deborah Johnson)," *Burning Spear,* June 1990.

24. Jeffrey Haas, *The Assassination of Fred Hampton,* 76.

25. Arthur Turco was also implicated in the Baltimore case, but he was eventually acquitted. Little else is known about Turco except for this case. He briefly practiced law in New York City and attempted to represent the Panther 21 defendants who had been arrested for plotting to blow up city buildings, but were later cleared. Shortly after the dissolution of the Patriots, he seemed to disappear from public view. Records kept by the New York State Bar Association show that he was disbarred in the mid-Seventies.

26. For a good account of the Panther 21 trial, see Murray Kempton, *The Briar Patch: The Trial of the Panther 21* (New York: Da Capo Press, 1997). See also, Bill Fesperman, "Patriot Party Attacked," *The Patriot,* March 21, 1970, 10; and Liberation News Service, "Young Patriots," in *The Movement Toward a New America,* Mitchell Goodman, ed. (New York: Pilgrim Press, 1970).

27. The charges against Seale for the Alex Rackley murder were eventually

dropped. See, Paul Bass and Douglas W. Rae, *Murder in the Model City: The Black Panthers, Yale and the Redemption of a Killer* (New York: Basic Books, 2006).

28. This and other stories of the Eugene chapter of the Patriots Party are documented in surveillance files now at the Portland City Archives. Thanks to author and journalist Jim Redden for pointing us toward them. Chuck Armsbury provided additional archival material, including a copy of the Genocide Complaint. Jaja Nkruma described the improbable growth of the Eugene Patriots in an interview over catfish sandwiches in Oakland. Part of this story can also be found in his essay *Short History of the Black Panther Party in the Eugene Oregon Chapter* on the Black Panthers archival website, http.itsabouttimebpp.com/Chapter_History/Eugene_Oregon_Chapter.html (last accessed May 4, 2011). Thanks to Daniel Burton-Rose for sharing notes about his research into this portion of Armsbury's history, now captured in the book *Guerrilla USA: The George Jackson Brigade and the Anti-Capitalist Underground of the 1970s* (Berkeley, CA: University of California Press, 2010).

29. The Prisoner Rights Movement in the U.S. is a powerful outgrowth of the Sixties upheaval. Good points of departure in this study include Eric Cummins, *The Rise and Fall of California's Radical Prison Movement* (Stanford, CA: Stanford University Press, 1994); Eric Mann, *Comrade George: An Investigation Into the Life, Political Thought and Assassination of George Jackson* (New York: Harper & Row, 1974); Jamie Bissonette, *When the Prisoners Ran Walpole: A True Story in the Movement for Prison Abolition* (Cambridge, MA: South End Press, 1974); Part I of Angela Y. Davis, *The Angela Y. Davis Reader*, Joy James, ed. (Malden, MA: Blackwell Publishers, 1998); and more recently, Dan Berger, *We Are the Revolutionaries: Visibility, Protest and Racial Formation in 1970s Prison Radicalism* (PhD Diss., University of Pennsylvania, 2010).

30. At the time, such legal work was made possible by inmates' access to law books and their ability to file complaints with the help of outside attorneys. McNeil's prisoners enjoyed a Writ Room, in which determined prisoners could learn the ropes of legal research.

31. Raymond Tackett interviewed by Peter M. Michels, "Aufstand in den Ghettos," *Zur Organisation d. Lumpenproletariats in d. USA.* (Frankfurt a.M., 1971): Fischer-Taschenbuch-Verl (1972, Hamburg). Translated for this book by Amber Tellez.

32. "Raymond Tackett Murdered in Kentucky," *Rising Up Angry*, February 11–March 4, 1973.

33. Among the only books to feature the Young Patriots are Philip S. Foner, *The Black Panthers Speak;* Bruce Franklin, *From the Movement Toward Revolution*; and Jeffrey Ogbar, *Black Power: Radical Politics and African American Identity*, each cited above.

Chapter 3: Pedagogy of the Streets

1. In May 1970 the *New York Times* published a poll reporting that more than three million U.S. college students thought revolution was necessary. While staggering, this number reflects only one sector of a much broader Left whose revolutionary outlook and impact was never captured in single statistic. As found in Max Elbaum, *Revolution in the Air: Sixties Radicals Turn to Lenin, Mao and Che* (London: Verso, 2002), 18.

2. For more on these events see, Ron Jacobs, *The Way the Wind Blew* (London: Verso, 1997).

3. As author Dan Berger summarized, "It was a split over class and race, aboveground versus underground, Communist party versus armed revolutionary movement—and more than a few strong egos were involved." See, Dan Berger, *Outlaws of America: The Weather Underground and the Politics of Solidarity* (Oakland, CA: AK Press, 2006), 87. Other good accounts of these debates and the end of SDS are included in Max Elbaum, *Revolution in the Air*; and Kirkpatrick Sale, *SDS*, cited above.

4. After the splits, RYM II returned to the Old Left's arena of class conflict to build revolutionary organization and multiracial unity among workers. Among them was JOIN's Steve Goldsmith who spent the next ten years organizing in a Midwest steel mill, and Mike Klonsky, a Chicago activist close to members of both JOIN and Rising Up Angry, who worked in various factories over the next decade. Meanwhile, the now-famous Weathermen set out to act as a pressure valve, forcing the FBI to pursue them rather than revolutionaries of color. Within a few months of the split at the SDS convention, Weather planted dynamite at the police memorial statue at Haymarket Square in Chicago, starting a five-day clash between police and protesters dubbed the Days of Rage. After the protests failed to produce the mass turnout Weather had hoped, the group refocused their efforts to build a small but decisive cadre of militant fighters. Some Weather members went underground. Over the next few years, the Weather Underground Organization played a role in at least two-dozen deliberate bombings of targets associated with the U.S. government or corporations. The only proven fatalities Weather ever caused were their own. For more on RYM II's history and participants, see Elbaum, *Revolution in the Air*. For more on the evolution of the Weather Underground, see Cathy Wilkerson, *Flying Close to the Sun: My Life and Times as a Weatherman* (New York: Seven Stories Press, 2007); as well as Berger, *Outlaws of America*; and Jacobs, *The Way the Wind Blew*.

5. Rising Up Angry's inclusion of Ireland as part of the Third World pantheon was part of a larger Left tradition of collaboration between U.S. and Irish radicals. Leaders in the Irish movement were deeply influenced by the southern Civil Rights Movement, while U.S. radicals drew

inspiration from Ireland's history of resistance to British rule, especially during the twentieth century. Irish leaders like James Connolly, a Marxist, radicalized the Irish struggle by asserting that nationalism would only be revolutionary if the end goal was socialism. This was an important distinction for Sixties radicals, as well. As Connolly wrote, "The Republic I would wish our fellow-countrymen to set before them as their ideal should be of such character that the mere mention of its name would at all times serve as a beacon-light to the oppressed of every land. . . . Nationalism without Socialism—without a reorganisation of society on the basis of a broader and more developed form of that common property which underlay the social structure of Ancient Erin—is only national recreancy." See James Connolly, *Collected Works, Vol. One* (Dublin: New Books, 1987), 304–305.

6. For an authoritative firsthand account of veterans who joined the antiwar movement, see Gerald Nicosia, *Home to War: A History of the Vietnam Veterans Movement* (New York: Three Rivers Press, 2001). Also view, *Sir! No Sir!*, DVD, directed by David Zeiger (Los Angeles: Displaced Films, 2006).

7. In the mid-twentieth century, a host of radical thinkers, most notably Antonio Gramsci, turned their attention to the power of culture in society. Gramsci coined the phrase "cultural hegemony" to describe the intricate web of tradition, media and mores that produce a "common sense" in working-class people. Simply put, hegemony is a shared sense of reality that builds compliance with the State and capitalism. Imprisoned by Mussolini in the 1930s and writing from an Italian prison, Gramsci could not have anticipated rock-and-roll as both a product of capitalism and a tool of revolutionaries. Rising Up Angry set out to break this compliance and create a popular culture of Left politics among the urban white working class.

8. The legendary rock band MC5 was an important vehicle for another white-led radical group at the time: the White Panther Party in Detroit. Founded by John Sinclair and Pun Plamondon in 1968 as a response to Huey Newton's suggestion that whites should organize a Panther Party of their own, the White Panthers eschewed the Serve the People breakfast programs and free clinics in favor of using rock-and-roll to launch a "total assault on culture." For their efforts they were rewarded with relentless FBI surveillance, an attempted frame-up for an explosion at a CIA office and, later, exile. Sinclair was sentenced to ten years in prison for possession of two joints. His case became a cause célèbre, with Sinclair Freedom Rallies attracting performers such as Stevie Wonder, Phil Ochs, Allen Ginsberg, Muddy Waters, Bob Seeger and the Stooges. At the pinnacle of the campaign, John Lennon recorded a protest song calling for Sinclair's release: *"If he'd been a soldier man / Shooting gooks in Vietnam / If he was the*

CIA / Selling dope and making hay / He'd be free, they'd let him be / Breathing air, like you and me" (Lyrics from Lennon's "John Sinclair," 1972).

9. The Boston Women's Health Collective's *Our Bodies, Ourselves* broke ground as the first publication to address women's bodies, sexuality and health care in a radical framework (it was originally named "Women and Their Bodies" and spanned 193 pages). Framed by both the assertion of women's liberation and the openness of the sexual revolution, the book brought questions about women's bodies and reproductive health out of the shadows. There have been numerous revised editions since the Seventies, including special editions on issues like menopause and pregnancy. To this day, *Our Bodies Ourselves*, now nearly 800 pages in length, is considered the leading source on health information "by and for women."

10. D&C means "dilation and curettage." For more on this work, see the excellent self-published document, *Jane: Documents from Chicago's Clandestine Abortion Service 1968–1973* (Chicago: Firestarter Press, 2004). See also the award-winning film *Jane: An Abortion Service*, DVD, directed by Nell Lundy and Kate Kirtz (Independent Television Service, 1995).

Chapter 4: Lightning on the Eastern Seaboard

1. Nixon's 1971 Executive Order 11625 set specific goals for a Minority Business Enterprise contracting program. For a brief summary of this history, see: "The History of Affirmative Action Policies," *In Motion Magazine*, October 12, 2003.

2. The growth of the New Right follows a complex path. The term "New Right" is often used as a synonym for the Christian or evangelical Right that rose to the national stage during the Seventies. Here, we use the term to encompass a rightward political shift (present in both political parties) marked by the growth of right-wing populism in reaction to civil rights and the War on Poverty expansion of social welfare. A concise and insightful explanation of the dynamics contributing to the rise of the Right appears in Maurice Isserman and Michael Kazin's *America Divided: The Civil War of the 1960s* (New York: Oxford University, 2000); and in Jean Hardisty, *Mobilizing Resentment: Conservative Resurgence from the John Birch Society to the Promise Keepers* (Boston: Beacon Press, 2000). For an expansive look at the history of right-wing populist movements in the U.S., see Chip Berlet and Matthew Lyons, *Right-Wing Populism in America: Too Close for Comfort* (New York: Guilford Press, 2000).

3. For an introduction to the role of white resentment and the resurgence of ethnic essentialism during this period, see Thomas J. Sugrue and John

D. Skrentny's article, "The White Ethnic Strategy" in *Rightward Bound: Making America Conservative in the 1970s,* Bruce J. Schulman and Julian E. Zelizer, eds. (Cambridge, MA: Harvard University Press, 2008).

4. Nelson Rockefeller didn't invent the War on Drugs—Richard Nixon did when he made the anti-drug agenda a central part of his presidency—but the Rockefeller Laws provided the blueprint for states to implement it. As the War on Drugs continued, the U.S. prison population spiked dramatically. By the year 2000, it reached a record two million people, most imprisoned for nonviolent crimes. Counting those on probation and parole, the total number of people in the system at the turn of this century was a shocking 6.4 million. Ten years later, it climbed again to 7.2 million. For additional information on the history of the Rockefeller Laws, see New York Civil Liberties Union, *The Rockefeller Drug Laws: Unjust, Irrational, Ineffective* (March 11, 2009).

5. Accounts of this incident vary greatly, especially on its exact year. 1779 is used here because it is the year cited in O4O literature. For one account, see Steven Rosswurm, *Arms, Country and Class: The Philadelphia Militia and the "Lower Sort" During the American Revolution, 1775-1783* (New Brunswick, NJ: Rutgers University Press, 1973).

6. While their work was considerable, O4O was not the only Left organization in Philadelphia to build a base with white working-class communities. The Philadelphia Workers Organizing Committee, a Marxist-Leninist organization, also sent a cadre into workplaces to organize laborers.

7. Paul Lyons's book *The People of This Generation: The Rise and Fall of the New Left in Philadelphia* (Philadelphia: University of Pennsylvania, 2003) covers this and other important moments in Philadelphia's Left tradition.

8. Robert Barrow is a pseudonym used at the participant's request.

9. Peter Binzen, *Whitetown USA* (New York: Vintage Books, 1970), 81.

10. Journalist Nora Sayre's firsthand account of Philadelphia's left offers both anecdotes and analysis, see Nora Sayre, *Sixties Going on Seventies*: Revised Edition (New York: Arbor House, 1996), 90. Originally published in 1973.

11. Several different versions of this quote appear in news articles. Some attribute it to his plans for anti-police protestors, but most agree he made the comment to a reporter during his bid for reelection in 1974. Of course this was just one of many inflammatory statements. Rizzo's excesses even shocked members of the political establishment. Former Philadelphia mayor and U.S. Senator Joseph Clark remarked at the time, "He's a stupid arrogant son of a bitch—and that's on the record." For a complete history of Rizzo's rise to power, there is no better book than Joseph Daughen and Peter Binzen, *The Cop Who Would Be King: Mayor Frank Rizzo* (Boston: Little, Brown, 1977).

12. Rizzo conducted the raid with no evidence that the Panthers were behind the killings, and none has surfaced since. The infamous photo by Elwood P. Smith was circulated worldwide. See Deborah Boiling, "He's Seen It All," *City Paper,* August 22-28, 2002.

13. Frank Rizzo quoted in *People Against Rizzo,* Evening Bulletin, Philadelphia Free Press supplement, September 15, 1971.

14. Sue Milligan is a pseudonym used at the participant's request.

15. According to the U.S. Census, Philadelphia's Black population doubled after World War II, and rose another ten percent during the Sixties, though all sides assume the population was undercounted. By 1970, the official estimate put Philadelphia at thirty-four percent African American.

16. *Frankenhauser v. Rizzo* later set the standard by which private citizens could demand police records. Stephen M. Ryals, *Discovery and Proof in Police Misconduct Cases* (Frederick, MD: Aspen Publishers, 2002), 173–180.

17. See Jack McKinney, "The Voices of Dissent in Kensington," *Philadelphia Daily News,* October 26, 1972.

18. Andrew J. Rotter, ed., *Light at the End of the Tunnel: A Vietnam War Anthology* (Lanham, MD: Rowman & Littlefield, Revised Edition, 1999), 138–139.

19. Telford Taylor, ". . . and of Deceit," *New York Times,* January 3, 1973.

20. For original accounts of these events, see "Casts of 17 Shows Give $10,000 for Bach Mai," *New York Times,* January 13, 1973; and Eileen Shanahan, "I.R.S. Disallows Tax Exemptions For Gifts to Hospital," *New York Times,* July 9, 1973.

21. Emerging from the Black Women's Caucus of SNCC, the Third World Women's Alliance broke new ground in pursuing an agenda that centralized gender, race and class issues as part of their work. Further, groups like Triple Jeopardy, the Puerto Rican Socialist Party and the Combahee River Collective laid the foundation for the emergence of influential women of color feminist theory rooted in early concepts of intersectionality. The importance of this political tradition is evident in the feminist canon, especially in the works of Toni Morrison, Alice Walker, Angela Davis, Trinh T. Minh-ha, Cherríe Moraga, Gloria Anzaldúa, Audre Lorde, bell hooks and many others. For the specific history of the Puerto Rican Socialist Party in Philadelphia, see Carmen Teresa Whalen, "Bridging Homeland and Barrio Politics: The Young Lords in Philadelphia," in *The Puerto Rican Movement: Voices From the Diaspora,* Andrés Torres and José E. Velázquez, eds. (Philadelphia: Temple University Press, 1998), 107–123.

22. O4O's Chris Robinson details this and other efforts by the group in the pamphlet *Plotting Directions: An Activist's Guide* (Philadelphia: Recon Publications, 1982).

23. From O4O's newspaper: "People Force PECO Backdown," *A Single Spark!*, Winter 1974.

24. For a detailed breakdown of Rizzo's campaign finances in both mayoral runs, see Joseph R. Daughen and Peter Binzen, *The Cop Who Would Be King*, cited above.

25. For more on this history see Russell Leigh Sharman, *The Tenants of East Harlem* (Berkeley, CA: University of California Press, 2007), 34–37.

26. For more on Fagiani's life during this period, see Gil Fagiani, "East Harlem and Vito Marcantonio: My Search for a Progressive Italian American Identity," *Voices in Italian Americana*, Volume 5, Number 2, (Fall 1994); and George De Stefano's *An Offer We Can't Refuse: the Mafia in the Mind of America* (New York: Faber & Faber, 2006), 282–284.

27. The term Synanon refers to an internationally utilized recovery and self-actualization method, which later devolved into a cult. Former members often faced retaliation, even escalating to attempted murder. See Rod Janzen, *The Rise and Fall of Synanon: A California Utopia* (New York: Nation, 2001), 40–43. See also Gil Fagiani, "An Italian American On the Left: Revolution and Ethnicity in the 1970s," in *Italian Americans in a Multicultural Society: Proceedings of the Symposium of the American Italian Historical Association 7*, Jerome Krase and Judith N. DeSena, eds. (1994), 218–222.

28. The battle for a better Lincoln Hospital is most vividly memorialized in Fitzhugh Mullan's *White Coat, Clenched Fist: The Political Education of An American Physician* (New York: Macmillan, 1976).

29. The Chicago chapter was known as the Young Lords Organization, while the New York chapter was known as the Young Lords Party. For an accessible introduction to the New York Lords see Miguel Melendez, *We Took the Streets: Fighting for Latino Rights with the Young Lords* (New York: St. Martin's Press, 2003).

30. See Juan Gonzalez, "Lincoln Hospital Emancipation Takeover," *New York Daily News*, October 1, 2008; as well as Fitzhugh Mullan, *White Coat, Clenched Fist*, cited above.

31. See Dan Berger, *Outlaws of America*, cited above.

32. Michael Tabor, *Capitalism Plus Dope Equals Genocide* (New York: Black Panther Party, no date).

33. White Lightning and the Panthers were right to suspect foul play. In 1996, *San Jose Mercury News* reporter Gary Webb published a series of articles that finally proved the CIA connection with the explosion of the crack epidemic. Webb documented how the CIA allowed a flood of cocaine into poor neighborhoods in order to finance anti-socialist covert action in Latin America. His work lent credence to anecdotal suspicions that the U.S. government had used similar tactics in Southeast Asia

during the Vietnam era. Not without critics, Webb later published a book on the same theme with extensive citations, *Dark Alliance: The CIA, the Contras, and the Crack Cocaine Explosion* (New York: Seven Stories Press, 1999).

34. Sasha Abramsky, *Hard Time Blues: How Politics Built a Prison Nation* (New York: St. Martin's Press, 2002), 67.

35. It took a while for Rockefeller's approach to catch on. In the 1970s even conservative Republicans advocated medical not punitive measures against drug addiction and championed rehabilitation. In 1970, President Nixon passed the Comprehensive Drug Abuse Prevention and Control Act, which repealed federal mandatory sentencing guidelines, yet within a decade, they had become part of the tough-on-crime toolbox and emulated in dozens of states.

36. For more on this history, see Jim Rooney, *Organizing in the South Bronx* (New York: SUNY Press, 1994), 44.

37. This practice allowed the same financial institutions to later buy up the buildings cheaply and redevelop the area at a profit. For original accounts of these events, see "Arson for Hate and Profit," *Time* magazine, October 31, 1977; and "Fire Attacks On Our Neighborhood," *White Lightning* newsletter, March 1975.

38. For more on El Comité see José E. Velázquez, "Another West Side Story: An Interview with Members of El Comité-MINH," in *The Puerto Rican Movement: Voices from the Diaspora,* Andrés Torres and José E. Velázquez, eds. (Philadelphia: Temple University Press, 1998), 88–106.

39. The term *vanguard* is an easily misused and misunderstood one. Lenin believed that in order for revolution to be possible, a single vanguard political party must be built to develop leadership among workers and provide political clarity during mass working-class rebellion. It was through a vanguard that revolution was possible by providing the continuity between periods of upsurge and decline. Among the U.S. Left a vanguard proved elusive. During the Depression, the Communist Party USA became the closest embodiment. They organized strikes, led militant anti-eviction efforts and mobilized the unemployed for relief. Their analysis of race could be simplistic ("Black and White, Unite and Fight"), but the Party's willingness to defend and organize Black workers set them apart from other parts of the white Left which rode the fence on the Jim Crow issue.

40. Thanks to Dan Sidorick, Sue Milligan and Jack Whalen some of this rare archival material was not destroyed.

41. See Gregory Jaynes, "Philadelphia's Message to Rizzo: 'Enough,'" *New York Times,* November 9, 1978.

42. James F. Clarity, "Out of Mayoral Race, Rizzo Plans Career as Guardian of White Rights," *New York Times,* November 8, 1978.

Epilogue

1. *The Combahee River Collective Statement*. 1977. Web archive in Library of Congress at, https://www.loc.gov/item/lcwaN0028151 (accessed March 20, 2021). Many thanks to Barbara Smith, Demita Frazier, and Beverly Smith, primary authors. See also, Taylor, Keeanga-Yamahtta. "Until Black Women Are Free, None of Us Will Be Free." *New Yorker*, July 20, 2020. https://www.newyorker.com/news/our-columnists/until-black-women-are-free-none-of-us-will-be-free.
2. Saul Alinsky, "Saul Alinsky, a Candid Conversation with a Feisty Radical Organizer," interview by Eric Norden, *Playboy Magazine*, March 1972.
3. Bob Lee, "Interview with Bob Lee," by James Tracy, *Area Magazine*, March 2008.
4. Thomas Ogozalek, Luisa Puig, and Spencer Piston, "White Trump voters are richer than they appear," *Washington Post*, November 12, 2019.
5. Pape, Robert and Ruby Kevin. "The Capitol Rioters Aren't Like Other Extremists." *The Atlantic*. February 2, 2021.
6. Mike James, "Getting Off the Interstate: Or, Back Home in Heartbreak, USA," *The Movement*, vol. 4, no. 8, September 1968, 5.
7. We are grateful for the many examples of anti-racist and multiracial organizing in this spirit. In the first edition, we mentioned Oregon's Bring the Ruckus, which did outreach at gun shows to counter anti-immigrant scapegoating. We looked to the Vermont Workers Center, the Excluded Workers Congress, and Jobs With Justice for their sophisticated approach to alliance building. In the tradition that led us to write this book (following the footnotes in the history of the New Left and Black Panthers), we hope readers will look further into the rich history of Rising Up Angry, Slim Coleman's Intercommunal Survival Committee in Chicago, the White Panthers in Detroit, and the Grassroots Organizing Work started by Bob and Dottie Zellner in New Orleans. Most of all, we look forward to seeing the stories future generations will tell about today's organizing in the heartland, from Rednecks for Black Lives and Southern Crossroads, to People's Action, and the long history of the Highlander Center.

Selected Bibliography

Alk, Howard, and Mike Gray, dir. 2000. *American Revolution 2*. Film. Chicago: Chicago Film Archives. https://vimeo.com/351632080

Armsbury, Chuck. 2019. *Odyssey of a Mother Country Radical*. Colville, WA: Charles Armsbury.

Bliss, Jenna, dir. 2018. *The People's Detox*. Film. New York.

Fernández, Johanna. 2020. *Young Lords: a Radical History*. Chapel Hill, NC: University of North Carolina Press.

Gitlin, Todd, and Nancy Hollander. 1971. *Uptown: Poor Whites in Chicago*. New York: Harper and Row.

James, Michael. 2019. *Rising Up Angry*. October 14. http://www.risingupangry.org

Santisteban, Ray, dir. 2019. *The First Rainbow Coalition*. Film. San Antonio, TX: Nantes Media LLC.

Thurman, Hy. 2020. *Revolutionary Hillbilly: Notes from the Struggle on the Edge of the Rainbow*. Berkeley, CA: Regent Press.

Williams, Jakobi. 2015. *From the Bullet to the Ballot: the Illinois Chapter of the Black Panther Party and Racial Coalition Politics in Chicago*. Chapel Hill: The University of North Carolina Press.

Index

JAMES TRACY is the chair of the Labor and Community Studies Department of City College of San Francisco. He is the co-author of *No Fascist USA! The John Brown Anti-Klan Committee and Lessons for Today's Movements* (City Lights/OpenMedia), author of *Dispatches Against Displacement: Field Notes From San Francisco's Housing Wars* (AK Press), and editor of *Avanti-Popolo: Italian-Americans Sail Beyond Columbus* (Manic D Press). He is an organizer who has been active in groups such as the San Francisco Community Land Trust and Jobs With Justice, and the American Federation of Teachers 2121. His articles have been featured in *Z Magazine*, *Shelterforce*, *Yes!*, and *48 Hills*. He is a co-founder of the Howard Zinn Book Fair and a host of the Books to the Barricades podcast. He lives in Oakland, California.

AMY SONNIE is a librarian, educator, and editor of the award-winning anthology, *Revolutionary Voices* (Alyson Books), which introduced the country to a rising generation of queer and transgender youth activism more than twenty years ago. As co-founder of the Center for Media Justice with Malkia Cyril and Jen Soriano, Amy helped build a national grassroots movement for digital equity and racial justice. She is the recipient of the Zoia Horn Intellectual Freedom Award for her leadership in public libraries, and continues to be active in movements for social justice. She earned a masters of Library and Information Science from San Jose State University, and a dual BA in Journalism and Women's Studies from Syracuse University. She lives in the San Francisco Bay Area.